REMARKS ON THE FOUNDATIONS OF MATHEMATICS

REMARKS
ON THE FOUNDATIONS
OF MATHEMATICS

By

LUDWIG WITTGENSTEIN

Edited by

G. H. von WRIGHT
R. RHEES
G. E. M. ANSCOMBE

Translated by
G. E. M. ANSCOMBE

Revised Edition

The MIT Press
Cambridge, Massachusetts,
and London, England

First MIT Press paperback edition, 1983

Revised edition published by The MIT Press, 1978;
published in Great Britain by Basil Blackwell, 1978.

First edition published in Great Britain by Basil Blackwell, 1956;
paperback of first edition published by The MIT Press, 1967.

Library of Congress catalog card number: 78-59781

ISBN 0-262-23080-2 (hard)
0-262-73067-7 (paper)

TABLE OF CONTENTS

Part I

Appendix I

Appendix II

Appendix III

Part III

Part IV

Part V

Part VI

Part VII

EDITORS' PREFACE TO THE
REVISED EDITION

THE posthumously published writings of Wittgenstein which first appeared in 1956 with the title "Remarks on the Foundations of Mathematics" almost all take their origin from the period September 1937–April 1944. Wittgenstein did not return to this subject matter in the last years of his life. On the other hand, he wrote a great deal on the philosophy of mathematics and logic from 1929 to about 1934. A considerable part of this—together with other material from these years—has been published under the titles "Philosophische Bermerkungen" (1964) and "Philosophische Grammatik" (1969).

The present revised edition of the "Remarks on the Foundations of Mathematics" contains the *whole* text of the first (1956) edition. In editing it we have thus left out nothing that was already in print. On the other hand, we have included additional material. Only Parts II and III of the first edition are here reprinted, practically unaltered, as Parts III and IV.

We have taken the second Appendix to Part I of the first edition, enlarged by a few additions from the MSS, and placed it as an independent Part II of this edition.

Part VI of the present edition is entirely new. The MS includes perhaps the most satisfactory presentation of Wittgenstein's thoughts on the problem of following a rule—one of his most frequently recurring themes. The MS (164) was written in the period 1941–1944; we have not been able to date it more precisely.[1] With the exception of a few remarks at the end, which do not quite fit in with the circle of problems that are otherwise the topic of the MS, it is here printed *in extenso*.

Part I is the earliest of this collection and to a certain extent it has a peculiar position. It is the only part that existed in typescript and is the most worked over of them all. The typescript itself goes back to manuscripts which were composed for the most part in the period from September 1937 to about the end of that year (117, 118, 119). But the remarks on negation form an exception; they stem from a MS belonging to about the turn of the year 1933–1934 (115).

In its original form the typescript that is the basis for Part I formed

[1] The numbering of Wittgenstein's manuscripts and typescripts follows that of the list given in the article "The Wittgenstein Papers" by G. H. von Wright in: *The Philosophical Review*, Vol. LXXVIII, 1969.

the second half of an earlier version of "Philosophical Investigations". Wittgenstein then split up this half of that version into clippings, supplied them with extensive alterations and additions, and only then constructed that order of the individual remarks that is reproduced here. In a notebook as late as 1944 he proposed a few alterations to this typescript. (See p. 80, n.)

The last section of the rearranged collection consisted of papers that had not been cut up, though there were many manuscript additions, and it is not quite clear whether Wittgenstein regarded them as belonging with the preceding text. This section deals with the concept of negation, and as we have already mentioned, it was written 3–4 years earlier than the remainder of Part I. Its content occurs in great part in the "Investigations" §§ 547–568. The editors left it out of the first edition, but have included it here as Appendix I to Part I.

The collection had two further appendices. They come from the same typescript as the second half of the (earlier) "Investigations"; nevertheless they were separated from the rest of the collection of clippings. The first deals with 'mathematical surprise'. The second discusses among other things Gödel's theories of the existence of un-provable but true propositions in the system of "Principia Mathema-tica." In the first edition we included only the second appendix, but here both are published (Appendices II and III.)

With the exception of a few remarks which Wittgenstein himself had left out in the arrangement of the clippings, what is here published as Part I comprises the whole content of the second half of the early version of "Philosophical Investigations."

It must have been Wittgenstein's intention also to attach appendices on Cantor's theory of infinity and Russell's logic to the contributions on problems of the foundations of mathematics that he planned to include in the "Philosophical Investigations." Under the heading 'Ad-ditions' he wrote a certain amount on the problems connected with set theory: about the diagonal procedure and the different kinds of number-concept. In the time from April 1938 to January 1939 he wrote a MS book where, together with other remarks on the philosophy of psy-chological concepts, he put in a good deal on probability and truth (Gödel) and also on infinity and kinds of number (Cantor). These writings he immediately continued in a notebook (162a and the be-ginning of 162b). In the later war-years too he occasionally comes back to these topics. The confrontation with Cantor was never brought to a terminus.

What is here published as Part II consists of the above-mentioned "Additions" in 117 and of a selection of remarks from 121. The whole presents an inconsiderable expansion of Appendix II of Part I of the earlier (1956) edition. The arrangement of sentences and paragraphs into numbered Remarks corresponds to the original text (which was not wholly the case in the 1956 edition). The sections have been numbered by the editors.

Wittgenstein's confrontation with Russell, that is to say with the thought of the derivability of mathematics from the calculi of logic, is found in Part III of this collection (Part II of the edition of 1956). These writings stem from the period from October 1939 to April 1940. The MS (122, continued in the second half of 117) was the most extensive of all the MSS which form the basis of this collection. Neither in style nor in content has it been perfected. The author keeps on renewing the attempt to elucidate his thoughts on the nature of mathematical proof: what it means, for example, to say that a proof must be surveyable; that it presents us with a new picture; that it creates a new concept; and the like. His effort is to declare "the motley of mathematics" and to make clear the connexion between the different techniques of calculation. In so striving he simultaneously sets his face against the idea of a "foundation" of mathematics, whether in the form of a Russellian calculus or in that of the Hilbertian conception of a meta-mathematics. The idea of contradiction and of a consistency proof is extensively discussed.

The editors were of the opinion that this manuscript contained a wealth of valuable thoughts as they are nowhere otherwise to be encountered in Wittgenstein's writings. On the other hand it also seemed clear to them that this MS could not be published unabridged. Thus a selection was requisite. The task was difficult, and the editors are not entirely satisfied with the result.

In the autumn of 1940 Wittgenstein began to occupy himself anew with the philosophy of mathematics and wrote something about the question of following a rule. These writings (MS 123) are not published here. In May 1941 the work was taken up again and soon led to investigations from which a considerable selection is published here as Part VII.

The first part of Part VII (§§ 1–23) was mostly written in June 1941. It discusses the relation between mathematical and empirical propositions, between calculation and experiment, treats the concept of contradiction and consistency anew and ends in the neighbourhood of the

Gödelian problem. The second half was written in the spring of 1944. It deals principally with the concept of following a rule, of mathematical proof and logical inference, and with the connexion between proof and concept formation in mathematics. There are here numerous points of contact, on the one side with the manuscripts of the intervening period (Parts IV and V) and with thoughts in the "Philosophical Investigations" on the other. §§ 47–60 essentially form an earlier version of what can now be found in the "Investigations" §§ 209 to 237. The sequence of the remarks is different here; and some have not been taken up into the later version.—Both halves of this Part VII were in the same MS book, which is one of the indications that the author regarded them as belonging together.

Part V is taken from two MSS (126 and 127) belonging to the years 1942 and 1943—while Part IV derives mainly from one MS (125) from the year 1942, with some additions from the two MSS on which Part V is based. Much on these two parts has the character of "preliminary studies" for the second half of Part VII; but they also contain a wealth of material that the author did not use there.

In Part V Wittgenstein discusses topics that connect up with Brouwer and Intuitionism: the law of excluded middle and mathematical existence; the Dedekind cut and the extensional and intensional way of looking at things in mathematics. In the second half of this part there are remarks on the concept of generality in mathematics and especially on a theme that makes its appearance still more strongly in Part VII: the role of concept-formation and the relation between concept and truth in mathematics.

The chronological arrangement of the material has the consequence that one and the same theme is sometimes treated in different places. If Wittgenstein had put his remarks together into a book, he would presumably have avoided many of these repetitions.

It must once more be emphasized: Part I and, practically speaking also Part VI, but only these, are complete reproductions of texts of Wittgenstein's. Thus what is here published as Parts II, III, IV, V and VII is a *selection* from extensive MSS. In their preface to the first edition the editors conjectured that it might be desirable later to print what they had omitted. They are still of the same opinion—but also of the opinion that the time has not yet come to print the whole of Wittgenstein's MSS on these and other topics.

The editors alone are responsible for the numbering of the selected paragraphs. (Even in Part I.) But the articulation of the writing into "remarks"—here separated from one another by larger gaps—is Wittgenstein's own. With a few exceptions we did not want to interfere with the order of the sections. Nevertheless we have sometimes (especially at the end of Part IV and V) brought together material belonging to the same subject matter from different places.

The list of contents and the index are meant to help the reader to look over the whole and to make it easier to look things up. We alone are responsible for the thematic articulation of the material indicated in the list of contents.

I

Circa 1937–1938

1. We use the expression: "The steps are determined by the formula . . .". How is it used?—We may perhaps refer to the fact that people are brought by their education (training) so to use the formula $y = x^2$, that they all work out the same value for y when they substitute the same number for x. Or we may say: "These people are so trained that they all take the same step at the same point when they receive the order 'add 3' ". We might express this by saying: for these people the order "add 3" completely determines every step from one number to the next. (In contrast with other people who do not know what they are to do on receiving this order, or who react to it with perfect certainty, but each one in a different way.)

On the other hand we can contrast different kinds of formula, and the different kinds of use (different kinds of training) appropriate to them. Then we *call* formulae of a particular kind (with the appropriate methods of use) "formulae which determine a number y for a given value of x", and formulae of another kind, ones which "do not determine the number y for a given value of x. ($y = x^2 + 1$ would be of the first kind, $y > x^2 + 1$, $y = x^2 \pm 1$, $y = x^2 + z$ of the second.) The proposition "The formula . . . determines a number y" will then be a statement about the form of the formulae—and now we must distinguish such a proposition as "The formula which I have written down determines y", or "Here is a formula which determines y", from one of the following kind: "The formula $y = x^2$ determines the number y for a given value of x". The question "Is the formula written down there one that determines y?" will then mean the same as "Is what is there a formula of this kind or that?"—but it is not clear off-hand what we are to make of the question "Is $y = x^2$ a formula which determines y for a given value of x?" One might address this question to a pupil in order to test whether he understands the use of the word "to determine"; or it might be a mathematical problem to work out whether there was only one variable on the right-hand side of the formula, as e.g. in the case: $y = (x^2 + z)^2 - z(2x^2 + z)$.

2. "The way the formula is meant determines which steps are to be taken." What is the criterion for the way the formula is meant? Presumably the way we always use it, the way we were taught to use it.

We say, for instance, to someone who uses a sign unknown to us: "If by '$x!2$' you mean x^2, then you get this value for y, if you mean $\sqrt{x}$, that one".—Now ask yourself: how does one *mean* the one thing or the other by "$x!2$"?

That will be how meaning it can determine the steps in advance.

3. *How do I know* that in working out the series $+ 2$ I must write

"20004, 20006"

and not

"20004, 20008"?

—(The question: "How do I know that this colour is 'red'?" is similar.)

"But you surely know for example that you must always write the *same* sequence of numbers in the units: 2, 4, 6, 8, 0, 2, 4, etc."—Quite true: the problem must already appear in this sequence, and even in *this* one: 2, 2, 2, 2, etc.—For how do I know that I am to write "2" after the five hundredth "2"? i.e. that 'the same figure' in that place is "2"? And if I know it *in advance*, what use is this knowledge to me later on? I mean: how do I know what to do with this earlier knowledge when the step actually has to be taken?

(If intuition is needed to continue the series $+ 1$, then it is also needed to continue the series $+ 0$.)

"But do you mean to say that the expression '+ 2' leaves you in doubt what you are to do e.g. after 2004?"—No; I answer "2006" without hesitation. But just for that reason it is superfluous to suppose that this was determined earlier on. My having no doubt in face of the question does *not* mean that it has been answered in advance.

"But I surely also know that whatever number I am given I shall be able, straight off and with certainty, to give the next one.—Certainly my dying first is excluded, and a lot of other things too. But my being so certain of being able to go on is naturally very important.—

4. "But then what does the peculiar inexorability of mathematics consist in?"—Would not the inexorability with which two follows one and three two be a good example?—But presumably this means: follows in the *series of cardinal numbers*; for in a different series something different follows. And isn't *this* series just *defined* by this sequence?—"Is that supposed to mean that it is equally correct whichever way a person counts, and that anyone can count as he pleases?"— We should presumably not call it "counting" if everyone said the numbers one after the other *anyhow*; but of course it is not simply a question of a name. For what we call "counting" is an important part of our life's activities. Counting and calculating are not—e.g.—simply a pastime. Counting (and that means: counting like *this*) is a technique that is employed daily in the most various operations of our lives. And that is why we learn to count as we do: with endless practice, with merciless exactitude; that is why it is inexorably insisted that we shall all say "two" after "one", "three" after "two" and so on.—But is this counting only a *use*, then; isn't there also some truth corresponding to this sequence?" The *truth* is that counting has proved to pay.— "Then do you want to say that 'being true' means: being usable (or

useful)?"—No, not that; but that it can't be said of the series of natural numbers—any more than of our language—that it is true, but: that it is usable, and, above all, *it is used*.

5. "But doesn't it follow with logical necessity that you get two when you add one to one, and three when you add one to two? and isn't this inexorability the same as that of logical inference?"—Yes! it is the same.—"But isn't there a truth corresponding to logical inference? Isn't it *true* that this follows from that?"—The proposition: "It is true that this follows from that" means simply: this follows from that. And how do we use this proposition?—What would happen if we made a different inference—*how* should we get into conflict with truth?

How should we get into conflict with truth, if our footrules were made of very soft rubber instead of wood and steel?—"Well, we shouldn't get to know the correct measurement of the table."—You mean: we should not get, or could not be sure of getting, *that* measurement which we get with our rigid rulers. So if you had measured the table with the elastic rulers and said it measured five feet by our usual way of measuring, you would be wrong; but if you say that it measured five feet by your way of measuring, that is correct.—"But surely that isn't measuring at all!"—It is similar to our measuring and capable, in certain circumstances, of fulfilling 'practical purposes'. (A shop-keeper might use it to treat different customers differently.)

If a ruler expanded to an extraordinary extent when slightly heated, we should say—in normal circumstances—that that made it *unusable*. But we could think of a situation in which this was just what was wanted. I am imagining that we perceive the expansion with the naked eye; and we ascribe the same numerical measure of length to bodies in rooms of different temperatures, if they measure the same by the ruler which to the eye is now longer, now shorter.

It can be said: What is here called "measuring" and "length" and "equal length", is something different from what we call those things. The use of these words is different from ours; but it is *akin* to it; and we too use these words in a variety of ways.

6. We must get clear what inferring really consists in: We shall perhaps say it consists in the transition from one assertion to another. But does this mean that inferring is something that takes place when we are making a transition from one assertion to another, and so *before* the second one is uttered—or that inferring consists in making the one assertion follow upon the other, that is, e.g., in uttering it after the other? Misled by the special use of the verb "infer" we readily imagine that inferring is a peculiar activity, a process in the medium of the understanding, as it were a brewing of the vapour out of which the deduction arises. But let's look at what happens here.—There is a transition from one proposition to another *via* other propositions, that is, a chain of inferences; but we don't need to talk about this; for it presupposes another kind of transition, namely that from one link of the chain to the next. Now a process of forming the transition may occur between the links. There is nothing occult about this process; it is a derivation of one sentence from another according to a rule; a comparison of both with some paradigm or other, which represents the schema of the transition; or something of the kind. This may go on on paper, orally, or 'in the head'.—The conclusion may however also be drawn in such a way that the one proposition is uttered after the other, without any such process; or the process may consist merely in our saying "Therefore" or "It follows from this", or something of the kind. We call it a "conclusion" when the inferred proposition *can* in fact be derived from the premise.

7. Now what does it mean to say that one proposition *can* be derived from another by means of a rule? Can't anything be derived from anything by means of *some* rule—or even according to any rule, with a suitable interpretation? What does it mean for me to say e.g.: this number can be got by multiplying these two numbers? This is a rule telling us that we must get this number if we multiply *correctly*; and we can obtain this rule by multiplying the two numbers, or again in a different way (though any procedure that leads to this result might be called 'multiplication'). Now I am said to have multiplied when I have carried out the multiplication 265 × 463, and also when I say: "twice four is eight", although here no calculating procedure led to the product (which, however, I could also have *worked out*). And so we also say a conclusion is drawn, where it is not calculated.

8. But still, I must only infer what really *follows*!—Is this supposed to mean: only what follows, going by the rules of inference; or is it supposed to mean: only what follows, going by *such* rules of inference as somehow agree with some (sort of) reality? Here what is before our minds in a vague way is that this reality is something very abstract, very general, and very rigid. Logic is a kind of ultra-physics, the description of the 'logical structure' of the world, which we perceive through a kind of ultra-experience (with the understanding e.g.). Here perhaps inferences like the following come to mind: "The stove is smoking, so the chimney is out of order again". (And *that* is how this conclusion is drawn! Not like this: "The stove is smoking, and whenever the stove smokes the chimney is out of order; and so . . .".)

9. What we call 'logical inference' is a transformation of our expression. For example, the translation of one measure into another. One edge of a ruler is marked in inches, the other in centimetres. I

measure the table in inches and go over to centimetres *on the ruler*.—
And of course there is such a thing as right and wrong in passing
from one measure to the other; but what is the reality that 'right'
accords with here? Presumably a *convention*, or a *use*, and perhaps our
practical requirements.

10. "But doesn't e.g. '*fa*' have to follow from '$(x).fx$' if '$(x).fx$' is
meant in the way we mean it?"—And how does *the way* we mean it
come out? Doesn't it come out in the constant practice of its use?
and perhaps further in certain *gestures*—and similar things.——But it is
as if there were also something attached to the word "all", when *we*
say it; something with which a different use could not be combined;
namely, the *meaning*. " 'All' surely means: *all*!" we should like to say,
when we have to explain this meaning; and we make a particular
gesture and face.

Cut down all these trees!——But don't you understand what '*all*'
means? (He had left one standing.) How did he learn what 'all'
means? Presumably by practice.—And of course this practice did not
only bring it about that he *does this* on receiving the order—it sur-
rounded the word with a whole lot of pictures (visual and others) of
which one or another comes up when we hear and speak the word.
(And if we are supposed to give an account of what the 'meaning' of
the word is, we first pull out *one* from this mass of pictures—and then
reject it again as non-essential when we see that now this, now that,
picture presents itself, and sometimes none at all.)

One learns the meaning of "all" by learning that '*fa*' follows from
'$(x).fx$'.—The exercises which drill us in the use of this word, which
teach its meaning, always make it natural to rule out any exception.

11. For how do we *learn* to infer? Or don't we learn it?

Does a child know that an affirmative follows from a double negative?—And how does one *shew* him that it does? Presumably by shewing him a process (a double inversion, two turns through 180° and similar things) which he then takes as a picture of negation.

And the meaning of '$(x).fx$' is made clear by our insisting on 'fa' 's following from it.

12.   "From '*all*', if it is meant *like this, this* must surely follow!"—If it is meant like *what*? Consider how you mean it. Here perhaps a further picture comes to your mind—and that is all you have got.—No, it is not true that it *must*—but it *does* follow: we *perform* this transition.

And we say: If this does not follow, then it simply wouldn't be *all*—and that only shews how we react with words in such a situation.—

13.   It strikes us as if something else, something over and above the *use* of the word "all", must have changed if 'fa' is no longer to follow from '$(x).fx$'; something attaching to the word itself.

Isn't this like saying: "If this man were to act differently, his character would have to be different". Now this may mean something in some cases and not in others. We say "behaviour flows from character" and that is how use flows from meaning.

14.   This shews you—it might be said—how closely certain gestures, pictures, reactions, are linked with a constantly practised use.

'The picture forces itself on us . . . .' It is very interesting that pictures do *force* themselves on us. And if it were not so, how could such a sentence as "What's done cannot be undone" mean anything to us?

15. It is important that in our language—our natural language— 'all' is a fundamental concept and 'all but one' less fundamental; i.e. there is not a *single* word for it, nor yet a characteristic gesture.

16. The *point* of the word "all" is that it admits no exception.— True, that is the point of its use in our language; but the kinds of use we feel to be the 'point' are connected with the role that such-and-such a use has in our whole life.

17. When we ask what inferring consists in, we hear it said e.g.: "If I have recognized the truth of the propositions . . ., then I am justified in further writing down . . .".—In what sense justified? Had I no right to write that down before?—"Those propositions convince me of the truth of this proposition." But of course that is not what is in question either.—"The mind carries out the special activity of logical inference according to these laws." That is certainly interesting and important; but then, is it true? Does the mind always infer according to *these* laws? And what does the special activity of inferring consist in?—This is why it is necessary to look and see how we carry out inferences in the practice of language; what kind of procedure in the language-game inferring is.

For example: a regulation says "All who are taller than five foot six are to join the . . . section". A clerk reads out the men's names and heights. Another allots them to such-and-such sections.—"N.N. five foot nine." "So N.N. to the . . . section." That is inference.

18.   Now, what do we call 'inferences' in Russell or Euclid? Am I to say: the transitions from one proposition to the next one in the proof? But where is the *passage* to be found?—I say that in Russell one proposition follows from another if the one can be derived from the other according to the position of both in a proof and the appended signs—when we read the book. For reading this book is a game that has to be learnt.

19.   One is often in the dark about what following and inferring really consists in; what kind of fact, and what kind of procedure, it is. The peculiar use of these verbs suggests to us that following is the existence of a connexion between propositions, which connexion we follow up when we infer.   This comes out very instructively in Russell's account (*Principia Mathematica*). That a proposition $\vdash q$ follows from a proposition $\vdash p \supset q.p$ is here a fundamental law of logic:

$$\vdash p \supset q.p. \supset .\vdash q \,^1$$

Now this, one says, justifies us in inferring $\vdash q$ from $\vdash p \supset q.p$.   But what does 'inferring', the procedure that is now justified, consist in?   Surely in this: that in some language-game we utter, write down (etc.), the one proposition as an assertion after the other; and how can the fundamental law justify me in *this*?

20.   Now Russell wants to say: "*This* is how I am going to infer, and it is *right*".   So he means to tell us how he means to infer: this is done by a *rule* of inference. How does it run? That this proposition implies that one?——Presumably that in the proofs in this book a proposition like this is to come after a proposition like this.—But it is supposed to be a fundamental law of logic that it is

---

¹ *Principia Mathematica*: What is implied by a true premiss is true. Pp. (Eds.)

correct to infer in this way!—Then the fundamental law would have to run: "It is correct to infer . . . from . . ."; and this fundamental law should presumably be self-evident——in which case the rule itself will self-evidently be correct, or justified. "But after all this rule deals with sentences in a book, and that isn't part of logic!"—Quite correct, the rule is really only a piece of information that in this book only *this* transition from one proposition to another will be used (as it were a piece of information in the index); for the correctness of the transition must be evident where it is made; and the expression of the 'fundamental law of logic' is then the *sequence of propositions* itself.

21.   In his fundamental law Russell seems to be saying of a proposition: "It already follows—all I still have to do is, to infer it". Thus Frege somewhere says that the straight line which connects any two points is really already there before we draw it; and it is the same when we say that the transitions, say in the series + 2, have really already been made before we make them orally or in writing—as it were tracing them.

22.   One might reply to someone who said this: Here you are using a picture. One *can determine* the transitions which someone is to make in a series, by doing them for him first. E.g. by writing down in another notation the series which he is to write, so that all that remains for him to do is to translate it; or by actually writing it down very faint, and he has to trace it. In the first case we can also say that we don't write down *the* series that he has to write, and so that we do not ourselves make the transitions of that series; but in the second case we shall certainly say that the series which he is to write is already there. We should also say this if we *dictate* what he has to write down, although then we are producing a series of sounds and he a series of

written signs. It is at any rate a sure way of *determining* the transitions that someone has to make, if we in some sense make them first.—If, therefore, we determine these transitions in a quite different sense, namely, by subjecting our pupil to such a training as e.g. children get in the multiplication tables and in multiplying, so that all who are so trained do random multiplications (not previously done in the course of being taught) in the same way and with results that agree—if, that is, the transitions which someone is to make on the order 'add 2' are so determined by training that we can predict with certainty how he will go, even when he has never up to now taken *this* step—then it may be natural to us to use this as a picture of the situation: the steps are all already taken and he is just writing them down.

23. "But we surely infer this proposition from that because it actually follows! We ascertain that it follows."—We ascertain that what is written here follows from what is written there. And this proposition is being used *temporally*.

24. Separate the feelings (gestures) of agreement, from what you *do* with the proof.

25. But how about when I ascertain that this pattern of lines:

 (a)

is like-numbered with this pattern of angles:

(b)

(I have made the patterns memorable on purpose) by correlating them:

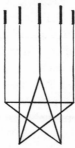

(c)

Now what do I ascertain when I look at this figure? What I see is a star with threadlike appendages.—

26.   But I can make use of the figure like this: five people stand arranged in a pentagon; against the wall are wands, like the strokes in (a); I look at the figure (c) and say: "I can give each of the people a wand".

I could regard figure (c) as a schematic *picture* of my giving the five men a wand each.

27.   For if I first draw some arbitrary polygon:

and then some arbitrary series of strokes

$$|\,|\,|\,|\,|\,|\,|\,|\,|\,|\,|\,|\,|\,|\,|\,|\,|\,|\,|\,|\,|\,|\,|\,|\,|\,|\,|\,|\,|\,|\,|\,|\,|\,|\,|\,|\,|\,|\,|$$

I can find out by correlating them whether I have as many angles in the top figure as strokes in the bottom one. (I do not know how it would turn out.) And so I can also say that by drawing projection-lines I have ascertained that there are as many strokes at the top of figure (c) as the star beneath has points. (Temporally!) In this way of taking it the figure is not like a mathematical proof (any more than it is a mathematical proof when I divide a bag of apples among a group of people and find that each can have just *one* apple).

I can however conceive figure (c) as a mathematical proof. Let us give names to the shapes of the patterns (a) and (b): let (a) be called a "hand", H, and (b) a "pentacle", P. I have proved that H has as many strokes as P has angles. And this proposition is once more non-temporal.

28.   A proof—I might say—is a *single* pattern, at one end of which are written certain sentences and at the other end a sentence (which we call the 'proved proposition'.)

To describe such a pattern we may say: in it the proposition . . . follows from. . . . This is one way of describing a *design*, which might also be for example an ornament (a wallpaper design). I can say, then, "In the proof on that blackboard the proposition p follows from q and r", and that is simply a description of what can be seen there. But it is not the mathematical proposition that p follows from q and r. That has a different application. It says—as one might put it—that it makes sense to speak of a proof (pattern) in which p follows from q and r. Just as one can say that the proposition "white is lighter than black" asserts that it makes sense to speak of two objects, the lighter one white and the other black, but not of two objects, the lighter one black and the other white.

29.   Let us imagine that we had given a paradigm of 'lighter' and 'darker' in the shape of a white and a black patch, and now, so to speak, we use it to deduce that red is darker than white.

30.   The proposition proved by (c) now serves as a new prescription for ascertaining numerical equality: if one set of objects has been arranged in the form of a hand and another as the angles of a pentacle, we say the two sets are equal in number.

31.   "But isn't that merely because we have already correlated H and P and seen that they are the same in number?"—Yes, but if they were so in one case, how do I know that they will be so again now?— "Why, because it is of the *essence* of H and P to be the same in number."—But how can you have brought *that* out by correlating them? (I thought the counting or correlation merely yielded the result that these two groups before me were—or were not—the same in number.) —"But now, if he has an H of things and a P of things, and he actually correlates them, it surely isn't *possible* for him to get any result but that they are the same in number.—And that it is not possible can surely be seen from the proof."—But *isn't* it possible? If, e.g., he—as someone else might say—omits to draw one of the correlating lines. But I admit that in an enormous majority of cases he will always get the same result, and, if he did not get it, would think something had put him out. And if it were not like this the ground would be cut away from under the whole proof. For we decide to use the proof-picture instead of correlating the groups; we do *not* correlate them, but *instead* compare the groups with those of the proof (in which indeed two groups are correlated with one another).

32. I might also say as a result of the proof: "From now on an *H* and a *P* are called 'the same in number' ".

Or: The proof doesn't *explore* the essence of the two figures, but it does express what I am going to count as belonging to the essence of the figures from now on.——I deposit what belongs to the essence among the paradigms of language.

The mathematician creates *essences*.

33. When I say "This proposition follows from that one", that is to accept a rule. The acceptance is *based* on the proof. That is to say, I find this chain (this figure) acceptable as a *proof*.——"But could I do otherwise? Don't I *have* to find it acceptable?"—Why do you say you have to? Because at the end of the proof you say e.g.: "Yes—I have to accept this conclusion". But that is after all only the expression of your unconditional acceptance.

I.e. (I believe): the words "I have to admit this" are used in *two kinds* of case: when we have got a proof—and also with reference to the individual steps of the proof.

34. And how does it come out that the proof *compels* me? Well, in the fact that once I have got it I go ahead in such-and-such a way, and refuse any other path. All I should further say as a final argument against someone who did not want to go that way, would be: "Why, don't you see . . .!"—and that is no *argument*.

35. "But, if you are right, how does it come about that all men (or at any rate all normal men) accept these patterns as proofs of these propositions?"—It is true, there is great—and interesting—agreement here.

36.   Imagine you have a row of marbles, and you number them with
Arabic numerals, which run from 1 to 100; then you make a big gap
after every 10, and in each 10 a rather smaller gap in the middle with
5 on either side: this makes the 10 stand out clearly as 10; now you
take the sets of 10 and put them one below another, and in the middle
of the column you make a bigger gap, so that you have five rows
above and five below; and now you number the rows from 1 to 10.—
We have, so to speak, done drill with the marbles.   I can say that
we have unfolded properties of the hundred marbles.—But now
imagine that this whole process, this experiment with the hundred
marbles, were filmed. What I now see on the screen is surely not an
experiment, for the picture of an experiment is not itself an experiment.—But I see the 'mathematically essential' thing about the process
in the projection too! For here there appear first a hundred spots,
and then they are arranged in tens, and so on and so on.
    Thus I might say: the proof does not serve as an experiment; but it
does serve as the picture of an experiment.

37.   Put two apples on a bare table, see that no one comes near
them and nothing shakes the table; now put another two apples on
the table; now count the apples that are there. You have made an
experiment; the result of the counting is probably 4. (We should
present the result like this: when, in such-and-such circumstances, one
puts first 2 apples and then another 2 on a table, mostly none disappear
and none get added.)   And analogous experiments can be carried out,
with the same result, with all kinds of solid bodies.—This is how our
children learn sums; for one makes them put down three beans and
then another three beans and then count what is there. If the result
at one time were 5, at another 7 (say because, *as we should now say*, one
sometimes got added, and one sometimes vanished of itself), then the
first thing we said would be that beans were no good for teaching

sums. But if the same thing happened with sticks, fingers, lines and most other things, that would be the end of all sums.

"But shouldn't we then still have 2 + 2 = 4?"—This sentence would have become unusable.

38.   "You only need to look at the figure

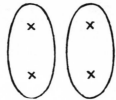

to see that 2 + 2 are 4."—Then I only need to look at the figure

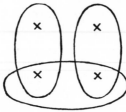

to see that 2 + 2 + 2 are 4.

39.   What do I convince anyone of, if he has followed the film projection of the experiment with the hundred marbles?

One might say, I convince him that it happened like that.—But this would not be a mathematical conviction.——But can't I say: *I impress a procedure on him*? This procedure is the regrouping of 100 things in 10 rows of 10. And this procedure can *as a matter of fact* always be carried out again. And he can rightly be convinced of that.

40. And that is how the proof (25) impresses a procedure on us by drawing projection-lines: the procedure of one-one correlation of the *H* and the *P*.—"But doesn't it also *convince* me of the fact that this[1] correlation is *possible?*"—If that is supposed to mean: you can always carry it out—, then that doesn't have to be true at all. But the drawing of the projection-lines convinces us that there are as many lines above as angles below; and it supplies us with a model to use in correlating such patterns.—"But surely what the model shews in this way is that it does work, not that it did work this time? In the sense in which it wouldn't have worked if the top figure had been | | | | | | instead of | | | | |"—How is that? doesn't it work then? Like *this* e.g.:

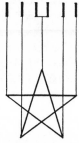

This figure too could be used to prove something. It could be used to shew that groups of these forms *cannot* be given a 1-1 correlation.[2] 'A 1-1 correlation is impossible here' means, e.g., "these figures and 1-1 correlation don't fit together."

"I didn't mean it like that!"—Then shew me how you mean it, and I'll do it.

But can't I say that the figure shews *how* such a correlation is possible —and mustn't it for that reason also shew *that* it is possible?—

---

[1] Is 'this correlation' here the correlation of the patterns in the proof itself? A thing cannot be at the same time the measure and the thing measured. (Note in margin.)

[2] On the strength of the figure I shall e.g. try to effect one correlation, but not the other, and shall say that that one is not possible. (Note in margin.)

41. Now what was the point of our proposal to attach names to the five parallel strokes and the five-pointed star? What is done by their having got names? It will be a means of indicating something about the kind of use these figures have. Namely—that we recognize them as such-and-such at a glance. To do so, we don't count their strokes or angles; for us they are typical shapes, like knife and fork, like letters and numerals.

Thus, when given the order "Draw an *H*" (for example)—I can produce this shape immediately.—Now the proof teaches me a way of correlating the two shapes. (I should like to say that it is not merely these individual figures that are correlated in the proof, but the *shapes themselves*. But this surely only means that these shapes are well impressed on my mind; are impressed as paradigms.) Now isn't it possible for me to get into difficulties when I want to correlate the shapes *H* and *P*—say by there being an angle too many at the bottom or a stroke too many at the top?—"But surely not, if you have really drawn *H* and *P* again!—And that can be proved; look at this figure."

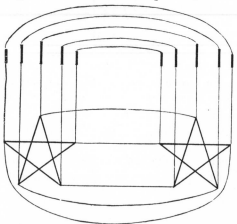

—This figure teaches me a new way of checking whether I have really drawn the same figures; but can't I still get into difficulties when I now want to use this model as a guide? But I say that I am certain I shall not normally get into any difficulties.

42.   There is a puzzle which consists in making a particular figure, e.g. a rectangle, out of given pieces. The division of the figure is such that we find it difficult to discover the right arrangement of the parts. Let it for example be this:

What do you discover when you succeed in arranging it?—You discover a position—of which you did not think before.—Very well; but can't we also say: you find out that these triangles can be arranged like this?—But 'these triangles': are they the actual ones in the rectangle above, or are they triangles which have yet to be arranged like that?

43.   If you say: "I should never have thought that these shapes could be arranged like that", we can't point to the solution of the puzzle and say: "Oh, you didn't think the pieces could be arranged like that?"—You would reply: "I mean, I didn't think of this way of arranging them at all".

44.   Let us imagine the physical properties of the parts of the puzzle to be such that they can't come into the desired position. Not, however, that one feels a resistance if one tries to put them in this

position; but one simply tries everything else, only not *this*, and the pieces don't get into this position by accident either. This position is as it were excluded from space. As if there were e.g. a 'blind spot' in our brain here.—And *isn't* it like this when I believe I have tried all *possible* arrangements and have always passed this one by, as if bewitched?

Can't we say: the figure which shews you the solution removes a blindness, or again changes your geometry? It as it were shews you a new dimension of space. (As if a fly were shewn the way out of the fly-bottle.)

45.   A demon has cast a spell round this position and excluded it from our space.

46.   The new position has as it were come to be out of nothingness. Where there was nothing, now there suddenly is something.

47.   In what sense has the solution shewn you that such-and-such can be done? Before, you could *not* do it—and now perhaps you can.—

48.   I said, "I accept such-and-such as proof of a proposition"—but is it possible for me *not* to accept the figure shewing the arrangement of the pieces as proof that these pieces can be arranged to have this periphery?

49.   But now imagine that one of the pieces is lying so as to be the *mirror-image* of the corresponding part of the pattern. Now you want to arrange the figure according to the pattern; you see it must work, but you never hit on the idea of turning the piece over, and you find that you do not succeed in fitting the puzzle together.

50.   A rectangle can be made of two parallelograms and two triangles.   Proof:

A child would find it difficult to hit on the composition of a rectangle with these parts, and would be surprised by the fact that two sides of the parallelograms make a straight line, when the parallelograms are, after all, askew. It might strike him as if the rectangle came out of these figures by something like magic. True, he has to admit that they do form a rectangle, but it is by a trick, by a distorted arrangement, in an unnatural way.

I can imagine the child, after having put the two parallelograms together in *this* way, not believing his eyes when he sees that they fit like *that*. '*They don't look* as if they fitted together like that.' And I could imagine its being said: It's only through some hocus-pocus that it looks to us as if *they* yielded the rectangle—in reality they have changed their nature, they aren't the parallelograms any more.

51.   "You admit *this*—then you must admit *this* too."—He *must* admit it—and all the time it is possible that he does not admit it! You want to say: "if he *thinks*, he must admit it".

"I'll shew you why you have to admit it."—I shall bring a case before your eyes which will determine you to judge this way if you think about it.

52.   Now, how can the manipulations of the proof make him admit anything?

53.   "Now you will admit that 5 consists of 3 and 2."

I will only admit it, if that is not to admit anything. Except—that I want to use *this picture*.

54.   One might for example take this figure

as a proof of the fact that 100 parallelograms arranged like this must yield a straight strip. Then, when one actually does put 100 together, one gets e.g. a slightly curved strip.—But the proof has determined us to use this picture and form of expression: if they don't yield a straight strip, they were not accurately constructed.

55. Just think, how can the picture (or procedure) that you shew me now oblige me always to judge in such-and-such a way?

If what we have here is an experiment, then surely *one* is too little to bind me to any judgment.

56. The one who is offering the proof says: "Look at this figure. What shall we say about it? Surely that a rectangle consists of . . .?—"

Or again: "Now, surely you call this a 'parallelogram' and this a 'triangle', and *this* is what it is like for one figure to consist of others".

57. "Yes, you have convinced me that a rectangle always consists of . . ."—Should I also say: "Yes, you have convinced me that *this* rectangle (the one in the proof) consists of . . ."? For wouldn't this be the more modest proposition, which you ought to grant even if perhaps you don't yet grant the general proposition? But oddly enough if *that* is what you grant, you seem to be granting, not the more modest geometrical proposition, but what is not a proposition of geometry at all. Of course not—for as regards the rectangle in the proof he didn't convince me of anything. (I shouldn't have been in any doubt about this figure, if I had seen it previously.) As far as concerns this figure I acknowledged everything of my own accord. And he merely used it to make me realize something.—But on the other hand, if he didn't convince me of anything as regards this rectangle, then how has he convinced me of a property of other rectangles?

58. "True, this shape doesn't look as if it could consist of two skew parts."

What are you surprised at? Surely not at seeing this figure. It is something *in* the figure that surprises me.—But there isn't anything going on in the figure!

What surprises me is the way straight and skew go together. It makes me as it were dizzy.

59. But I do actually say: "I have convinced myself that this figure can be constructed with these pieces", e.g. I have seen a picture of the solution of the puzzle.

Now if I say this to somebody it is surely supposed to mean: "Just try: these bits, properly arranged, really do yield the figure". I want to encourage him to do something and I forecast that he will succeed. And the forecast is founded on the ease with which we can construct the figure from the pieces as soon as we know *how*.

60. You say you are astonished at what the proof shews you. But are you astonished at its having been possible to draw these lines? No. You are only astonished when you tell yourself that two bits like this *yield* this shape. When, that is, you think yourself into the situation of seeing the result after having expected something different.

61. "*This* follows inexorably from *that*."—True, in this demonstration this issues from that.

This is a demonstration for whoever acknowledges it as a demonstration. If anyone *doesn't* acknowledge it, doesn't go by it as a demonstration, then he has parted company with us even before anything is said.

62.

Here we have something thats looks inexorable—. And yet it can be 'inexorable' only in its consequences! For otherwise it is nothing but a picture.

What does the action at a distance—as it might be called—of this pattern consist in?

63. I have read a proof—and now I am convinced.—What if I straightway forgot this conviction?

For it is a peculiar procedure: I *go through* the proof and then accept its result.—I mean: this is simply what we *do*. This is use and custom among us, or a fact of our natural history.

64. 'If I have *five*, then I have *three* and *two*.'——But how do I know that I have five?—Well, if it looks like this: | | | | | .—And is it also certain that when it looks like *this*, I can always split it up into groups like *those*?

It is a fact that we can play the following game: I teach someone what a group of two, three, four, or five, is like, and I teach him how to put strokes into one-to-one correspondence; then I always make him carry out the order "Draw a group of five" twice—and then I teach him to carry out the order: "Correlate these two groups"; and here it proves that he practically *always* correlates the strokes without remainder.

Or again: it is a fact that I *practically never* get into difficulties in correlating what I have drawn as groups of five.

65. I have to assemble the puzzle, I try it this way and that, am doubtful whether I shall do it. Next someone shows me a picture of the solution, and I say without any sort of doubt—"Now I can do it!" —Then am I *certain* to do it now?—The fact, however, is: I don't have any doubt.

Suppose someone now asked: "What does the action at a distance of the picture consist in?"—In the fact that I apply it.

66. *In* a demonstration we *get agreement* with someone. If we do not, then we've parted ways before ever starting to communicate in this language.

It is not essential that one should talk the other over by means of the demonstration. Both might see it (read it), and accept it.

67. "But you can see—there can't be any doubt, that a group like *A* consists essentially of one like *B* and one like *C*."—I too say—i.e.

this is how I too express myself—that the group drawn there consists of the two smaller ones; but I don't know whether every group which I should call the same in kind (or form) as the first will necessarily be composed of two groups of the same kind as the smaller ones.—— But I believe that it will probably always be so (perhaps experience has taught me this), and that is why I am willing to accept the rule: I will say that a group is of the form *A* if and only if it can be split up into two groups like *B* and *C*.

68.   And this too is how the drawing (50) works as a proof. "True enough! Two parallelograms together do make this shape!" (That is very much as if I were to say: "Actually, a curve can consist of straight bits.")—I shouldn't have thought it. Thought what? That the parts of this figure yield this figure? No, not *that*. For that doesn't mean anything.—My surprise is only when I think of myself unwittingly fitting the top parallelogram on to the bottom one, and then seeing the result.

69.   And it could be said: What the proof made me realize—*that's* what can surprise me.

70.   For why do I say that the figure (50) makes me realize something any more than this one:

After all it too shews that two bits like that yield a rectangle. "But that isn't interesting", we want to say. And why is it uninteresting?

71.   When one says: "This shape consists of these shapes"—one is thinking of the shape as a fine drawing, a fine frame of this shape, on which, as it were, things which have this shape are stretched. (Compare Plato's conception of properties as ingredients of a thing.)

72. "This shape consists of these shapes. You have shewn the essential property of this shape."—You have shewn me a new *picture*.

It is as if *God* had constructed them like that.——*So we are employing a simile*. The *shape* becomes an ethereal entity which has this shape; it is as if it had been constructed like this once for all (by whoever put the essential properties into things). For if the shape is to be a thing consisting of parts, then the pattern-maker who made the shape is he who also made light and dark, colour and hardness, etc. (Imagine someone asking: "The shape . . . is made up of these parts; who made it? You?")

The word "being" has been used for a sublimed ethereal kind of existence. Now consider the proposition "Red *is*" (e.g.). Of course no one ever uses it; but if I had to invent a use for it all the same, it would be this: as an introductory formula to statements which went on to make use of the word "red". When I pronounce the formula I look at a sample of the colour red.

One is tempted to pronounce a sentence like "red *is*" when one is looking attentively at the colour; that is, in the same *situation* as that in which one observes the existence of a thing (of a leaflike insect, for example).

And I want to say: when one uses the expression, "the proof has taught me—shewn me—that this is the case", one is still using this simile.

73. I could also have said: it is not the property of an object that is ever 'essential', but rather the mark of a concept.

74. "If the form of the group was the same, then it must have had the same aspects, the same possibilities of division. If it has different ones then it isn't the same form; perhaps it somehow made the same

impression on you; but it is the *same form* only if you can divide it up in the same way."

It is as if this expressed the essence of form.—I say, however: if you talk about *essence*—, you are merely noting a convention. But here one would like to retort: there is no greater difference than that between a proposition about the depth of the essence and one about— a mere convention. But what if I reply: to the *depth* that we see in the essence there corresponds the *deep* need for the convention.

Thus if I say: "It's as if this proposition expressed the *essence* of form"—I mean: it is as if this proposition expressed a property of the entity *form*!—and one can say: the entity of which it asserts a property, and which I here call the entity 'form', is the picture which I cannot help having when I hear the word "form".

75. But what sort of properties of the hundred marbles did you unfold, or display?[1]——Well, that these things can be done with them. ——But *what* things? Do you mean that you were able to move them about like that, that they weren't glued on to the table top?——Not so much that, as that they have gone into these formations without any loss or addition.——So you have shewn the physical properties of the row. But why did you use the expression "unfolded"? You would not have spoken of unfolding the properties of a bar of iron by shewing that it melts at such and such a temperature. And mightn't you as well say that you unfolded the properties of our memory for numbers, as the properties of the row (e.g.)? For what you really do *unfold*, or *lay out*, is the row of marbles.—And you shew e.g. that if a row looks thus and thus, or is numbered with roman numerals in this way, it can be brought into that other memorable arrangement in a simple way, and without addition or loss of any marble. But this could after all equally well have been a psychological experiment shewing that you *now* find memorable certain patterns into which 100 spots are made merely by shifting them about.

---

[1] See above, § 36. (Eds.)

"I have shewn what can be done with 100 marbles."—You have shewn that *these* 100 marbles (or those marbles over there), can be laid out in this way. The experiment was one of laying out (as opposed say to one of burning).

And the psychological experiment might for example have shewn how easy it is for you to be deceived: i.e. that you don't notice if marbles are smuggled into or out of the row. One could also say *this*: I have shewn what can be made of a row of 100 spots by means of apparent shifts,—what figures can be got out of it by apparent shifts.—But what did I unfold in this case?

76. Imagine it were said: we unfold the properties of a polygon by using diagonals to take the sides together three at a time. It then proves to be a figure with 24 angles. Do I want to say I have unfolded a property of the 24-angled polygon? No. I want to say I have unfolded a property of this polygon (the one drawn here). I now know that there is drawn here a figure with 24 angles.

Is this an experiment? It shews me e.g. what kind of polygon is drawn here now. What I did can be called an experiment in counting.

But what if I perform such an experiment on a pentagon, which I can already take in at a glance?——Well, let us assume for a moment that I could not take it in at a glance,—which (e.g.) may be the case if it is very big. Then drawing the diagonals would be a way of finding out that this is a pentagon. I could once more say I had unfolded the properties of the polygon drawn here.——Now if I can take it in at a glance then surely nothing *about it* can be changed. It was, perhaps, superfluous to unfold this property, as it is superfluous to count two apples which are before my eyes.

Ought I to say now: "It was an experiment again, but I was certain of the result"? But am I certain of the result in the way I am certain of the result of the electrolysis of a mass of water? No, but in another way. If the electrolysis of the liquid did not yield . . . , I should consider myself crazy, or say that I no longer have any idea what to say.

Imagine I were to say: "Yes, here is a square,—but still let's look and see whether a diagonal divides it into two triangles". Then I draw the diagonal and say: "Yes, here we have two triangles". Here I should be asked: Couldn't you *see* that it could be divided into two triangles? Have you only just convinced yourself that there is a square here; and why trust your eyes now rather than before?

77. Exercises: Number of notes—the internal property of a tune; number of leaves—the external property of a tree. How is this connected with the identity of the concept? (Ramsey.)

78. If someone splits up four marbles into two and two, puts them together again, splits them up again and so on, what is he shewing us? He is impressing on us a physiognomy and a typical alteration of this physiognomy.

79. Think of the possible postures of a puppet. Or suppose you had a chain of, say, ten links, and you were shewing what kind of characteristic (i.e. memorable) figures it can be made into. Let the links be numbered; in this way they become an easily memorable structure even when they lie in a straight line.

So I impress characteristic positions and movements of this chain on you.

If I now say: "Look, *this* can be made of it too" and display it, am I shewing you an experiment?—It may be; I am shewing for example that it can be got into this shape: but that you didn't doubt. And what interests you is not something to do with this individual chain.—But all the same isn't what I am displaying a property of this chain? Certainly: but I only display such movements, such transformations, as are of a memorable kind; and it interests you to *learn* these transformations. But the reason why it interests you is that it is so easy to reproduce them again and again in different objects.

80. The words "look what I can make with it—" are indeed the same as I should use if I were shewing what I can make with a lump of clay, for example. E.g. that I am clever enough to make such things with this lump. In another case: that this material can be dealt with like *this*. Here I should hardly be said to be 'drawing your attention to' the fact that I can do this, or that the material can stand this;—while in the case of the chain one would say: I draw your attention to the fact that this can be done with it.—For you could also have *imagined* it. But of course you can't get to know any property of the material by imagining.

The experimental character disappears when one looks at the process simply as a memorable picture.

81. What I unfold may be said to be the *role* which '100' plays in our calculating system.

82. (I once wrote: "In mathematics process and result are equivalent.")[1]

---

[1] Cf. *Tractatus* 6. 1261: In logic process and result are equivalent. (Eds.)

83.   And yet I feel that it is a property of '100' that it is, or can be, produced in this way. But then how can it be a property of the structure '100' to be produced in this way, if e.g. it didn't get produced in this way at all? If no one multiplied in this way? Surely only if one could say, it is a property of this sign to be the subject of this rule. For example it is the property of '5' to be the subject of the rule '3 + 2 = 5'. For only as the subject of the rule is this number *the* result of the addition of the other numbers.

But suppose I now say: it is a property of the number . . . to be the result of the addition of . . . according to the rule . . . ?—So it is a property of the number that it arises when we apply this rule to these numbers. The question is: should we call it 'application of the rule', if this number were *not* the result? And that is the same question as: "What do you understand by 'application of this rule': what you e.g. do with it (and you may apply it at one time in this way, at another in that), or is 'its application' otherwise explained?"

84.   "It is a property of this number that this process leads to it."— But, mathematically speaking, a process does not lead to it; it is the end of a process (is itself part of the process).

85.   But why do I feel that a property of the row is unfolded, is shewn? —Because I alternately look at what is shewn as essential and as non-essential to the row. Or again: because I think of these properties alternately as external and as internal. Because I alternately take something as a matter of course and find it noteworthy.

86.   "You surely unfold the properties of the hundred marbles

when you shew what can be made of them."—Can be made of them *how*? For, that it *can* be made of them no one has doubted, so the point must be the *kind of way* it is produced from them. But look at that, and see whether it does not perhaps itself presuppose the result.—

For suppose that in *that way* you got one time this and another time a different result; would you accept this? Would you not say: "I must have made a mistake; the *same* kind of way would always have to produce the same result". This shows that you are incorporating the result of the transformation into the kind of way the transforming is done.

87.   Exercise: am I to call it a fact of experience that *this* face turns into *that* through *this* alteration? (How must '*this* face', '*this* alteration' be explained so as to . . . ?)

88.   One says: this division *makes it clear* what kind of row of marbles we have here. Does it make it clear what kind of row it *was* before the division, or does it make it clear what kind of row it is now?

89.   "I can see at a glance how many there are." Well, how many are there? Is the answer "*so* many"?—(pointing to the group of objects). How does the answer go, though? There are '50', or '100', etc.

90.   "The division makes it clear to me what kind of row it is." Well, what kind of row is it? Is the answer "*this* kind"? How does a significant answer run?

91. Now I am surely also unfolding the geometrical properties of this chain, if I display the transformations of another, similarly constructed, chain. What I do, however, does not shew what I can in fact do with the first one, if it in fact should prove inflexible or in some other way physically unsuitable.

So after all I cannot say: I unfold the *properties of this chain*.

92. Can one unfold properties of the chain which it doesn't possess at all?

93. I measure a table; it is one yard long.—Now I put one yardstick up against another yardstick. Am I measuring it by doing that? Am I finding out that the second yardstick is a yard long? Am I making the same experiment of measuring, only with the difference that I am certain of the outcome?

94. And when I put the ruler up against the table, am I always measuring the table; am I not sometimes checking the ruler? And in what does the distinction between the one procedure and the other consist?

95. The experiment of laying a row out may shew us, among other things, how many marbles the row consists of, or on the other hand that we can move these (say) 100 marbles in such-and-such ways.

But when we calculate how the row can be laid out, the calculation shews us what we call a 'transformation merely by laying out'.

96. Examine this proposition: it is not an *empiral fact* that the tangent of a visual curve partly coincides with the curve; and if a figure shews this, then it does not do so as the result of an experiment.

It could also be said: here you can see that segments of a continuous visual curve are straight.——But ought I not to have said:—"Now you call this a 'curve'.—And do you call this little bit of it 'curved' or 'straight'? —Surely you call it a 'straight line'; and the curve contains this bit."

But why should one not use a new name for visual stretches of a curve which themselves exhibit no curvature?

"But the experiment of drawing these lines has shewn that they do not touch at a *point*."——That *they* do not touch at a point? How are '*they*' defined? Or again: can you point to a picture of what it is like for them to 'touch at a point'? Why shouldn't I simply say the experiment has yielded the result that they, i.e. a curved and a straight line, touch one another? For *isn't* this what I call a "touching" of such lines?

97. Let us draw a circle composed of black and white segments getting smaller and smaller.

"Which is the first of these segments—going from left to right—that strikes you as straight?" Here I am making an experiment.

98.   What if someone were to say "Experience tells me that this line

is curved"?—Here it would have to be said that the words "this line" mean the line drawn on the paper. The experiment can actually be made, one can show this line to different people and ask: "What do you see, a straight line or a curved one?"—

But suppose someone were to say: "I am now imagining a curved line", whereupon we tell him: "So you see that the line is a curved one" —what kind of sense would that make?

One can however also say: "I am imagining a circle made of black and white segments; one is big and curved, the ones that come after it keep on getting smaller, the sixth is quite straight". Where is the experiment here?

I can *calculate* in the medium of imagination, but not experiment.

99.   What is the characteristic use of the derivation procedure as a *calculation*—as opposed to its use as an experiment?

We regard the calculation as demonstrating an *internal property* (a property of the *essence*) of the structures. But what does that mean?

The following might serve as a model of an 'internal property':

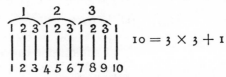

Now when I say: 10 strokes necessarily consist of 3 times 3 strokes and 1 stroke—that does not mean: if there are 10 strokes there, then

they have always got these figures and loops round them.—But if I
put them in, I say that I was only demonstrating the nature of the group
of strokes.—But are you certain that the group did not change while
you were writing those symbols in?—"I don't know; but *a* definite
number of strokes was there; and if it was not 10 then it was another
number, and in that case it simply had different properties.—"

100.   One says: calculation 'unfolds' the property of a hundred.—
What does it really mean to say that 100 consists of 50 and 50? One
says: the contents of the box consist of 50 apples and 50 pears. But if
someone were to say: "The contents of the box consist of 50 apples and
50 apples"—, to begin with we shouldn't know what he meant.—If one
says: "The contents of the box consist of twice 50 apples", this means
either that there are two compartments each containing 50 apples; or
what is in question is, say, a distribution in which each person is
supposed to get 50 apples, and now I hear that two people can be given
their share out of this box.

101.   "The 100 apples in this box consist of 50 and 50"—here the
non-temporal character of 'consist' is important. For it doesn't mean
that *now*, or just for a time, they consist of 50 and 50.

102.   For what is the characteristic mark of 'internal properties'?
That they persist always, unalterably, in the whole that they constitute;
as it were independently of any outside happenings. As the construction of a machine on paper does not break when the machine itself
succumbs to external forces.—Or again, I should like to say that they
are not subject to wind and weather like physical things; rather are they
unassailable, like shadows.

103. When we say: "This proposition follows from that one" here again "to follow" is being used *non-temporally*. (And this shews that the proposition does not express the result of an experiment.)

104. Compare "White is lighter than black". This expression too is non-temporal and it too expresses the existence of an *internal* relation.

105. "But this relation *holds*"—one would like to say. The question is: has this proposition a use—and what use? For at the moment all I know is that a picture comes before my mind as I say it (but that does not guarantee the use for me) and that the words form an English sentence. But it sticks out that the words are being used otherwise here than in the everyday case of a useful statement. (As, say, a wheelwright may notice that the statements that he ordinarily makes about what is circular and straight are of a different kind from what are to be found in Euclid.) For we say: this *object* is lighter than that one, or the colour of this thing is lighter than the colour of that one, and in this case something is lighter now and may be darker later on.

Whence comes the feeling that "white is lighter than black" expresses something about the *essence* of the two colours?—

But is this the right question to ask? For what do we mean by the 'essence' of white or black? We think perhaps of 'the inside', 'the constitution', but this surely makes no sense here. We also say e.g.: "It is part of white to be lighter than . . .".

Is it not like this: the picture of a black and a white patch

serves us *simultaneously* as a paradigm of what we understand by "lighter" and "darker" and as a paradigm for "white" and for "black". Now darkness 'is part of' black *inasmuch as* they are *both* represented by this patch. It is dark *by* being black.—But to put it better: it *is called* "black" and hence in our language "dark" too. That connexion, a connexion of the paradigms and the names, is set up in our language. And our proposition is non-temporal because it only expresses the connexion of the words "white", "black" and "lighter" with a paradigm.

Misunderstandings can be avoided by declaring it nonsense to say: "the colour of this body is brighter than the colour of that one"; what would have to be said is "this body is brighter than that one". I.e. the former way of putting it is excluded from our language.

Whom do we tell "White is lighter than black"? What information does it give?

106.   But can't I believe the geometrical proposition even without a proof, for example on someone else's assurance?—And what does the proposition lose in losing its proof?—Here I presumably ought to ask: "What can I do with it?", for that is the point. *Accepting* the proposition on someone else's assurance—how does my doing this come out? I may for example use it in further calculating operations, or I use it in judging some physical fact. If someone assures me, for example, that 13 × 13 are 196 and I believe him, then I shall be surprised that I can't arrange 196 nuts in 13 rows of 13 each, and I shall perhaps assume that the nuts have increased of themselves.

But I feel a temptation to say: one can't *believe* that 13 × 13 = 196, one can only *accept* this number mechanically from somebody else. But why should I not say I believe it? For is believing it a mysterious act with as it were an underground connexion with the correct calculation? At any rate I can *say*: "I believe it", and act accordingly.

One would like to ask: "What are you doing in believing that $13 \times 13 = 196$?" And the answer may be: Well, that will depend on whether, for instance, you did the sum and made a slip of the pen in doing so,—or whether somebody else did it, but you yourself know how such a calculation is done,—or whether you cannot multiply but know that the product is the number of people to be found in 13 rows of 13 each,—in short it depends on what you can do with the equation $13 \times 13 = 196$. For testing it is doing something with it.

107.   The thing is, if one thinks of an arithmetical equation as the expression of an internal relation, then one would like to say: "You can't believe at all that 13×13 yields *this*, because that isn't a multiplication of 13 by 13, or is not a case of something *yielded*, if 196 comes at the end." But that means that one is not willing to use the word "believe" for the case of a calculation and its result,—or is willing only in the case in which one has a correct calculation before one.

108.   "What are you believing if you believe $13 \times 13 = 196$?"— How deep do you penetrate, one might say, with your belief, into the relation of these numbers? For—one wants to say—you cannot be penetrating all the way, or you could not believe it.

But when have you penetrated into the relations of the numbers? Just while you say that you believe . . . ? You will not take your stand on that—for it is easy to see that this appearance is merely produced by the superficial form of our grammar (as it might be called).

109.   For I want to say: "One can only *see* that $13 \times 13 = 169$, and even that one can't *believe*. And one can—more or less blindly—accept a rule". And what am I doing if I say this? I am *drawing a line* between

the *calculation* with its result (that is to say a particular picture, a particular model), and an experiment with its outcome.

110.   I should like to say: "When I believe that $a \times b = c$—and I do sometimes have such beliefs—do say that I have them—I am not believing the mathematical proposition, for that comes at the end of a proof, is the end of a proof; I am believing that this is the formula that comes in such-and-such a place, which I shall obtain in such-and-such a way, and so on".—And this does sound as if I were penetrating the process of believing such a proposition. Whereas I am merely—in an unskilful fashion—pointing to the *fundamental* difference, together with an apparent similarity, between the roles of an arithmetical proposition and an empirical proposition.

For in certain circumstances I do *say*: "I believe that $a \times b = c$". What do I *mean* by this?—What I *say*!——But what *is* interesting is the question in what circumstances I say this and what is characteristic of them in contrast to those of a statement like: "I believe it is going to rain". For what preoccupies us is this contrast. What we require is a picture of the employment of mathematical propositions and of sentences beginning "I believe that . . .", where a mathematical proposition is the object of belief.

111.   "But you surely don't believe a mathematical proposition." —That means: 'Mathematical proposition' signifies a role for the proposition, a function, in which believing does not occur.

Compare: "If you say: 'I believe that castling takes place in such and such a way', then you are not believing the rule of chess, but believing e.g. that a rule of chess runs like *that*".

112. "One can't *believe* that the multiplication 13 × 13 yields 169, because the result is part of the calculation."—What am I calling "the multiplication 13 × 13"? Only the correct pattern of multiplication, at the end of which comes 169? Or a 'wrong multiplication' too?

How is it established which pattern is the multiplication 13 × 13? —Isn't it *defined* by the rules of multiplication?—But what if, using these rules, you get different results to-day from what all the arithmetic books say? Isn't that possible? —"Not if you apply the rules as *they* do!" Of course not! But that is a mere pleonasm. And where does it say how they are to be applied—and if it does say somewhere, where does it say how *that* is to be applied? And that does not mean only: in what book does it say, but also: in what *head*?—What then is the multiplication 13 × 13—or what am I to take as a guide in multiplying —the rules, or the multiplication that comes in the arithmetic books—— if, that is, these two do not agree?—Well, it never in fact happens that somebody who has learnt to calculate goes on obstinately getting different results, when he does a given multiplication, from what comes in the arithmetic books. But if it should happen, then we should declare him abnormal, and take no further account of his calculation.

113. "But am I not compelled, then, to go the way I do in a chain of inferences?"—Compelled? After all I can presumably go as I choose!—"But if you want to remain in accord with the rules you *must* go this way."—Not at all, I call *this* 'accord'.—"Then you have changed the meaning of the word 'accord', or the meaning of the rule."—No;—who says what 'change' and 'remaining the same' mean here?

However many rules you give me—I give a rule which justifies *my* employment of your rules.

114. We might also say: when we *follow* the laws of inference (inference-rules) then following always involves interpretation too.

115. "But you surely can't suddenly make a different application of the law now!"—If my reply is: "Oh yes of course, *that* is how I was applying it!" or: "Oh! *That's* how I ought to have applied it—!"; then I am playing your game. But if I simply reply: "Different?—But this surely *isn't* different!"—what will you do? That is: somebody may reply like a rational person and yet not be playing our game.[1]

116. "Then according to you everybody could continue the series as he likes; and so infer *any*how!" In that case we shan't call it "continuing the series" and also presumably not "inference". And thinking and inferring (like counting) is of course bounded for us, not by an arbitrary definition, but by natural limits corresponding to the body of what can be called the role of thinking and inferring in our life.

For we are at one over this, that the laws of inference do not compel him to say or to write such and such like rails compelling a locomotive. And if you say that, while he may indeed *say* it, still he can't *think* it, then I am only saying that that means, not: try as he may he can't think it, but: it is for us an essential part of 'thinking' that—in talking, writing, etc.—he makes *this sort* of transition. And I say further that the line between what we include in 'thinking' and what we no longer include in 'thinking' is no more a hard and fast one than the line between what is still and what is no longer called "regularity".

Nevertheless the laws of inference can be said to compel us; in the

---

[1] The last sentence added in March, 1944. (Eds.)

same sense, that is to say, as other laws in human society. The clerk who infers as in (17) *must* do it like that; he would be punished if he inferred differently. If you draw different conclusions you do indeed get into conflict, e.g. with society; and also with other practical consequences.

And there is even something in saying: he can't *think* it. One is trying e.g. to say: he can't fill it with personal content; he can't really *go along with it*—personally, with his intelligence. It is like when one says: this sequence of notes makes no sense, I can't sing it with expression. I cannot *respond* to it. Or, what comes to the same thing here: I don't respond to it.

"If he says it"—one might say—"he can only say it without thinking". And here it merely needs to be noticed that 'thoughtless' talk and other talk do indeed sometimes differ as regards what goes on in the talker, his images, sensations and so on while he is talking, but that this accompaniment does not constitute the thinking, and the lack of it is not enough to constitute 'thoughtlessness'.

117.   In what sense is logical argument a compulsion?—"After all you grant *this* and *this*; so you must also grant *this*!" That is the way of compelling someone. That is to say, one can in fact compel people to admit something in this way.—Just as one can e.g. compel someone to go over there by pointing over there with a bidding gesture of the hand.

Suppose in such a case I point with two fingers at once in different directions, thus leaving it open to the man to go in which of the two directions he likes,—and another time I point in only *one* direction; then this can also be expressed by saying: my first order did not compel him to go just in *one* direction, while the second one did. But this is a statement to tell us what kind of orders I gave; not the way they operate, not whether they do in fact compel such-and-such a person, i.e. whether he obeys them.

118.   It looked at first as if these considerations were meant to shew that 'what seems to be a logical compulsion is in reality only a psychological one'—only here the question arose: am I acquainted with both kinds of compulsion, then?!

Imagine that people used the expression: "The law § . . . punishes a murderer with death". Now this could only mean: this law runs so and so. That form of expression, however, might force itself on us, because the law is an instrument when the guilty man is brought to punishment.—Now we talk of 'inexorability' in connexion with people who punish. And here it might occur to us to say: "The law is *inexorable*—men can let the guilty go, the law executes him". (And even: "the law *always* executes him".)—What is the use of such a form of expression?—In the first instance, this proposition only says that such-and-such is to be found in the law, and human beings sometimes do not go by the law. Then, however, it does give us a picture of a single inexorable judge, and many lax judges. That is why it serves to express respect for the law. Finally, the expression can also be so used that a law is called inexorable when it makes no provision for a possible act of grace, and in the opposite case it is perhaps called 'discriminating'.

Now we talk of the 'inexorability' of logic; and think of the laws of logic as inexorable, still more inexorable than the laws of nature. We now draw attention to the fact that the word "inexorable" is used in a variety of ways. There correspond to our laws of logic very general facts of daily experience. They are the ones that make it possible for us to keep on demonstrating those laws in a very simple way (with ink on paper for example). They are to be compared with the facts that make measurement with a yardstick easy and useful. This suggests the use of precisely these laws of inference, and now it is *we* that are inexorable in applying these laws. Because we '*measure*'; and it is part of measuring for everybody to have the same measures. Besides this, however, inexorable, i.e. *unambiguous* rules of inference can be distinguished from ones that are not unambiguous, I mean from such as leave an alternative open to us.

119. "But I can infer only what actually does follow."—That is to
say: what the logical machine really does produce. The logical machine
—that would be an all-pervading ethereal mechanism.—We must give
warning against this picture.

Imagine a material harder and more rigid than any other. But if a
rod made of this stuff is brought out of the horizontal into the vertical,
it shrinks; or it bends when set upright and at the same time it is so hard
that there is no other way of bending it.—(A mechanism made of this
stuff, say a crank, connecting-rod and crosshead. The different way
the crosshead would move.)

Or again: a rod bends if one brings a certain mass near it; but it is
completely rigid in face of all forces that we subject it to. Imagine that
the guide-rails of the crosshead bend and then straighten again as the
crank approaches and retreats. My assumption would be, however,
that no particular external force is necessary to cause this. This
behaviour of the rails would give an impression as of something alive.

When we say: "If the parts of the mechanism were quite rigid, they
would move so and so", what is the criterion for their being quite
rigid? Is it that they resist certain forces? Or that they do move so
and so?

Suppose I say: "This is the law of motion of the crosshead (the
correlation of its position and the position of the crank perhaps) when
the lengths of the crank and connecting-rod remain constant". This
presumably means: If the crank and crosshead keep these relative
positions, I say that the length of the connecting-rod remains constant.

120. "If the parts were perfectly rigid this is how they would
move"; is that a hypothesis? It seems not. For when we say: "Kinematics describes the movements of the mechanism on the assumption
that its parts are completely rigid", on the one hand we are admitting
that this assumption never squares with reality, and on the other hand it

is not supposed to be in any way doubtful that completely rigid parts would move in this way. But whence this certainty? The question here is not really one of certainty but of something stipulated by us. We do not *know* that bodies would move in these ways if (by such and such criteria) they were quite rigid; but (in certain circumstances) we should certainly *call* 'rigid' such parts as did move in those ways.— Always remember in such a case that geometry (or kinematics) does not specify any method of measuring when it talks about the same, or constant, length.

When therefore we call kinematics the theory, say, of the movement of perfectly rigid parts of a mechanism, on the one hand this contains an indication as to (mathematical) method—we stipulate certain distances as the lengths of machine parts that do not alter—and on the other hand an *indication* about the application of the calculus.

121. The hardness of the logical *must*. What if one were to say: the *must* of kinematics is much harder than the causal *must* compelling a machine part to move like *this* when another moves like *this*?—

Suppose we represented the movement of the 'perfectly rigid' mechanism by a cinematographic picture, a cartoon film. Suppose this picture were said to be *perfectly hard*, and this meant that we had taken this picture as our method of description—whatever the facts may be, however the parts of the real mechanism may bend or expand.

122. The machine (its structure) as symbolizing its action: the action of a machine—I might say at first—seems to be there in it from the start. What does that mean?—

If we know the machine, everything else, that is its movement, seems to be already completely determined.

"We talk as if these parts *could* only move in this way, as if they could not do anything else."

How is this—do we forget the possibility of their bending, breaking off, melting, and so on? Yes; in *many* cases we don't think of that at all. We use a machine, or the picture of a machine, to symbolize a particular action of the machine. For instance, we give someone such a picture and assume that he will derive the movement of the parts from it. (Just as we can give someone a number by telling him that it is the twenty-fifth in the series 1, 4, 9, 16, ...)

"The machine's action seems to be in it from the start" means: you are inclined to compare the future movements of the machine in definiteness to objects which are already lying in a drawer and which we then take out.

But we do not say this kind of thing when we are concerned with predicting the actual behaviour of a machine. Here we do not in general forget the possibility of a distortion of the parts and so on.

We do talk like that, however, when we are wondering at the way we can use a machine to symbolize a given way of moving—since it can also move in quite *different* ways.

Now, we might say that a machine, or the picture of it, is the first of a series of pictures which we have learnt to derive from this one.

But when we remember that the machine could also have moved differently, it readily seems to us as if the way it moves must be contained in the machine-as-symbol far more determinately than in the actual machine. As if it were not enough here for the movements in question to be empirically determined in advance, but they had to be really—in a mysterious sense—already *present*. And it is quite true: the movement of the machine-as-symbol is predetermined in a different sense from that in which the movement of any given actual machine is predetermined.

123.   "It is as if we could grasp the whole use of the word in a flash."
Like *what* e.g.?—Can't the use—in a certain sense—be grasped in a
flash? And in *what* sense can it not? The point is, that it is as if we
could 'grasp it in a flash' in yet another and much more direct sense
than that.—But have you a model for this? No. It is just that this
expression suggests itself to us. As the result of crossing similes.

124.   You have no model of this superlative fact, but you are
seduced into using a *super-expression*.

125.   When does one have the thought: the possible movements of
a machine are already there in it in some mysterious way?—Well, when
one is doing philosophy. And what leads us into thinking that? The
way we talk about machines. We say, for example, that a machine *has*
(*possesses*) such-and-such possibilities of movement; we speak of the
ideally rigid machine which *can* only move in such-and-such a way.——
What is this *possibility* of movement? It is not the *movement*, but it does
not seem to be the mere physical *conditions* for moving either, e.g.
that there is a certain space between socket and pin, the pin not fitting
too tight in the socket. For while this is the *empirical* condition for
movement, one could also imagine it to be otherwise. The possibility
of a movement is, rather, supposed to be a shadow of the movement
itself. But do you know of such a shadow? And by a shadow I do
not mean some picture of the movement; for such a picture would
not necessarily be a picture of just *this* movement. But the possibility
of this movement must be the possibility of just this movement. (See
how high the seas of language run here!)
   The waves subside as soon as we ask ourselves: how do we use the

phrase "possibility of movement" when we are talking about a given machine?—But then where did our queer ideas come from? Well, I shew you the possibility of a movement, say by means of a *picture* of the movement: 'so possibility is something which is like reality'. We say: "It isn't moving yet, but it already has the possibility of moving"— 'so possibility is something very near reality'. Though we may doubt whether such-and-such physical conditions make this movement possible, we never discuss whether *this* is the possibility of this or of that movement: 'so the possibility of the movement stands in a unique relation to the movement itself; closer than that of a picture to its subject'; for it can be doubted whether a picture is the picture of this thing or that. We say "Experience will shew whether this gives the pin this possibility of movement", but we do not say "Experience will shew whether this is the possibility of this movement": 'so it is not an empirical fact that this possibility is the possibility of precisely this movement'.

We pay attention to the expressions we use concerning these things; we do not understand them, however, but misinterpret them. When we do philosophy we are like savages, primitive people, who hear the expressions of civilized men, put a false interpretation on them, and then draw queer conclusions from it.

Imagine someone not understanding our past tense: "he has had it".—He says: " 'he *has*'—that's present, so the proposition says that in some sense the past is present."

126. "But I don't mean that what I do now (in grasping a sense) determines the future use *causally* and as a matter of experience, but that in a *queer* way, the use itself is in some sense present." But of course it is, 'in *some* sense'! (And don't we also say: "the events of the years that are past are present to me"?) Really the only thing wrong with what you say is the expression "in a queer way". The rest is

correct; and the sentence only seems queer when one imagines a different language-game for it from the one in which we actually use it. (Someone once told me that as a child he had wondered how a tailor *'sewed a dress'*—he thought this meant that a dress was produced *just by sewing*, by sewing one thread on to another.)

127.   In our failure to understand the use of a word we take it as the expression of a queer *process*. (As we think of time as a queer medium, of the mind as a queer kind of being.)

The difficulty arises in all these cases through mixing up "is" and "is called".

128.   The connexion which is not supposed to be a causal, experiential one, but much stricter and harder, so rigid even, that the one thing somehow already *is* the other, is always a connexion in grammar.

129.   How do I know that this picture is my image of the *sun*?—I *call* it an image of the sun. I *use* it as a picture of the *sun*.

130.   "It's as if we could grasp the whole use of the word in a flash." —And that is just what we say we do. That is to say: we sometimes describe what we do in these words. But there is nothing astonishing, nothing queer, about what happens. It becomes queer when we are led to think that the future development must in some way already be

present in the act of grasping the use and yet isn't present.—For we say that there isn't any doubt that we understand the word . . ., and on the other hand its meaning lies in its use. There is no doubt that I now want to play *chess*, but chess is the game it is in virtue of *all its rules* (and so on). Don't I know, then, which game I wanted to play until I *have* played it? Or are all the rules contained in my act of intending? Is it experience that tells me that this sort of play usually follows this act of intention? So is it impossible for me to be certain what I am intending to do? And if that is nonsense, what kind of super-strong connexion exists between the act of intending and the thing intended?——Where is the connexion effected between the sense of the expression "Let's play a game of chess" and all the rules of the game?—Well, in the list of rules of the game, in the teaching of it, in the day-to-day practice of playing.

131.   The laws of logic are indeed the expression of 'thinking habits' but also of the habit of *thinking*. That is to say they can be said to shew: how human beings think, and also *what* human beings call "thinking".

132.   Frege calls it 'a law about what men take for true' that 'It is impossible for human beings . . . to recognize an object as different from itself".[1]—When I think of this as impossible for me, then I think of *trying* to do it. So I look at my lamp and say: "This lamp is different from itself". (But nothing stirs.) It is not that I see it is false, I can't do anything with it at all. (Except when the lamp shimmers in sunlight; then I can quite well use the sentence to

---

[1] *Grundgesezte der Arithmetik* I, xviii. (Eds.)

express that.) One can even get oneself into a thinking-cramp, in which one *does* someone trying to think the impossible and not succeed-ing. Just as one can also *do* someone trying (vainly) to draw an object to himself from a distance by mere willing (in doing this one makes e.g. certain faces, as if one were trying, by one's expression, to give the thing to understand that it should come here.)

133. The propositions of logic are 'laws of thought', 'because they bring out the essence of human thinking'—to put it more correctly: because they bring out, or shew, the essence, the technique, of thinking. They shew what thinking is and also shew kinds of thinking.

134. Logic, it may be said, shews us what we understand by 'proposition' and by 'language'.

135. Imagine the following queer possibility: we have always gone wrong up to now in multiplying 12 × 12. True, it is unintelligible how this can have happened, but it has happened. So everything worked out in this way is wrong!——But what does it matter? It does not matter at all!—And in that case there must be something wrong in our idea of the truth and falsity of arithmetical propositions.

136. But then, is it impossible for me to have gone wrong in my calculation? And what if a devil deceives me, so that I keep on over-looking something however often I go over the sum step by step? So that if I were to awake from the enchantment I should say: "Why, was I blind?"—But what difference does it make for me to 'assume'

this? I might say: "Yes to be sure, the calculation is wrong—but that is how I calculate. And this is what I now call adding, and this 'the sum of these two numbers'."

137.   Imagine someone bewitched so that he calculated:

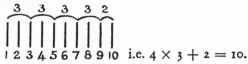

Now he is to apply this calculation. He takes 3 nuts four times over, and then 2 more, and he divides them among 10 people and each one gets *one* nut; for he shares them out in a way corresponding to the loops of the calculation, and as often as he gives someone a second nut it disappears.

138.   One might also say: in a proof you advance from one proposition to another; but do you also accept a check on whether you have gone right?—Or do you merely say "It *must* be right" and measure everything else by the proposition you arrive at?

139.   For if *that* is how it is, then you are only advancing from one picture to another.

140.   It might be practical to measure with a ruler which had the property of shrinking to, say, half its length when it was taken from this room to that. A property which would make it useless as a ruler in other circumstances.

It might be practical, in certain circumstances, to leave numbers out when you were counting a set: to count them: 1, 2, 4, 5, 7, 8, 10.

141.   What goes on when someone tries to make a shape coincide with its mirror-image by moving it about in the plane, and does not succeed? He puts them one on top of the other in various ways; looks at the parts that don't coincide; is dissatisfied; says perhaps: "But it *must* work", and puts the figures together again in another way.

What happens when someone tries to lift a weight and does not succeed because the weight is too heavy? He assumes such and such a posture, takes hold of the weight, tenses such and such muscles, and then lets go and perhaps shews dissatisfaction.

How does the geometrical, logical impossibility of the first task come out?

"Well, he could surely have shewn, in a picture or in some other way, what the thing he is attempting in the second case looks like." But he asserts that he can do that in the first case too by putting two similar *congruent* figures together so that they coincide.—What are we to say now? That the two examples are different? But so are the picture and the reality in the second case.

142.   What we are supplying are really remarks on the natural history of man: not curiosities however, but rather observations on facts which no one has doubted and which have only gone unremarked because they are always before our eyes.

143.   We teach someone a method of sharing out nuts among

people; a part of this method is multiplying two numbers in the decimal system.

We teach someone to build a house; and at the same time how he is to obtain a sufficient quantity of material, boards, say; and for this purpose a technique of calculation. The technique of calculation is part of the technique of house-building.

People pile up logs and sell them, the piles are measured with a ruler, the measurements of length, breadth and height multiplied together, and what comes out is the number of pence which have to be asked and given. They do not know 'why' it happens like this; they simply do it like this: that is how it is done.—Do these people not calculate?

144. If somebody calculates like this must he utter any 'arithmetical *proposition*'? Of course, we teach children the multiplication tables in the form of little *sentences*, but is that essential? Why shouldn't they simply: *learn to calculate*? And when they can do so haven't they learnt arithmetic?

145. But in that case how is the *foundation* of a calculating procedure related to the calculation itself?

146. "Yes, I understand that this proposition follows from that." —Do I understand *why* it follows or do I only understand *that* it follows?

147. Suppose I had said: those people pay for wood on the *ground of calculation*; they accept a calculation as proof that they have to pay so much.—Well, that is simply a description of their procedure (of their behaviour).

148. Those people—we should say—sell timber by cubic measure ——but are they right in doing so? Wouldn't it be more correct to sell it by weight—or by the time that it took to fell the timber—or by the labour of felling measured by the age and strength of the woodsman? And why should they not hand it over for a price which is independent of all this: each buyer pays the same however much he takes (they have found it possible to live like that). And is there anything to be said against simply giving the wood away?

149. Very well; but what if they piled the timber in heaps of arbitrary, varying height and then sold it at a price proportionate to the area covered by the piles?

And what if they even justified this with the words: "Of course, if you buy more timber, you must pay more"?

150. How could I shew them that—as I should say—you don't really buy more wood if you buy a pile covering a bigger area?—I should, for instance, take a pile which was small by their ideas and, by laying the logs around, change it into a 'big' one. This *might* convince them—but perhaps they would say: "Yes, now it's a *lot* of wood and costs more"—and that would be the end of the matter.—We should presumably say in this case: they simply do not mean the same by "a lot of wood" and "a little wood" as we do; and they have a quite different system of payment from us.

151. (A society acting in this way would perhaps remind us of the Wise Men of Gotham.)

152. Frege says in the preface to the *Grundgesetze der Arithmetik*[1]: "... here we have a hitherto unknown kind of insanity"—but he never said what this 'insanity' would really be like.

153. What does people's agreement about accepting a structure as a proof consist in? In the fact that they use words as *language*? As what we call "language".

Imagine people who used money in transactions; that is to say coins, looking like our coins, which are made of gold and silver and stamped and are also handed over for goods——but each person gives just what he pleases for the goods, and the merchant does not give the customer more or less according to what he pays. In short this money, or what looks like money, has among them a quite different role from among us. We should feel much less akin to these people than to people who are not yet acquainted with money at all and practise a primitive kind of barter.—"But these people's coins will surely also have some purpose!"—Then has everything that one does a purpose? Say religious actions—.

It is perfectly possible that we should be inclined to call people who behaved like this insane. And yet we don't call everyone insane who acts similarly within the forms of our culture, who uses words 'without purpose'. (Think of the coronation of a King.)

154. Perspicuity is part of proof. If the process by means of which I get a result were not surveyable, I might indeed make a note that this number is what comes out—but what fact is this supposed to confirm for me? I don't know 'what is *supposed* to come out'.

---

[1] ibid., I, XVI.

155.   Would it be possible that people should go through one of
our calculations to-day and be satisfied with the conclusions, but
to-morrow want to draw quite different conclusions, and other ones
again on another day?

Why, isn't it imaginable that it should *regularly* happen like that:
that when we make *this* transition one time, the next time, '*just for
that reason*', we make a different one, and therefore (say) the next
time the first one again? (As if in some language the colour which is
called "red" one time is for that reason called another name the next
time, and "red" again the next time after that and so on; people might
find this natural. It might be called a need for variety.)

[*Note in margin:* Are our laws of inference eternal and immutable?]

156.   Isn't it like this: so long as one thinks it can't be otherwise,
one draws logical conclusions. This presumably means: so long as
such-and-such is not brought in question at all.

The steps which are not brought in question are logical inferences.
But the reason why they are not brought in question is not that they
'certainly correspond to the truth'—or something of the sort,—no, it
is just this that is called 'thinking', 'speaking', 'inferring', 'arguing'.
There is not any question at all here of some correspondence between
what is said and reality; rather is logic *antecedent* to any such correspondence; in the same sense, that is, as that in which the establishment of
a method of measurement is *antecedent* to the correctness or incorrectness of a statement of length.

157.   Is it experimentally settled whether one proposition can
be derived from another?—It looks as if it were. For I write down
certain sequences of signs, am guided in doing so by certain paradigms
—in doing which it is indeed essential that no sign should get over-

looked or otherwise lost—and of what I get in this procedure I say: it follows.——One argument against this is: If 2 and 2 apples add up to only 3 apples, i.e. if there are 3 apples there after I have put down two and again two, I don't say: "So after all 2 + 2 are not always 4"; but "Somehow one must have gone".

158.   But how am I making an experiment when I merely *follow* a proof which has already been written out? It might be said: "When you look at this chain of transformations,—*don't they strike you as being in agreement* with the paradigms?".

159.   So if this is to be called an experiment it is presumably a psychological one. For the appearance of agreement may of course be founded on sense-deception. And so it sometimes is when we make a slip in calculating.

One also says: "This is my result". And what shews that this is *my* result is presumably an experiment.

160.   One might say: the result of the experiment is that at the end, having reached the result of the proof, I say with conviction: "Yes, that's right".

161.   Is a calculation an experiment?—Is it an experiment for me to get out of bed in the morning? But might it not be an experiment,—to shew whether I have the strength to raise myself up after so and so many hours' sleep?

And how does the action fall short of being this experiment?—Merely by not being carried out with this purpose, i.e. in connexion with an investigation of this kind. It is the use that is made of something that turns it into an experiment.

Is an experiment in which we observe the acceleration of a freely falling body a physical experiment, or is it a psychological one shewing what people see in such circumstances?—Can't it be either? Doesn't it depend on its *surroundings*: on what we do with it, say about it?

162.   If a proof is conceived as an experiment, at any rate the result of the experiment is not what is called the result of the proof. The result of the calculation is the proposition with which it concludes; the result of the experiment is that from these propositions, by means of these rules, I was led to this proposition.

163.   But our interest does not attach to the fact that such-and-such (or all) human beings have been led this way by these rules (or have gone this way); we take it as a matter of course that people—'if they can think correctly'—go *this* way. We have now been given a *road*, as it were by means of the footsteps of those who have gone this way. And the traffic now proceeds on this road—to various purposes.

164.   Certainly experience tells me how the calculation comes out; but that is not all there is to my accepting it.

165.   I learned empirically that this came out this time, that it usually does come out; but does the proposition of mathematics say

that? I learned empirically that this is the road I travelled. But is *that* the mathematical statement?—What does it say, though? What relation has it to these empirical propositions? The mathematical proposition has the dignity of a rule.

So much is true when it's said that mathematics is logic: its moves are from rules of our language to other rules of our language. And this gives it its peculiar solidity, its unassailable position, set apart.

(Mathematics deposited among the standard measures.)

166. What, then—does it just twist and turn about within these rules?—It forms ever new rules: is always building new roads for traffic; by extending the network of the old ones.

167. But then doesn't it need a sanction for this? Can it extend the network *arbitrarily*? Well, I could say: a mathematician is always inventing new forms of description. Some, stimulated by practical needs, others, from aesthetic needs,—and yet others in a variety of ways. And here imagine a landscape gardener designing paths for the layout of a garden; it may well be that he draws them on a drawing-board merely as ornamental strips without the slightest thought of someone's sometime walking on them.

168. The mathematician is an inventor, not a discoverer.

169. We know by experience that when we count anything off on the fingers of one hand, or on some group of things that looks like this | | | | |, and say: I, you, I, you, etc., the first word is also the last.

"But doesn't it *have* to be like that, then?"——Well, is it unimaginable for someone to see the group | | | | | (e.g.) as the group | | ‖ | | with the two middle strokes fused, and should accordingly count the middle stroke twice? (True, it is not the usual case.—)

170. But how about when I draw someone's attention for the first time to the fact that the result of counting off is determined in advance by the beginning, and he understands and says: "Yes, of course,— that's how it has to be". What sort of knowledge is this?—He e.g. drew himself the schema:

$$\text{I} \quad \text{Y} \quad \text{I} \quad \text{Y} \quad \text{I}$$
$$\vert \quad \vert \quad \vert \quad \vert \quad \vert$$

and his reasoning is e.g.: "*That*'s what it's like when I count off.—So it has to. . . ."

(171. Connected with this: We should sometimes like to say "There must surely be a reason why—in a movement of a sonata, for example— just *this* theme follows that one." What we should acknowledge as a reason would be a certain relation between the themes, a kinship, a contrast or the like.—But we may even construct such a relation: an operation, so to speak, that produces the one theme from the other; but this serves only when this relation is one that we are familiar with. So it is as if the sequence of these themes had to correspond to a paradigm that is already present in us.

Similarly one might say of a picture that shews two human figures: "There must be a reason why precisely *these* two faces make such an impression upon us." That means: we should like to find this impression from the pair of faces again somewhere else—in another region.— But could we?

One might ask: what arrangement of themes together has a *point*, and what has *no* point? Or again: *Why* has this arrangement a point and *this* one none? That may not be easy to say! Often we may say: "This one corresponds to a gesture, this one doesn't.")[1]

---

[1] This remark came at the end of the cut-up typescript which is the source of this Part I and the following Appendix I. (Cf. Preface, p. 33). But its place in the collection of cuttings is not quite clear—and for that reason the editors did not include the remark in the first edition. It is uncertain whether the words "Connected with this" relate to the preceding remarks 169 and 170. The remark was put between brackets in the typescript too. (Eds.)

APPENDIX I
(1933–1934)

1. Might I not say that two words—let's write them "non" and "ne"—had the same meaning, that they were both negation signs—but

$$\text{non non } p = p$$

and

$$\text{ne ne } p = \text{ne } p$$

(In spoken language a double negation very often means a negation.) But then why do I call them both "negations"? What have they in common with one another? Well, it is clear that a great part of their employment is common. But that does not solve our problem. For we should after all like to say: "It must also hold for both of them that the double negation is an affirmation, at least if the doubling is thought of appropriately". But *how?*—Well, as for example we expressed it using brackets:

$$(\text{ne ne})p = \text{ne } p, \qquad \text{ne}(\text{ne } p) = p$$

We think at once of an analogous case in geometry: "Two half turns added together cancel one another out," "Two half turns added together make one half turn."

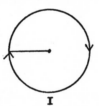

I   II

It just depends how we add them. (Whether we put them side by side or one after the other.)

2. (Here we stumble on a remarkable and characteristic phenomenon in philosophical investigation: The difficulty—I might say—isn't one

of finding the solution; it is one of recognizing something as the solution. We have already said everything. Not something that follows from this; no, just *this* is the solution!

This, I believe, hangs together with our wrongly expecting an explanation; whereas a description is the solution of the difficulty, if we give it the right place in our consideration. If we dwell upon it and do not try to get beyond it.)

3. "That's already all there is to say about it." *Taking* "non non p" as the negation of the negated proposition in the particular case is, say, giving an explanation of the kind "non non p = non (non p)".

4. "If 'ne' is a negation, then 'ne ne p' must be the same as p, if only it is taken appropriately."

"If one takes 'ne ne p' as negating p, one must be taking the doubling in a different way."

One would like to say: "'Doubling' *means* something different in this case and *that's* why it yields a negation here;" and so, its yielding a negation here is the consequence of this difference of nature. "Now I mean it as a strengthening", one would say. *We* use the expression of meaning to assess meaning.[1]

5. When I was uttering the double negation, what may it have

---

[1] Several alternatives to the last sentence were indicated in the MS. "We fix our eye on the expression of meaning." "*We* investigate the expression of meaning." "We focus on the *expression* of meaning." "Focus on the expression of meaning." (Eds.)

consisted in that I meant it as a strengthening? In the circumstances in which I use the expression, perhaps in the image that comes before my mind as I use it or which I employ, in my tone of voice (as I can even reproduce the brackets in "ne (ne p) in my tone of voice). In that case, meaning the doubling as a strengthening corresponds to pronouncing it as a strengthening. The activity of meaning the doubling as a cancellation was e.g., putting brackets.—"Yes, but these brackets themselves may have a variety of roles; for who says that they are to be taken as brackets in the ordinary sense in 'non (non p)' and not for example the first as a hyphen between the two 'non's and the second as the full stop for the sentence? No one says it. And haven't you yourself replaced your conception by words? What the brackets mean will come out in their use; and in another sense perhaps lies in the rhythm of the optical impression of 'non (non p)'.

6.   Am I now to say: the meanings of "non" and "ne" are *somewhat* different? That they are different species of negation?—That no one would say. For it would be objected, in that case won't "do not go into this room" perhaps fail to mean exactly the same as usual if we set up the rule that "not not" is to be used as a negation?—But this might be countered: "If the two propositions 'ne p' and 'non p' say exactly the same, then how can 'ne ne' not mean exactly the same as 'non non'?" But here we are presupposing a symbolism—i.e., we are taking it as a model—in which from "ne p = non p" it follows that "ne" and "non" are used in the same way in all cases.

Turning through 180° and negation are in fact the same in the particular case, and the application of 'non non p = p' is of the same kind as the application of a particular geometry.

7. What does one mean by saying: 'ne ne *p*', even if by convention it means 'ne *p*', *could* also be used as a cancelled negation?—One would like to say: "with the meaning that we have given it, 'ne' could cancel itself, if only we apply it right." What does one mean by that? (The two half turns in the same direction could cancel one another, if they are put together appropriately.) "The *movement* of the negation 'not' is capable of cancelling itself." But where is this movement? One would like of course to speak of a mental movement of negation, for the execution of which the sign 'ne' merely gives the signal.

8. We can imagine human beings with a 'more primitive' logic, in which only for certain sentences is there anything corresponding to our negation: say for such as contain no negation. In the language of these people, then, a sentence like "He is going into this house" could be negated; but they would understand a doubling of the negation as mere repetition, never as cancelling the negation.

9. The question whether negation had the same meaning for these people as for us would be analogous to the question whether the digit '2' means the same, for people whose number series ends with 5, as it does for us.

10. Suppose I were to ask: When we pronounce the proposition "this rod is 1 metre long" and 'here is 1 soldier', is it quite apparent to us that "1" has different meanings here?—It is not at all apparent. Especially when we say a sentence like: "On every 1 metre there stands 1 soldier, every 2 metres 2 soldiers, and so on." Asked, "Do you

mean the same by the two ones?" we should reply: "of course I mean the same:—*one*" (perhaps holding up one finger).

11.   Whoever calls " $\sim \sim p = p$ " (or again " $\sim \sim p \equiv p$ ") a "necessary proposition of logic" (not a stipulation about the method of presentation that we adopt) also has a tendency to say that this proposition proceeds from the meaning of negation. When double negation is used as negation in some dialect, as in "he found nothing nowhere", we are inclined to say: *really* that would mean that he found something everywhere. Let us consider what this "really" means.

12.   Suppose we had two systems for measuring length; in both a length is expressed by a numeral, followed by a word that gives the system of measurement. One system designates a length as "*n* foot" and foot is a unit of length in the ordinary sense; in the other system a length is designated by "*n* W" and

$$1 \text{ foot} = 1 \text{ W}$$

But: 2 W = 4 foot,   3 W = 9 foot and so on.

So the sentence "this post is 1 W long" says the same as "this post is 1 foot long".
Question: Have "W" and "foot" the same meaning in these two sentences?

13.   The question is framed wrong. One sees this when we express identity of meaning by means of an equation. Then the question has to run: "Does W = foot or not?"—The sentences in which these signs occur disappear in this way of looking at it. Of course in this terminology one can just as little ask whether "is" means the same as "is";

but one *can* ask whether "ε" means the same as "=". What we *said* was: 1 foot = 1 W, but: foot ≠ W.

14. Has "ne" the same meaning as "non"?—Can I replace "non" by "ne"?—"Well, I can in certain places, but not in others."—But I wasn't asking about that. My question was: can one, without any further qualification, use "ne" in place of "non"?—No.

15. "'ne' and 'non' mean exactly the same in this case."—And *what* do they mean?—"Well, one is *not* to do such and such."—But by saying this you have only said that in this case ne˙ p = non p and that we don't deny.

When you explain: ne ne p = ne p, non non p = p, you are indeed using the two words in different ways; and if one holds on to the conception that what they yield in certain combinations 'depends' on their meaning, or the meaning that they carry around with them, then one has to say that they must have different meanings if, compounded in the same way, they may yet yield different results.

16. One would like to speak of the *function* of the word, of what it does, in this sentence. As of the function of a lever in a machine. But what does this function consist in? How does it come to light? For there isn't anything hidden, is there? We see the whole sentence all right. The function must reveal itself in the course of the calculus.

But one wants to say: "'non' *does* the same with the proposition 'p' as 'ne' does: it reverses it". But that is just "non p = ne p" in other words.[1] Over and over the thought, the picture, that what we

---

[1] [Marginal note:] What is meant by "ne non p" and "non ne p"?

see of the sign is only the exterior of some inner thing in which the real operations of meaning run on.

17.   But if the use of a sign is its meaning is it not remarkable that I say the word "is" gets used with two different meanings (as 'ε' and '$=$') and should not like to say that its meaning is its use as copula and as sign of identity?

One would like to say that these two kinds of use do not yield a *single* meaning; the personal union through the same word is inessential, is mere accident.

18.   But how can I decide what is an essential and what is an inessential, accidental feature of the notation? Is there a reality behind the notation, then, which its grammar is aiming at?

Think of a similar case in a game: In draughts a king is distinguished by putting two pieces one on top of the other. Won't one say that it is inessential to draughts that this is the way a king is distinguished?

19.   Let us say: the meaning of a piece (a figure) is its role in the game.—Now before the start of any chess-game let it be decided by lot which of the players gets white. For this purpose one player holds a king in each closed hand and the other chooses one of the hands at random. Will it be reckoned as part of the role of the king in chess that it is used for drawing by lot?

20. Thus even in a game I am inclined to distinguish between essential and inessential. The game, I should like to say, does not just have rules; it has a point.

21. What is the word the same for? For in the calculus we make no use of this identity! What do both players have the same pieces for? But what does "making use of the identity" mean here? For isn't it a use, if we do use the same word?

22. Here it looks now as if the use of the same word, the same piece, had a *purpose*—if the identity was not accidental, not inessential. And as if the purpose were that one should recognize the piece and be able to tell how to play. Is it a physical or a logical possibility that is in question here? If the latter, then the identity of the pieces does indeed belong to the game.

23. The game is supposed to be defined by the rules! So if a rule of the game prescribes that the kings are to be taken for choosing by lot before the game starts then that belongs essentially to the game. What objection might be made to this?—That one does not see the point of this rule. As, say, one wouldn't see the point of a prescription either, that required one to turn any piece round three times before making a move with it. If we found this rule in a board-game, we should be surprised, and form conjectures about the origin, the purpose, of such a rule. ("Is this prescription supposed to prevent one from moving without consideration?")

24.   "If I understand the character of the game right," I might say, "this is not essential to it."

25.   But let us think of the two offices joined in one person as an old convention.

26.   One says: the use of the same word is inessential *here*, because the identity of the shape of the word does not here serve to mediate a transition.   But in saying that one is merely describing the character of the game that one wants to play.

27.[1]   "What does the word 'a' mean in the sentence 'F(a)'?"   "What does the word 'a' mean in the sentence 'Fa' which you have just spoken?"   "What does the word .... mean in this sentence?"

---

[1] This remark was in handwriting on the back of the page. (Eds.)

II—2 FOUNDATIONS OF MATHEMATICS III

APPENDIX II

1. The surprising may play two completely different parts in mathematics.

One may see the value of a mathematical train of thought in its bringing to light something that surprises us:—because it is of great interest, of great importance, to see how such and such a kind of representation of it makes a situation surprising, or astonishing, even paradoxical.

But different from this is a conception, dominant at the present day, which values the surprising, the astonishing, because it shews the depths to which mathematical investigation penetrates;—as we might measure the value of a telescope by its shewing us things that we'd have had no *inkling* of without this instrument. The mathematician says as it were: "Do you see, this is surely important, this you would never have known without me." As if, by means of these considerations, as by means of a kind of higher experiment, astonishing, nay *the most* astonishing facts were brought to light.

2. But the mathematician is not a discoverer: he is an inventor.

"The demonstration has a surprising result!"—If you are surprised, then you have not understood it yet. For surprise is not legitimate here, as it is with the issue of an experiment. *There*—I should like to say—it is permissible to yield to its charm; but not when the surprise comes to you at the end of a chain of inference. For here it is only a sign that unclarity or some misunderstanding still reigns.

"But why should I not be surprised that I have been led *hither*?"— Imagine you had a long algebraic expression before you; at first it looks as if it could not be essentially shortened; but then you see a possibility of shortening it and now it goes on until the expression is shrunk into a compact form. May we not be surprised at this result? (Something similar happens in playing Patience.) Certainly, and it is a pleasant surprise; and it is of psychological interest, for it shows a phenomenon of failure to command a clear view and of the change of aspect of a seen complex. It is interesting that one does not always see in this complex that it can be shortened in this way; but if we are able to survey the way of shortening it, the surprise disappears.

When one says that one just is surprised at having been led *to this*, that does not represent the situation quite correctly. For one surely has this surprise only when one does not yet know the way. Not when one has the whole of it before one's eyes. The fact that this way, that I have completely in view, begins where it begins and ends where it ends, that's no surprise. The surprise and the interest, then, come, so to speak, from outside. I mean: one can say "This mathematical investigation is of great psychological interest" or "of great physical interest."

3.   I keep on being astonished at this turn of the theme; though I have heard it countless times and know it by heart. It is perhaps its *sense* to arouse astonishment.

What is it supposed to mean, then, when I say "You *oughtn't* be astonished?"

Think of mathematical puzzles. They are framed because they surprise: that is their whole sense.

I want to say: You ought not to believe that there is something hidden here, into which one can get no insight—as if we had walked through an underground passage and now come up somewhere into the light, without being able to tell how we got here, or how the entry of the tunnel lay in relation to its exit.

But then how was it possible for us to fancy this at all? What is there about a calculation that is like a movement underground? What can have suggested this picture to us? I believe it is this: no daylight

falls on these steps; that we understand the starting point and the end
of the calculation in a sense in which we do not understand the remaining course of the calculation.

4.   "There's no mystery here!"—but then how can we have so
much as believed that there was one?—Well, I have retraced the path
over and over again and over and over again been surprised; and I
never had the idea that here one can *understand* something.—So "There's
no mystery here!" means "Just look about you!"

5.   Isn't it as if one saw a sort of turning up of a card in a calculation?
One mixed up the cards; one doesn't know what was going on among
them; but in the end this card came out on top, and this means that
rain is coming.

6.   The difference between casting lots and counting out before a
game. But might not naive people even when it is a serious matter use
counting out instead of choosing a man by lot?

7.   What is someone doing when he makes us realize that in counting
out the result is already fixed?

8.   I want to say: "We don't command a clear view of what we
have done, and that is why it strikes us as mysterious. For now there
is a result in front of us and we no longer know how we got there,

it is not perspicuous to us, but we say (we have learnt to say): "this is how it has to be"; and we accept it—and marvel at it. Might we not imagine the following case: Someone has a series of orders of the form "You must now do such and such", each one written on a card. He mixes these cards up together, reads the one that comes out on top and says: so I *must* do *that?*—For the reading of a written order now makes a particular impression, has a particular effect on him. And so equally has the reaching of the conclusion of an inference. —However, one might perhaps break the spell of such an order, by bringing it clearly before the man's eyes again *how* he arrived at these words, and comparing what happened here with other cases—by saying, e.g.: "After all, no one has given you the order!"

And isn't it like *that*, when I say "There's no mystery here"?— Indeed, in a certain sense he had not believed that there was a mystery in the case. But he was under the *impression* of mystery (as the other was under the *impression* of an order). In *one* sense he was indeed acquainted with the situation, but he related to it (in feeling and in action) 'as if there were something else involved'—as we would say.

9. "A definition surely only takes you one step further back, to something that is not defined." What does that tell us? Did anyone not know that?—No—but may he not have lost sight of it?

10. Or: "If you write

'1, 4, 9, 16. . . .',

you have merely written down four numbers and four dots"—what are you bringing to our notice here? Could anyone think anything else? It would also be natural to say: "You have written nothing there except four numerals and a fifth sign—the dots." Well didn't he know this? Still, he might say, mightn't he, "I never really looked on the dots as *one* further sign in this series of signs—but rather as a way of suggesting further numerals."

11.   Or suppose someone gets us to notice that a line, in Euclid's sense, is a boundary of two coloured surfaces, and not a mark? and a point the intersection of such colour boundaries and not a dot? (How often has it been said that you cannot imagine a point.)

12.   It is possible for one to live, to think, in the fancy that things are thus and so, without *believing* it; that is to say, when one is asked, then one knows, but if one does not have to answer the question one does *not* know, but acts and thinks according to another opinion.

13.   For a form of expression makes us act thus and so. When it dominates our thinking, then in spite of all objections we should like to say: "But surely it *is* so in some sense." Although the 'some sense' is just what matters. (Roughly like the way it signifies a man's dishonesty when we say "He's *not* a *thief*".)

APPENDIX III

1.   It is easy to think of a language in which there is not a form for questions, or commands, but question and command are expressed in the form of statements, e.g. in forms corresponding to our: "I should like to know if . . ." and "My wish is that . . .".

No one would say of a question (e.g. whether it is raining outside) that it was true or false. Of course it is English to say so of such a sentence as "I want to know whether . . .". But suppose this form were always used instead of the question?—

2.   The great majority of sentences that we speak, write and read, are statement sentences.

And—you say—these sentences are true or false. Or, as I might also say, the game of truth-functions is played with them. For assertion is not something that gets added to the proposition, but an essential feature of the game we play with it. Comparable, say, to that characteristic of chess by which there is winning and losing in it, the winner being the one who takes the other's king.   Of course, there could be a game in a certain sense very near akin to chess, consisting in making the chess moves, but without there being any winning and losing in it; or with different conditions for winning.

3.   Imagine it were said: A command consists of a proposal ('assumption') and the commanding of the thing proposed.

4.   Might we not do arithmetic without having the idea of uttering arithmetical *propositions*, and without ever having been struck by the similarity between a multiplication and a proposition?

Should we not shake our heads, though, when someone shewed us a multiplication done wrong, as we do when someone tells us it is raining, if it is not raining?—Yes; and here is a point of connexion. But we also make gestures to stop our dog, e.g. when he behaves as we do not wish.

We are used to saying "2 times 2 is 4", and the verb "is" makes this into a proposition, and apparently establishes a close kinship with everything that we call a 'proposition'. Whereas it is a matter only of a very superficial relationship.

5.   Are there true propositions in Russell's system, which cannot be proved in his system?—What is called a true proposition in Russell's system, then?

6.   For what does a proposition's *being true* mean? *'p' is true = p.* (That is the answer.)

So we want to ask something like: under what circumstances do we assert a proposition? Or: how is the assertion of the proposition used in the language-game? And the 'assertion of the proposition' is here contrasted with the utterance of the sentence e.g. as practice in elocution,—or as *part* of another proposition, and so on.

If, then, we ask in this sense: "Under what circumstances is a proposition asserted in Russell's game?" the answer is: at the end of one of his proofs, or as a 'fundamental law' (Pp.). There is no other way in this system of employing asserted propositions in Russell's symbolism.

7. "But may there not be true propositions which are written in this symbolism, but are not provable in Russell's system?"—'True propositions', hence propositions which are true in *another* system, i.e. can rightly be asserted in another game. Certainly; why should there not be such propositions; or rather: why should not propositions —of physics, e.g.—be written in Russell's symbolism? The question is quite analogous to: Can there be true propositions in the language of Euclid, which are not provable in his system, but are true?—Why, there are even propositions which are provable in Euclid's system, but are *false* in another system. May not triangles be—in another system— similar (*very* similar) which do not have equal angles?—"But that's just a joke! For in that case they are not 'similar' to one another in the same sense!"—Of course not; and a proposition which cannot be proved in Russell's system is "true" or "false" in a different sense from a proposition of *Principia Mathematica*.

8. I imagine someone asking my advice; he says: "I have constructed a proposition (I will use '*P*' to designate it) in Russell's symbolism, and by means of certain definitions and transformations it can be so interpreted that it says: '*P* is not provable in Russell's system'. Must I not say that this proposition on the one hand is true, and on the other hand is unprovable? For suppose it were false; then it is true that it is provable. And that surely cannot be! And if it is proved, then it is proved that it is not provable. Thus it can only be true, but unprovable."

Just as we ask: " 'provable' in what system?", so we must also ask: " 'true' in what system?" 'True in Russell's system' means, as was said: proved in Russell's system; and 'false in Russell's system' means: the opposite has been proved in Russell's system.—Now what does your "suppose it is false" mean? *In the Russell sense* it means 'suppose the opposite is proved in Russell's system'; *if that is your assumption*, you will now presumably give up the interpretation that it is unprovable. And by 'this interpretation' I understand the translation into this English sentence.—If you assume that the proposition is provable in Russell's system, that means it is true *in the Russell sense*, and the interpretation "*P* is not provable" again has to be given up. If you assume that the proposition is true in the Russell sense, *the same* thing follows. Further: if the proposition is supposed to be false in some other than the Russell sense, then it does not contradict this for it to be proved in Russell's system. (What is called "losing" in chess may constitute winning in another game.)

9. For what does it mean to say that *P* and "*P* is unprovable" are the same proposition? It means that these *two* English sentences have a *single* expression in such-and-such a notation.

10. "But surely *P* cannot be provable, for, supposing it were proved, then the proposition that it is not provable would be proved." But if this were now proved, or if I believed—perhaps through an error—that I had proved it, why should I not let the proof stand and say I must withdraw my interpretation "*unprovable*"?

11. Let us suppose I prove the unprovability (in Russell's system) of *P*; then by this proof I have proved *P*. Now if this proof were one in Russell's system—I should in that case have proved at once that it belonged and did not belong to Russell's system.—That is what comes of making up such sentences.—But there is a contradiction here!— Well, then there is a contradiction here. Does it do any harm here?

12.   Is there harm in the contradiction that arises when someone says: "I am lying.—So I am not lying.—So I am lying.—etc."? I mean: does it make our language less usable if in this case, according to the ordinary rules, a proposition yields its contradictory, and vice versa?— the proposition *itself* is unusable, and these inferences equally; but why should they not be made?—It is a profitless performance!—It is a language-game with some similarity to the game of thumb-catching.

13.   Such a contradiction is of interest only because it has tormented people, and because this shews both how tormenting problems can grow out of language, and what kind of things can torment us.

14.   A proof of unprovability is as it were a geometrical proof; a proof concerning the geometry of proofs. Quite analogous e.g. to a proof that such-and-such a construction is impossible with ruler and compass. Now such a proof contains an element of prediction, a physical element. For in consequence of such a proof we say to a man: "Don't exert yourself to find a construction (of the trisection of an angle, say)—it can be proved that it can't be done". That is to say: it is essential that the proof of unprovability should be capable of being applied in this way. It must—we might say—be a *forcible reason* for giving up the search for a proof (i.e. for a construction of such-and-such a kind).

A contradiction is unusable as such a prediction.

15.   Whether something is rightly called the proposition "*X* is unprovable" depends on how we prove this proposition. The proof

alone shews what counts as the criterion of unprovability. The proof
is part of the system of operations, of the game, in which the proposition is used, and shews us its 'sense'.

Thus the question is whether the 'proof of the unprovability of *P*'
is here a forcible reason for the assumption that a proof of *P* will not
be found.

16. The proposition "*P* is unprovable" has a different sense after-
wards—from before it was proved.

If it is proved, then it is the terminal pattern in the proof of unprovability.—If it is unproved, then *what* is to count as a criterion of
its truth is not yet *clear*, and—we can say—its sense is still veiled.

17. Now how am I to take *P* as having been proved? By a proof of
unprovability? Or in some other way? Suppose it is by a proof of
unprovability. Now, in order to see *what* has been proved, look at the
proof. Perhaps it has here been proved that such-and-such forms of
proof do not lead to *P*.—Or, suppose *P* has been proved in a direct
way—as I should like to put it—and so in that case there follows the
proposition "*P* is unprovable", and it must now come out how this
interpretation of the symbols of *P* collides with the fact of the proof,
and why it has to be given up here.

Suppose however that not-*P* is proved.—Proved *how*? Say by *P*'s
being proved directly—for from that follows that it is provable, and
hence not-P. What am I to say now, "*P*" or "not-*P*"? Why not both?
If someone asks me "Which is the case, *P*, or not-*P*?" then I reply: *P*
stands at the end of a Russellian proof, so you write *P* in the Russellian
system; on the other hand, however, it is then provable and this is
expressed by not-*P*, but this proposition does not stand at the end of
a Russellian proof, and so does not belong to the Russellian system.

——When the interpretation "*P* is unprovable" was given to *P*, this proof of *P* was not known, and so one cannot say that *P* says: *this* proof did not exist.——Once the proof has been constructed, this has created a *new situation*: and now we have to decide whether we will call *this* a proof (a *further* proof), or whether we will still call *this* the statement of unprovability.

Suppose not-*P* is directly proved; it is therefore proved that *P* can be directly proved! So this is once more a question of interpretation—unless we now also have a direct proof of *P*. If it were like that, well, that is how it would be.

(The superstitious dread and veneration by mathematicians in face of contradiction.)

18.   "But suppose, now, that the proposition were *false*—and hence provable?"—Why do you call it 'false'? Because you can see a proof?—Or for other reasons? For in that case it doesn't matter. For one can quite well call the Law of Contradiction false, on the grounds that we very often make good sense by answering a question "Yes and no". And the same for the proposition '$\sim\sim p = p$' because we employ double negation as a *strengthening* of the negation and not merely as its cancellation.

19.   You say: "..., so *P* is true and unprovable". That presumably means: "Therefore *P*". That is all .right with me——but for what purpose do you write down this 'assertion'? (It is as if someone had extracted from certain principles about natural forms and architectural style the idea that on Mount Everest, where no one can live, there belonged a châlet in the Baroque style. And how could you make the truth of the assertion plausible to me, since you can make no use of it except to do these bits of legerdemain?

20.   Here one needs to remember that the propositions of logic are so constructed as to have *no* application as *information* in practice. So it could very well be said that they were not *propositions* at all; and one's writing them down at all stands in need of justification. Now if we append to these 'propositions' a further sentence-like structure of another kind, then we are all the more in the dark about what kind of application this system of sign-combinations is supposed to have; for the mere *ring of a sentence* is not enough to give these connexions of signs any meaning.

PART II

1. How far does the diagonal method prove that there is a number which—let's say—is not a square root? It is of course extremely easy to shew that there are numbers that aren't square roots—but how does *this* method shew it?

Have we a general concept of what it means to shew that there is a number that is not included in this infinite set?

Let us suppose that someone had been given the task of naming a number different from every $\sqrt{n}$; but that he knew nothing of the diagonal procedure and had named the number $\sqrt[3]{2}$; and had shewn that it was not a value of $\sqrt{n}$. Or that he had said: assume that $\sqrt{2} = 1.4142 \ldots$ and subtract 1 from the first decimal, but have the rest of the places agree with $\sqrt{2}$. 1.3142 cannot be a value of $\sqrt{n}$.

2. "Name a number that agrees with $\sqrt{2}$ at every second decimal place." What does this task demand? The question is: is it performed by the answer: It is the number got by the rule: develop $\sqrt{2}$ and add 1 or −1 to every second decimal place?

It is the same as the way the task: *Divide an angle into three* can be regarded as carried out by laying 3 equal angles together.

3. If someone savs: "Shew me a number different from all these",
and is given the rule of the diagonal for answer, why should he not
say: "But I didn't mean it like that!"? What you have given me is a
rule for the step-by-step construction of numbers that are successively
different from each of these.

"But why aren't you willing to call this too a method of calculating
a number?"—But what is the method of calculating, and what the
result, here? You will say that they are *one*, for it makes sense now to
say: the number *D* is bigger than ... and smaller than ...; it can
be squared etc. etc.

Is the question not really: What can this number be *used* for? True,
that sounds queer.—But what it means is: what are its mathematical
surroundings?

4. So I am comparing methods of calculating—only here there are
certainly very different ways of making comparisons. However, I am
supposed in some sense to be comparing the *results* of the methods
with one another. But this is enough to make everything unclear,
for in one sense they don't each have a single result, or it is not clear
in advance what is to be regarded here as *the* result in each case. I
want to say that here we are afforded every opportunity of twisting
and turning the meanings.

5. Let us say—not: "This method gives a result", but rather: "it
gives an infinite series of results". How do I compare infinite series
of results? Well, there are very different things that I may call doing
that.

6.   The motto here is always: Take a *wider* look round.

7.   The result of a calculation expressed verbally is to be regarded with suspicion. The *calculation* illumines the meaning of the expression in words. It is the *finer* instrument for determining the meaning. If you want to know what the verbal expression means, look at the calculation; not the other way about. The verbal expression casts only a dim general glow over the calculation: but the calculation a brilliant light on the verbal expression. (As if you wanted to compare the heights of two mountains, not by the technique of measurement of heights, but by their apparent relation when looked at from below.)

8.   "I want to shew you a method by which you can serially *avoid* all these developments." The diagonal procedure is such a method.— "So it produces a series that is different from all of these." Is that right?—Yes; if, that is, you want to apply these words to the described case.

9.   How would it be with the following method of construction? The diagonal number is produced by addition or subtraction of 1, but whether to add or subtract is only found out by continuing the original series to several places. Suppose it were now said: the development of the diagonal series never catches up with the development of the other series:—certainly the diagonal series avoids each of those series when it encounters it, but that is no help to it, as the development of the other series is again ahead of it. Here I can surely say: There is *always* one of the series for which it is not determined whether or not it is different from the diagonal series. It may be said: they run after one another to infinity, but the original series is always ahead.

"But your rule already reaches to infinity, so you already know quite precisely that the diagonal series will be different from any other!"—

10.   It means nothing to say: "*Therefore* the X numbers are not denumerable". One might say something like this: I call number-concept X non-denumerable if it has been stipulated that, whatever numbers falling under this concept you arrange in a series, the diagonal number of this series is also to fall under that concept.

11.   Since my drawing is after all only the *indication* of infinity, why must it be like this

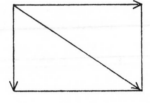

and not like this

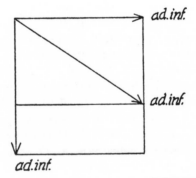

Here what we have is different pictures; and to them correspond different ways of talking. But does anything useful emerge if we have a dispute about the justification of *them*? What is important must reside somewhere else; even though these pictures fire our imagination most strongly.

12.   What can the concept 'non-denumerable' be used for?

13.   Surely—if anyone tried day-in day-out 'to put all irrational numbers into a series' we could say: "Leave it alone; it means nothing; don't you see, if you established a series, I should come along with the diagonal series!" This might get him to abandon his undertaking. Well, that would be useful. And it strikes me as if this were the whole and proper purpose of this method. It makes use of the vague notion of this man who goes on, as it were idiotically, with his work, and it brings him to a stop by means of a picture. (But one could get him to resume his undertaking by means of another picture.)

14.   The procedure exhibits something—which can in a very vague way be called the demonstration that *these* methods of calculation cannot be ordered in a series. And here the meaning of "*these*" is just kept vague.

15.   A clever man got caught in this net of language! So it must be an interesting net.

16.   The mistake begins when one says that the cardinal numbers can be ordered in a series. For what concept has one of this ordering? One has of course a concept of an infinite series, but here that gives

us at most a vague idea, a guiding light for the formation of a concept. For the concept itself is *abstracted* from this and from other series; or: the expression stands for a certain analogy between cases, and it can e.g. be used to define provisionally a domain that one wants to talk about.

That, however, is not to say that the question: "Can the set R be ordered in a series?" has a clear sense. For this question means e.g.: Can one do something with these formations, corresponding to the ordering of the cardinal numbers in a series? Asked: "Can the real numbers be ordered in a series?" the conscientious answer might be: "For the time being I can't form any precise idea of that".—"But you can order the roots and the algebraic numbers for example in a series; so you surely understand the expression!"—To put it better, I *have got* certain analogous formations, which I call by the common name 'series'. But so far I haven't any certain bridge from these cases to that of 'all real numbers'. Nor have I any general method of trying whether such-and-such a set 'can be ordered in a series'.

Now I am shewn the diagonal procedure and told: "Now here you have the proof that this ordering can't be done here". But I can reply: "I don't know—to repeat—what it is that *can't be done* here". Though I can see that you want to shew a difference between the use of "root", "algebraic number", etc. on the one hand, and "real number" on the other. Such a difference as e.g. this: roots are called "real numbers", *and so too* is the diagonal number formed from the roots. And similarly for all series of real numbers. For this reason it makes no sense to talk about a "series of all real numbers", just because the diagonal number for each series is also called a "real number".—Would this not be as if any row of books were itself ordinarily called a book, and now we said: "It makes no sense to speak of 'the row of all books', since this row would itself be a book."

17. Here it is very useful to imagine the diagonal procedure for the
production of a real number as having been well-known before the
invention of set theory, and familiar even to school-children, as indeed
might very well have been the case. For this changes the aspect of
Cantor's discovery. The discovery might very well have consisted
merely in the interpretation of this long familiar elementary calculation.

18. For this kind of calculation is itself useful. The question set
would be perhaps: write down a decimal number which is different
from the numbers:

> 0.1246798...
> 0.3469876...
> 0.0127649...
> 0.3426794...
> ....(Imagine a long series.)

The child thinks to itself: how am I to do this, when I should have to
look at all the numbers at once, to prevent what I write down from
being one of them? Now the method says: Not at all: change the first
place of the first number, the second of the second one etc. etc., and
you are sure of having written down a number that does not coincide
with any of the given ones. The number got in this way might always
be called the diagonal number.

19. The dangerous, deceptive thing about the idea: "The real
numbers cannot be arranged in a series", or again "The set ... is not
denumerable" is that it makes the determination of a concept—concept
formation—look like a fact of nature.

20. The following sentence sounds sober: "If something is called a
series of real numbers, then the expansion given by the diagonal

procedure is also called a 'real number', and is moreover said to be different from all members of the series".

21.   Our suspicion ought always to be aroused when a proof proves more than its means allow it. Something of this sort might be called 'a puffed-up proof'.

22.   The usual expression creates the fiction of a procedure, a method of ordering which, though applicable here, nevertheless fails to reach its goal because of the number of objects involved, which is greater even than the number of all cardinal numbers.

If it were said: "Consideration of the diagonal procedure shews you that the *concept* 'real number' has much less analogy with the concept 'cardinal number' than we, being misled by certain analogies, are inclined to believe", that would have a good and honest sense. But just the *opposite* happens: one pretends to compare the 'set' of real numbers in magnitude with that of cardinal numbers. The difference in kind between the two conceptions is represented, by a skew form of expression, as difference of extension. I believe, and hope, that a future generation will laugh at this hocus pocus.

23.   The sickness of a time is cured by an alteration in the mode of life of human beings, and it was possible for the sickness of philosophical problems to get cured only through a changed mode of thought and of life, not through a medicine invented by an individual.

Think of the use of the motor-car producing or encouraging certain sicknesses, and mankind being plagued by such sickness until, from some cause or other, as the result of some development or other, it abandons the habit of driving.

24. For how do we make use of the proposition: "There is no greatest cardinal number"? When and on what occasion woud it be said? This use is at any rate quite different from that of the mathematical proposition '25 × 25 = 625'.

25. First and foremost, notice that we ask this question at all; this points to the fact that the answer is not ready to hand.

Moreover, if one tries to answer the question in a hurry, it is easy to trip up. The case is like that of the question: what experience shews us that our space is three-dimensional?

26. We say of a *permission* that it has no end.

27. And it can be said that the permission to play language-games with cardinal numbers has no end. This would be said e.g. to someone to whom we were teaching our language and language-games. So it would again be a grammatical proposition, but of an *entirely* different kind from '25 × 25 = 625'. It would however be of great importance if the pupil were, say, inclined to expect a definitive end to this series of language-games (perhaps because he had been brought up in a different culture).

28. Why should we say: The irrational numbers cannot be ordered? —We have a method by which to upset any order.

29. Cantor's diagonal procedure does not shew us an irrational

number different from all in the system, but it gives sense to the mathematical proposition that the number so-and-so is different from all those of the system. Cantor could say: You can prove that a number is different from all the numbers in the system *by* proving that it differs in its first place from its first number and in its second place from its second number and so on.

Cantor is saying something about the multiplicity of the concept "Real number different from all the ones of a system".

30.   Cantor shews that if we have a system of expansions it makes sense to speak of an expansion that is different from them all.—But that is not enough to determine the grammar of the word "expansion".

31.   Cantor gives a sense to the expression "expansion which is different from all the expansions in a system", by proposing that an expansion should be so called when it can be proved that it is diagonally different from the expansions in a system.

32.   Thus it can be *set* as a question: Find a number whose expansion is diagonally different from those in this system.

33.   It might be said: Besides the rational points there are *diverse systems* of irrational points to be found in the number line.

There is no system of irrational numbers—but also no super-system, no 'set of irrational numbers' of higher-order infinity.

34.   Cantor defines a *difference of higher order*, that is to say a difference of an expansion from a *system* of expansions. This definition can be used so as to shew that a number is in this sense different from a system of numbers: let us say π from the system of algebraic numbers. But we cannot very well say that the rule of altering the places in the diagonal in such-and-such a way is as such proved different from the rules of the system, because this rule is itself of 'higher order'; for it *treats of* the alteration of a system of rules, and for that reason it is not clear in advance in which cases we shall be willing to declare the expansion of *such a* rule different from all the expansions of the system.

35.   'These considerations may lead us to say that $2^{\aleph_0} > \aleph_0$.'
That is to say: we can *make* the considerations lead us to that.
Or: we can say *this* and give *this* as our reason.
But if we do say it—what are we to do next? In what practice is this proposition anchored? It is for the time being a piece of mathematical architecture which hangs in the air, and looks as if it were, let us say, an architrave, but not supported by anything and supporting nothing.

36.   Certain considerations may lead us to say that 10^{10} souls fit into a cubic centimetre. But why do we nevertheless not say it? Because it is of no use. Because, while it does conjure up a picture, the picture is one with which we cannot go on to do anything.

37.   The proposition is worth as much as its grounds are.
It supports as much as the grounds that support it do.

38. An interesting question is: what is the connexion of $\aleph_0$ with the cardinal numbers whose number it is supposed to be? $\aleph_0$ would obviously be the *predicate "infinite series"* in its application to the series of cardinal numbers and to similar mathematical formations. Here it is important to grasp the relationship between a series in the non-mathematical sense and one in the mathematical sense. It is of course clear that in mathematics we do *not* use the word "series of numbers" in the sense "series of numerical signs", even though, of course, there is also a connexion between the use of the one expression and of the other. A railway is not a railway train; nor is it something similar to a railway train. A 'series' in the mathematical sense is a method of construction for series of linguistic expressions.

Thus we have a grammatical class "infinite sequence", and equivalent with this expression a word whose grammar has (a certain) similarity with that of a numeral: "infinity" or "$\aleph_0$". This is connected with the fact that among the calculi of mathematics we have a technique which there is a certain justice in calling "1–1 correlation of the members of two infinite series", since it has a similarity to such a mutual correlation of the members of what are called 'finite' classes.

From the fact, however, that we have an employment for a *kind* of numeral which, as it were, gives the number of the members of an infinite series, it does not follow that it also makes some kind of sense to speak of the number of the concept 'infinite series'; that we have *here* some kind of employment for something like a numeral. For there is no grammatical technique suggesting employment of such an expression. For I can of course form the expression: "class of all classes which are equinumerous with the class 'infinite series'" (as also: "class of all angels that can get on to a needlepoint") but this expression is empty so long as there is no employment for it. Such an employment is not: yet to be discovered, but: still to be *invented*.

39.   Imagine that I put a playing-board divided into squares in front of you, and put pieces like chess pieces on it—and stated: "This piece is the '*King*', these are the '*Knights*', these the '*Commoners*'.—So far that's all we know about the game; but that's always something.—And perhaps more will be discovered."

40.   "Fractions cannot be arranged in an order of magnitude."— First and foremost, this sounds extremely interesting and remarkable.

It sounds interesting in a quite different way from, say, a proposition of the differential calculus. The difference, I think, resides in the fact that *such* a proposition is easily associated with an application to physics, whereas *this* proposition belongs simply and solely to mathematics, seems to concern as it were the natural history of mathematical objects themselves.

One would like to say of it e.g.: it introduces us to the mysteries of the mathematical world. *This* is the aspect against which I want to give a warning.

41.   When it looks as if . . ., we should look out.

42.   When, on hearing the proposition that the fractions cannot be arranged in a series in order of magnitude, I form the picture of an unending row of things, and between each thing and its neighbour new things appear, and more new ones again between each of these things and its neighbour, and so on without end, then certainly there is something here to make one dizzy.

But once we see that this picture, though very exciting, is all the same not appropriate; that we ought not to let ourselves be trapped by the words "series", "order", "exist", and others, we shall fall back on the *technique* of calculating fractions, about which there is no longer anything *queer*.

43.   The fact that in a technique of calculating fractions the expression "the next greatest fraction" has no sense, that we have not given it any sense, is nothing to marvel at.

44.   If we apply a technique of continuous interpolation of fractions, we shall not be willing to call any fraction the "next biggest".

45.   To say that a technique is unlimited does *not* mean that it goes on without ever stopping—that it increases immeasurably; but that it lacks the institution of the end, that it is not finished off. As one may say of a sentence that it is not finished off if it has no period. Or of a playing-field that is unlimited, when the rules of the game do not prescribe any boundaries—say by means of a line.

46.   For the point of a new technique of calculation is to supply us with a *new* picture, *a new form of expression*; and there is nothing so absurd as to try and describe this new schema, this new kind of scaffolding, by means of the old expressions.

47.   What is the function of such a proposition as: "A fraction has not a next biggest fraction but a cardinal number has a next biggest cardinal number"? Well, it is as it were a proposition that compares two games. (Like: in draughts pieces jump over one another, but not in chess.)

48. We call something "constructing the next biggest cardinal number" but nothing "constructing the next biggest fraction".

49. How do we compare games? By describing them—by describing one as a variation of another—by describing them and *emphasizing* their differences and analogies.

50. "In draughts there isn't a King"—what does this mean? (It sounds childish.) Does it mean that none of the pieces in draughts is called "King"; and if we did call one of the pieces that, would there be a King in draughts? But what about *this* proposition: "In draughts all the pieces have the same rights, but not in chess"? Whom am I telling this? One who already knows both games, or else someone who does not yet know them. Here it looks as if the first one stands in no need of our information and the second can do nothing with it. But suppose I were to say: "See! In draughts all the pieces have the same rights, . . ." or better still: "See! In these games all the pieces have the same rights, in those not." But what does such a proposition do? It introduces a new *concept*, a new ground of classification. I teach you to answer the question: "Name games of the first sort" etc. But in a similar way it would be possible to set questions like: "Invent a game with a King".

51. 'We cannot arrange fractions in a series in order of magnitude but we *can* order them in an infinite series.'

If someone did not know this, what has he now learnt? He has learnt a new kind of calculation, e.g.: "Determine the number of the fraction . . .".

52. He learns this technique—but doesn't he also learn that there is such a technique?

I have indeed, in an important sense, learned that there is such a technique; that is, I have got to know a technique which can now be applied to all sorts of other things.

53. 'What would you call *this*?'

	1	2	3	4	·	·	·
1	1	3	6	10	·		
2	2	5	9	·			
3	4	8	·				
4	7	·					
·	·						

Surely "a method of numbering the pairs of numbers"? And might I not also say: "of ordering pairs of numbers in a series"?

54. Now does mathematics teach me that I can order the pairs of numbers in a series? Can I say: it teaches me that I can do *this*? For does it make sense to say that I teach a child that it is possible to multiply—by teaching him to multiply? It would rather be natural to say I teach him that it is possible to multiply fractions, after he has learned to multiply cardinal numbers together. For now, it might be said, he knows what "multiplying" means. But wouldn't this be misleading too?

55. If someone says I have proved the proposition that we can order pairs of numbers in a series, it should be answered that this is not a mathematical proposition, since one doesn't calculate with the words "we", "can", "the", "pairs of numbers", etc. The proposition

"one can . . ." is rather a mere approximate description of the technique one is teaching, say a not unsuitable *title*, a heading to this chapter. But a title with which it is not possible to *calculate*.

56.   But, you say, this is just what the logical calculus of Frege and Russell does: in it every word that is spoken in mathematics has exact significance, is an element of the calculus. Thus in this calculus we can really prove that "multiplying is possible". Very well, now it is a mathematical proposition; but who says that anything can be done with this proposition? Who says *what* use it can be? For its sounding interesting is not enough.

Just because when we are teaching we may use the proposition "So you see, we can order the fractions in a series", don't say that we have any other use for this proposition than of attaching a memorable picture to this sort of calculation.

If the interest here attaches to the proposition that has been proved, then it attaches to a picture which has an extremely weak justification, but which fascinates us by its queerness, like e.g. the picture of the "direction" of time. It produces a slight reeling of one's thoughts.

57.   Here I can only say: depart as quickly as possible from this picture, and see the interest of this calculation in its application. (It is as if we were at a masked ball at which every calculation appears in a queer guise.)

58.   "Ought the word 'infinite' to be avoided in mathematics?" Yes; where it appears to confer a meaning upon the calculus; instead of getting one from it.

59.   This way of talking: "But when one examines the calculus there is nothing infinite there" is of course clumsy—but it means: is it really necessary here to conjure up the picture of the infinite (of the enormously big)? And how is this picture connected with the *calculus*? For its connexion is not that of the picture | | | | with 4.

60.   To act as if one were disappointed to have found nothing infinite in the calculus is of course funny; but not to ask: what is the everyday employment of the word "infinite", which gives it its meaning for us; and what is its connexion with these mathematical calculi?

61.   Finitism and behaviourism are quite similar trends. Both say, but surely, all we have here is. . . . Both deny the existence of something, both with a view to escaping from a confusion.

62.   What I am doing is, not to shew that calculations are wrong, but to subject the *interest* of calculations to a test. I test e.g. the justification for still using the word . . . here. Or really, I keep on urging such an investigation. I shew that there is such an investigation and what there is to investigate there. Thus I must say, not: "We must not express ourselves like this", or "That is absurd", or "That is uninteresting", but: "Test the justification of this expression in this way". You cannot survey the justification of an expression unless you survey its employment; which you cannot do by looking at some facet of its employment, say a picture attaching to it.

PART III

1939-40

1. 'A mathematical proof must be perspicuous.' Only a structure whose reproduction is an easy task is called a "proof". It must be possible to decide with certainty whether we really have the same proof twice over, or not. The proof must be a configuration whose exact reproduction can be certain. Or again: we must be sure we can exactly reproduce what is essential to the proof. It may for example be written down in two different handwritings or colours. What goes to make the reproduction of a proof is not anything like an exact reproduction of a shade of colour or a hand-writing.

It must be easy to write down *exactly* this proof again. This is where a written proof has an advantage over a drawing. The essentials of the latter have often been misunderstood. The drawing of a Euclidian proof may be inexact, in the sense that the straight lines are not straight, the segments of circles not exactly circular, etc. etc. and at the same time the drawing is still an exact proof; and from this it can be seen that this drawing does not—e.g.—demonstrate that such a construction results in a polygon with five equal sides; that what it proves is a proposition of geometry, not one about the properties of paper, compass, ruler and pencil.

[Connects with: proof a *picture* of an experiment.]

2. I want to say: if you have a proof-pattern that cannot be taken in, and by a change in notation you turn it into one that can, then you are producing a proof, where there was none before.

Now let us imagine a proof for a Russellian proposition stating an addition like '$a + b = c$', consisting of a few thousand signs. You will say: Seeing whether this proof is correct or not is a purely external difficulty, of no mathematical interest. ("One man takes in easily what someone else takes in with difficulty or not at all" etc. etc..)

The assumption is that the definitions serve merely to abbreviate the expression for the convenience of the calculator; whereas they are part of the calculation. By their aid expressions are produced which could not have been produced without it.

3.   But how about the following: "While it is true that we cannot—in the ordinary sense—multiply 234 by 537 in the Russellian calculus, still there is a Russellian calculation corresponding to this multiplication."—What kind of correspondence is this? It might be like this: we can carry out this multiplication in the Russellian calculus too, only in a different symbolism,—just as, as we should certainly say, we can carry it out in a different number system. In that case, then, we could e.g. solve the practical problems for which we use that multiplication by means of the calculation in the Russellian calculus too, only in a more roundabout way.

Now let us imagine the cardinal numbers explained as $1, 1 + 1$, $(1 + 1) + 1, ((1 + 1) + 1) + 1$, and so on. You say that the definitions introducing the figures of the decimal system are a mere matter of convenience; the calculation 703000×40000101 could be done in that wearisome notation too. But is that true?—"Of course it's true! I can surely write down, construct, a calculation in that notation corresponding to the calculation in the decimal notation."—But how do I know that it corresponds to it? Well, because I have derived it from the other by a given method.—But now if I look at it again half an hour later, may it not have altered? For one cannot command a clear view of it.

Now I ask: could we also find out the truth of the proposition $7034174 + 6594321 = 13628495$ by means of a proof carried out in the first notation?—Is there such a proof of this proposition?—The answer is: no.

4. But still doesn't Russell teach us *one* way of adding?

Suppose we proved by Russell's method that $(\exists\ a \ldots g)$ $(\exists\ a \ldots l) \supset (\exists\ a \ldots s)$ is a tautology; could we reduce our result to $g + l$'s being s? Now this presupposes that I can take the three bits of the alphabet as representatives of the proof. But does Russell's proof shew this? After all I could obviously also have carried out Russell's proof with groups of signs in the brackets whose sequence made no characteristic impression on me, so that it would not have been possible to represent the group of signs between brackets by its last term.

Even assuming that the Russellian proof were carried out with a notation such as $x_1 x_2 \ldots x_{10} x_{11} \ldots x_{100} \ldots$ as in the decimal notation, and there were 100 members in the first pair of brackets, 300 in the second and 400 in the third, does the proof itself shew that $100 + 300 = 400$?—What if this proof led at one time to this result, and at another to a different one, for example $100 + 300 = 420$? What is needed in order to see that the result of the proof, if it is correctly carried out, always depends solely on the last figures of the first two pairs of brackets?

But still for small numbers Russell does teach us to add; for then we take the groups of signs in the brackets in at a glance and we can take *them* as numerals; for example '*xy*', '*xyz*', '*xyzuv*'.

Thus Russell teaches us a new calculus for reaching 5 from 2 and 3; and that is true even if we say that a logical calculus is only—frills tacked on to the arithmetical calculus.

The *application* of the calculation must take care of itself. And that is what is correct about 'formalism'.

The reduction of arithmetic to symbolic logic is supposed to shew the point of application of arithmetic, as it were the attachment by means of which it is plugged in to its application. As if someone were shewn, first a trumpet without the mouthpiece—and then the mouthpiece, which shews how a trumpet is used, brought into contact with the human body. But the attachment which Russell gives us is on the one hand too narrow, on the other hand too wide; too general and too special. The calculation takes care of its own application.

We extend our ideas from calculations with small numbers to ones with large numbers in the same kind of way as we imagine that, if the distance from here to the sun *could* be measured with a footrule, then we should get the very result that, as it is, we get in a quite different way. That is to say, we are inclined to take the measurement of length with a footrule as a model even for the measurement of the distance between two stars.

And one says, e.g. at school: "If we imagine rulers stretching from here to the sun . . ." and seems in this way to explain what we understand by the distance between the sun and the earth. And the use of such a picture is all right, so long as it is clear to us that we can measure the distance from us to the sun, and that we cannot measure it with footrules.

5.   Suppose someone were to say: "The only real proof of 1000 + 1000 = 2000 is after all the Russellian one, which shews that the expression . . . is a tautology"? For can I not prove that a tautology results if I have 1000 members in each of the two first pairs of brackets and 2000 in the third? And if I can prove that, then I can look at it as a proof of the arithmetical proposition.

In philosophy it is always good to put a *question* instead of an answer to a question.

For an answer to the philosophical question may easily be unfair; disposing of it by means of another question is not.

Then should I put a *question* here, for example, instead of the answer that that arithmetical proposition cannot be proved by Russell's method?

6.   The proof that $\overset{1}{(\ )}\,\overset{2}{(\ )} \supset \overset{3}{(\ )}$ is a tautology consists in always crossing out a term of the third pair of brackets for a term of (1) or (2). And there are many methods for such collating. Or one might even

say: there are many ways of establishing the success of a 1-1 correlation. One way, for example, would be to construct a star-shaped pattern for the left-hand side of the implication and another one for the right-hand side and then to compare these in their turn by making an ornament out of the two of them.

Thus the rule could be given: "If you want to know whether the numbers A and B together actually yield C, write down an expression of the form . . . and correlate the variables in the brackets by writing down (or trying to) the proof that the expression is a tautology".

My objection to this is *not* that it is arbitrary to prescribe just this way of collating, but that it cannot be established in this way that 1000 + 1000 = 2000.

7. Imagine that you had written down a 'formula' a mile long, and you shewed by transformation that it was tautologous ('if *it* has not altered meanwhile', one would have to say). Now we *count* the terms in the brackets or we divide them up and make the expression into one that can be taken in, and it comes out that there are 7566 terms in the first pair of brackets, 2434 in the second, 10000 in the third. Now have I proved that 2434 + 7566 = 10000?—That depends—one might say— on whether you are certain that the counting has really yielded the number of terms which stood between the brackets in the course of the proof.

Could one say: "Russell teaches us to write as many variables in the third pair of brackets as were in the first two together"? But really: he teaches us to write a variable in (3) for every variable in (1) and (2).

But do we learn from this what number is the sum of two given numbers? Perhaps it is said: "Of course, for in the third pair of brackets we have the paradigm, the prototype of the new number". But in what sense is | | | | | | | | | | | | | | | | | | the paradigm of a number? Consider how it can be used as such.

8. Above all, the Russellian tautology corresponding to the proposition $a + b = c$ does not shew us in what notation the number c is to be written, and there is no reason why it should not be written in the form $a + b$.—For Russell does not teach us the technique of, say, adding in the decimal system.—But could we perhaps derive it from his technique?

Let us just ask the following question: Can one derive the technique of the decimal system from that of the system 1, $1 + 1$, $(1 + 1) + 1$, etc.?

Could this question not also be formulated as follows: if one has one technique of calculation in the one system and one in the other,—how is it shewn that the two are equivalent?

9. "A proof ought to shew not merely that this is how it is, but this is how it has to be."

In what circumstances does counting shew this?

One would like to say: "When the figures and the thing being counted yield a memorable configuration. When this configuration is now used in place of any fresh counting."—But here we seem to be talking only of *spatial* configurations: but if we know a series of words by heart and then co-ordinate two such series, one to one, saying for example: "First—Monday; second—Tuesday; third—Wednesday;

etc."—can we not *prove* in this way that from Monday to Thursday is four days?

For the question is: What do we call a "memorable configuration"? What is the criterion for its being impressed on our minds? Or is the answer to that: "That we use it as a paradigm of identity!"?

10.   We do not make *experiments* on a sentence or a proof in order to establish its properties.

How do we reproduce, how do we copy, a proof?—Not e.g. by taking measurements of it.

Suppose a proof were so hugely long that it could not possibly be taken in? Or let us look at a different case: Let there be a long row of strokes engraved in hard rock which is our paradigm for the number that we call 1000. We call this row the proto-thousand and if we want to know whether there are a thousand men in a square, we draw lines or stretch threads. (1-1 correlation.)

Now here the sign of the number 1000 has the identity, not of a shape, but of a physical object. We could imagine a 'proto-hundred' similarly, and a proof, which we could not *take in at a glance*, that 10 × 100 = 1000.

The figure for 1000 in the system of 1 + 1 + 1 + 1 . . . cannot be recognized by its *shape*.

11. ||||||||||||||||||||||||||||||||| |||||||||||||||||
Is this pattern a proof of 27 + 16 = 43, because one reaches '27' if one counts the strokes on the left-hand side, '16' on the right-hand

side, and '43' when one counts the whole row?

Where is the queerness of calling the pattern the proof of this proposition? It lies in the kind of way this proof is to be reproduced or known again; in its not having any characteristic visual shape.

Now even if that proof has not any such visual shape, still I can copy (reproduce) it exactly—so isn't the figure a proof after all? I might e.g. have it engraved on a bit of steel and passed from hand to hand. So I should tell someone: "Here you have the proof that 27 + 16 = 43".—Well, can't one say *after all* that he proves the proposition with the aid of the pattern? Yes; but the pattern is not the proof.

This, however, would surely be called a proof of 250 + 3220 = 3470: one counts on from 250 and at the same time begins counting from 1 and co-ordinates the two counts:

$$251 \ldots\ldots 1$$
$$252 \ldots\ldots 2$$
$$253 \ldots\ldots 3$$
$$\text{etc.}$$
$$3470 \ldots\ldots 3220$$

That could be called a proof in 3220 steps. It is surely a proof—and can it be called perspicuous?

12. What is the invention of the decimal system really? The invention of a system of abbreviations——but what is the system of the abbreviations? Is it simply the system of the new signs or is it also a

system of applying them for the purpose of abbreviation? And if it is the latter, then it *is* a new way of looking at the old system of signs.

Can we start from the system of $1 + 1 + 1 \ldots$ and learn to calculate in the decimal system through mere abbreviations of the notation?

13.   Suppose that following Russell I have proved a proposition of the form $(\exists\, xyz \ldots)\,(\exists\, uvw \ldots) \supset (\exists\, abc \ldots)$—and now 'I make it perspicuous' by writing signs $x_1, x_2, x_3 \ldots$ over the variables—am I to say that following Russell I have proved an arithmetical proposition in the decimal system?

But for every proof in the decimal system there is surely a corresponding one in Russell's system!—How do we know there is? Let us leave intuition on one side.—But it can be proved.—

If a number in the decimal system is defined in terms of $1, 2, 3, \ldots$ $9, 0$, and the signs $0, 1 \ldots 9$ in terms of $1, 1 + 1, (1 + 1) + 1, \ldots$ can one then use the recursive explanation of the decimal system to reach a sign of the form $1 + 1 + 1 \ldots$ from any number?

Suppose someone were to say: Russellian arithmetic agrees with ordinary arithmetic up to numbers less than 10^{10}; but then it diverges from it. And now he produces a Russellian proof that $10^{10} + 1 = 10^{10}$. Now why should I not trust such a proof? How will anybody convince me that I must have miscalculated in the Russellian proof?

But then do I need a proof from another system in order to ascertain whether I have miscalculated in the first proof? Is it not enough for me to write down that proof in a way that makes it possible to take it in?

14. Is not my whole difficulty one of seeing how it is possible, without abandoning Russell's logical calculus, to reach the concept of the *set of variables* in the expression '(∃ *xyz* . . .)', where this expression cannot be taken in?—

Well, but it can be made surveyable by writing: (∃ x_1, x_2, x_3, etc.). And still there is something that I do not understand: the criterion for the identity of such an expression has now surely been changed: I now see in a different way that the set of signs in two such expressions is the same.

What I am tempted to say is: Russell's proof can indeed be continued step by step, but at the end one does not rightly know what one has proved—at least not by the old criteria. By making it possible to command a clear view of the Russellian proof, I prove something about this proof.

I want to say: one need not acknowledge the Russellian technique of calculation at all—and can prove by means of a different technique of calculation that there *must* be a Russellian proof of the proposition. But in that case, of course, the proposition is no longer based upon the Russellian proof.

Or again: its being possible to imagine a Russellian proof for every proved proposition of the form $m + n = l$ does not shew that the proposition is based on this proof. For it is conceivable that the Russellian proof of one proposition should not be distinguishable from the Russellian proof of another and should be called different only because they are the translations of two recognizably different proofs.

Or again: something stops being a proof when it stops being a paradigm, for example Russell's logical calculus; and on the other hand any other calculus which serves as a paradigm is acceptable.

15.   It is a fact that different methods of counting practically always agree.

When I count the squares on a chess-board I practically always reach '64'.

If I know two series of words by heart, for example numerals and the alphabet, and I put them into one-one correspondence:

a	1
b	2
c	3
etc.	

at '*z*' I practically always reach '26'.

There is such a thing as: knowing a series of words by heart. When am I said to know the poem ... by heart? The criteria are rather complicated. Agreement with a printed text is one. What would have to happen to make me doubt that I really know the *ABC* by heart? It is difficult to imagine.

But I use reciting or writing down a series of words from memory as a criterion for equality of numbers, equality of sets.

Ought I now to say: all that doesn't matter—logic still remains the fundamental calculus, only whether I have the same formula twice is of course differently established in different cases?

16.   It is not logic—I should like to say—that compels me to accept a proposition of the form (Ǝ   ) (Ǝ   ) ⊃ (Ǝ   ), when there are a million variables in the first two pairs of brackets and two million in the third. I want to say: logic would not compel me to accept any proposition at all in this case. Something *else* compels me to accept such a proposition as in accord with logic.

Logic compels me only so far as the logical calculus compels me.

But surely it is essential to the calculus with 1000000 that this number must be capable of resolution into a sum 1 + 1 + 1 ..., and in order to be certain that we have the right number of units before us, we can number the units: $\underset{1 \quad 2 \quad 3 \quad 4 \qquad\quad 1000000}{1 + 1 + 1 + 1 + \ldots + 1}$.   This notation would be like: '100,000.000,000' which also makes the numeral surveyable. And I can surely imagine someone's having a great sum of money in pennies entered in a book in which perhaps they appear as numbers of 100 places, with which I have to calculate. I should now begin to translate them into a surveyable notation, but still I should call them 'numerals', should treat them as a record of numbers. For I should even regard it as the record of a number if someone were to tell me that N has as many shillings as this vessel will hold peas. Another case again: "He has as many shillings as the Song of Songs has letters".

17.   The notation '$x_1, x_2, x_3, \ldots$' gives a shape to the expression '($\exists \ldots$)', and so to the R-proved tautology.

Let me ask the following question: Is it not conceivable that the 1-1 correlation could not be trustworthily carried out in the Russellian proof, that when, *for example*, we try to use it for adding, we regularly get a result contradicting the usual one, and that we blame this on fatigue, which makes us leave out certain steps unawares? And might we not then say:—if only we didn't get tired we should get the same result—? Because *logic* demands it? Does it demand it, then? Aren't we here rectifying logic by means of another calculus?

Suppose we took 100 steps of the logical calculus at a time and now got trustworthy results, while we don't get them if we try to take all the steps singly——one would like to say: the calculation is still based on unit steps, since 100 steps at a time is defined by means of unit steps.—But the definition says: to take 100 steps at a time is the same thing as . . ., and yet we take the 100 steps at a time and *not* 100 unit steps.

Still, in the shortened calculation I am obeying a *rule*——and how was this rule justified?—What if the shortened and the unshortened proof yielded different results?

18.   What I am saying surely comes to this: I can e.g. define '10' as '$1 + 1 + 1 + 1 \ldots$' and '100 $\times$ 2' as '$2 + 2 + 2 \ldots$' but I cannot therefore necessarily define '100 $\times$ 10' as '$10 + 10 + 10 \ldots$', nor yet as '$1 + 1 + 1 + 1 \ldots$.'

I can find out that 100 × 100 equals 10000 by means of a 'shortened' procedure. Then why should I not regard *that* as the original proof procedure?

A shortened procedure tells me what *ought* to come out with the unshortened one. (Instead of the other way round.)

19.   "But the calculation is surely based on the unit steps. . . ." Yes; but in a different way. For the procedure of proof is a different one.

I could say for example: 10 = 1 + 1 + 1 + 1 + 1 + 1 + 1 + 1 + 1 + 1 *and in like manner* 100 = 10 + 10 + 10 + 10 + 10 + 10 + 10 + 10 + 10 + 10. Have I not based the definition of 100 on the successive addition of 1? But in the same way as if I had added 100 units? Is there any need at all in my notation for a sign of the form— '1 + 1 + 1 . . .' with 100 components of the sum?

The danger here seems to be one of looking at the shortened procedure as a pale shadow of the unshortened one. The rule of counting is not counting.

20.   What does taking 100 steps of the calculus 'at once' consist in? Surely in one's regarding, not the unit step, but a different step, as decisive.

In ordinary addition of whole numbers in the decimal system we make steps in units, steps in tens, etc. Can one say that the procedure is founded on one of only making unit steps? One might justify it like this: the result of the addition does indeed look so—'7583'; but the explanation of this sign, its meaning, which must ultimately receive expression in its application too, is surely of this sort: $1 + 1 + 1 + 1 + 1$ and so on. But is it so? Must the numerical sign be explained in this way, or this explanation receive expression implicitly in its application? I believe that if we reflect it turns out that that is not the case.

Calculating with graphs or with a slide-rule.

Of course when we check the one kind of calculation by the other, we normally get the same result. But if there are several kinds—who says, if they do not agree, which is the proper method of calculation, with its roots at the source of mathematics?

21.   Where a doubt can make its appearance whether *this* is really the pattern of *this* proof, where we are prepared to doubt the identity of the proof, the derivation has lost its proving power. For the proof serves as a measure.

Could one say: it is part of proof to have an accepted criterion for the correct reproduction of a proof?

That is to say, e.g.: we must be able to be certain, it must hold as certain for us, that we have not overlooked a sign in the course of the

proof. That no demon can have deceived us by making a sign disappear without our noticing, or by adding one, etc.

One might say: When it can be said: "Even if a demon had deceived
us, still everything would be all right", then the prank he wanted to
play on us has simply failed of its purpose.

22.   Proof, one might say, does not merely shew *that* it is like this,
but: *how* it is like this. It shows *how* 13 + 14 yield 27.

"A proof must be capable of being taken in" means: we must be
prepared to use it as our guide-line in judging.

When I say "a proof is a picture"—it can be thought of as a cinematographic picture.

We construct the proof once for all.
A proof must of course have the character of a model.

The proof (the pattern of the proof) shews us the result of a procedure (the construction); and we are convinced that a procedure
regulated in *this* way always leads to this configuration.
(The proof exhibits a fact of synthesis to us.)

23.   When we say that a proof is a model,—we must, of course, not be saying anything new.

Proof must be a procedure of which I say: Yes, this is how it has to be; this must come out if I proceed according to this rule.

Proof, one might say, must originally be a kind of experiment—but is then taken simply as a picture.

If I pour two lots of 200 apples together and count them, and the result is 400, that is not a proof that 200 + 200 = 400. That is to say, we should not want to take this fact as a paradigm for judging all similar situations.

To say: "these 200 apples and these 200 apples come to 400"— means: when one puts them together, none are lost or added, they behave *normally*.

24.   "This is the model for the addition of 200 and 200"—not: "this is the model of the fact that 200 and 200 added together yield 400". The process of adding *did* indeed yield 400, but now we take this result as the criterion for the correct addition—or simply: for the addition—of these numbers.

The proof must be our model, our picture, of how these operations have *a result*.

The 'proved proposition' expresses what is to be read off from the proof-picture.

The proof is now our model of correctly counting 200 apples and 200 apples together: that is to say, it defines a new concept: 'the counting of 200 and 200 objects together'. Or, as we could also say: "a new criterion for nothing's having been lost or added".

The proof *defines* 'correctly counting together'.

The proof is our model for a particular *result's being yielded*, which serves as an object of comparison (yardstick) for real changes.

25.　　The proof convinces us of something——though what interests us is, not the mental state of conviction, but the applications attaching to this conviction.

For this reason the assertion that the proof convinces us of the truth of this proposition leaves us cold,—since this expression is capable of the most various constructions.

When I say: "the proof convinces me of something", still the proposition expressing this conviction need not be constructed in the proof. As e.g. we multiply, but do not necessarily write down the result in the form of the proposition '... × ... = ...' So we shall presumably say: the multiplication gives us this conviction without our ever uttering the *sentence* expressing it.

A psychological disadvantage of proofs that construct *propositions* is that they easily make us forget that the *sense* of the result is not to be read off from this by itself, but from the *proof*. In this respect the intrusion of the Russellian symbolism into the proofs has done a great deal of harm.

The Russellian signs veil the important forms of proof as it were to the point of unrecognizability, as when a human form is wrapped up in a lot of cloth.

26. Let us remember that in mathematics we are convinced of *grammatical* propositions; so the expression, the result, of our being convinced is that we *accept a rule*.

Nothing is more likely than that the verbal expression of the result of a mathematical proof is calculated to delude us with a myth.

27. I am trying to say something like this: even if the proved mathematical proposition seems to point to a reality outside itself, still it is only the expression of acceptance of a new measure (of reality).

Thus we take the constructability (provability) of this symbol (that is, of the mathematical proposition) as a sign that we are to transform symbols in such and such a way.

We have won through to a piece of knowledge in the proof? And the final proposition expresses this knowledge? Is this knowledge now independent of the proof (is the navel string cut)?—Well, the proposition is now used by itself and without having the proof attached to it.

Why should I not say: in the proof I have won through to a *decision*?

The proof places this decision in a system of decisions.

(I might of course also say: "the proof convinces me that this rule serves my purpose". But to say this might easily be misleading.)

28.   The proposition proved by means of the proof serves as a rule—and so as a paradigm. For we *go by* the rule.

But does the proof only bring us to the point of going by this rule (accepting it), or does it also shew us *how* we are to go by it?

For the mathematical proposition is to shew us what it makes SENSE to say.

The proof constructs a proposition; but the point is *how* it constructs it. Sometimes, for example, it first constructs a *number* and then comes the proposition that there is such a number. When we say that the construction must *convince* us of the proposition, that means that it must lead us to apply this proposition in such-and-such a way. That it must determine us to accept this as sense, that not.

29. What is in common between the purpose of a Euclidean construction, say the bisection of a line, and the purpose of deriving a rule from rules by means of logical inferences?

The common thing seems to be that by the construction of a sign I compel the acceptance of a sign.

Could we say: "mathematics creates new *expressions*, not new propositions"?
Inasmuch, that is, as mathematical propositions are instruments taken up into the language once for all—and their proof shews the place where they stand.

But in what sense are e.g. Russell's tautologies 'instruments of language'?

Russell at any rate would not have held them to be so. His mistake, if there was one, can however only have consisted in his not paying attention to their *application*.

The proof makes one structure generate another.

It exhibits the generation of one from others.

That is all very well—but still it does quite different things in different cases! What is the *interest* of this transition?

Even if I think of a proof as something deposited in the archives of language—who says *how* this instrument is to be employed, what it is for?

30. A proof leads me to say: this *must* be like this.——Now, I understand this in the case of a Euclidean proof or the proof of '25 times 25 = 625', but is it also like this in the case of a Russellian proof, e.g. of '⊢ $p \supset q \cdot p : \supset : q$'? What does 'it *must* be like this' mean here in contrast with 'it is like this'? Should I say: "Well, I accept this expression as a paradigm for all non-informative propositions of this form"?

I go through the proof and say: "Yes, this is how it *has* to be; I must fix the use of my language in *this* way".

I want to say that the *must* corresponds to a track which I lay down in language.

31.　When I said that a proof introduces a new concept, I meant something like: the proof puts a new paradigm among the paradigms of the language; like when someone mixes a special reddish blue, somehow settles the special mixture of the colours and gives it a name.

But even if we are inclined to call a proof such a new paradigm—what is the exact similarity of the proof to such a concept-model?

One would like to say: the proof changes the grammar of our language, changes our concepts. It makes new connexions, and it creates the concept of these connexions. (It does not establish that they are there; they do not exist until it makes them.)

32.　What concept is created by '$p \supset p$'? And yet I feel as if it would be possible to say that '$p \supset p$' serves as the sign of a concept.

'$p \supset p$' is a formula. Does a formula establish a concept? One can say: "by the formula . . . such-and-such follows from this". Or again: "such-and-such follows from this in the following way: . . ." But is that the sort of proposition I want? What, however, about: "Draw the consequences of this in the following way: . . ."?

33.　If I call a proof a model (a picture), then I must also be able to say this of a Russellian primitive proposition (as the egg-cell of a proof).

It can be asked: how did we come to utter the sentence '$p \supset p$' as a true assertion? Well, it was not used in practical linguistic inter-course,—but still there was an inclination to utter it in particular circumstances (when for example one was doing logic) *with conviction.*

But what about '$p \supset p$'? I see in it a degenerate proposition, which is on the side of truth.

I fix it as an important point of intersection of significant sentences. A pivotal point of our method of description.

34.   The construction of a proof begins with some signs or other, and among these some, the 'constants', must already have meaning in the language. In this way it is essential that 'v' and '$\sim$' already possess a familiar application, and the construction of a proof in *Principia Mathematica* gets its importance, its sense, from this. But the signs of the proof do *not* enable us to see this meaning.

The 'employment' of the proof has of course to do with that employ-ment of its signs.

35.   To repeat, in a certain sense even Russell's primitive propositions convince me.

Thus the conviction produced by a proof cannot simply arise from the proof-construction.

36.   If I were to see the standard metre in Paris, but were not

acquainted with the institution of measuring and its connexion with the standard metre—could I say, that I was acquainted with the concept of the standard metre?

Is a proof not also part of an institution in this way?

A proof is an instrument—but why do I say "an instrument of language"?

Is a calculation necessarily an instrument of language, then?

37. What I always do seems to be—to emphasize a distinction between the determination of a sense and the employment of a sense.

38. Accepting a proof: one may accept it as the paradigm of the pattern that arises when *these* rules are correctly applied to certain patterns. One may accept it as the correct derivation of a rule of inference. Or as a correct derivation from a correct empirical proposition; or as the correct derivation from a false empirical proposition; or simply as the correct derivation from an empirical proposition, of which we do not know whether it is true or false.

But now can I say that the conception of a proof as 'proof of constructability' of the proved proposition is in some sense a simpler, more primary, one than any other conception?

Can I therefore say: "Any proof proves *first and foremost* that this formation of signs must result when I apply these rules to these formations of signs"? Or: "The proof proves first and foremost that this formation can arise when one operates with these signs according to these transformation-rules".—

This would point to a geometrical application. For the proposition whose truth, as I say, is proved here, is a geometrical proposition—a proposition of grammar concerning the transformations of signs. It might for example be said: it is proved that it makes *sense* to say that someone has got the sign ... according to these rules from ... and ...; but no sense etc. etc.

Or again: when mathematics is divested of all content, it would remain that certain signs can be constructed from others according to certain rules.—

The least that we have to accept would be: that these signs etc. etc.—and accepting this is a basis for accepting anything else.

I should now like to say: the sequence of signs in the proof does not necessarily carry with it any kind of acceptance. If however it's to be a matter of accepting, this does not have to be 'geometrical' acceptance.

A proof could surely consist of only two steps: say one proposition '$(x).fx$' and one 'fa'—does the correct transition according to a rule play an important part here?

39.   *What* is unshakably certain about what is proved?

To accept a proposition as unshakably certain—I want to say—means to use it as a grammatical rule: this removes uncertainty from it.

"Proof must be capable of being taken in" really means nothing but: a proof is not an experiment. We do not accept the result of a proof because it results once, or because it often results. But we see in the proof the reason for saying that this *must* be the result.

What *proves* is not that this correlation leads to this result—but that we are persuaded to take these appearances (pictures) as models for what it is like if. . . . .

The proof is our new model for what it is like if nothing gets added and nothing taken away when we count correctly etc.. But these words shew that I do not quite know what the proof is a model of.

I want to say: with the logic of *Principia Mathematica* it would be possible to justify an arithmetic in which 1000 + 1 = 1000; and all that would be necessary for this purpose would be to doubt the sensible correctness of calculations. But if we do not doubt it, then it is not our conviction of the truth of logic that is responsible.

When we say in a proof: "This *must* come out"—then this is not for reasons that we do not *see*.

It is not our getting this result, but its being the end of this route, that makes us accept it.

What convinces us—*that* is the proof: a configuration that does not convince us is not the proof, even when it can be shewn to exemplify the proved proposition.

That means: it must not be necessary to make a physical investigation of the proof-configuration in order to shew us what has been proved.

40.   If we have a picture of two men, we do not say *first* that the one appears smaller than the other, and *then* that he seems to be further away. It is, one can say, perfectly possible that the one figure's being shorter should not strike us at all, but only its being behind. (This seems to me to be connected with the question of the 'geometrical' conception of proof.)

41.   "It (the proof) is the model for what is called such-and-such."

But what is the transition from '$(x).fx$' to 'fa' supposed to be a model for? At most for how inferences can be drawn from signs like '$(x).fx$'. I thought of the model as a justification, but here it is not a justification. The pattern $(x).fx \therefore fa$ does not *justify* the conclusion. If we want to talk about a justification of the conclusion, it lies outside this schema of signs.

And yet there is something in saying that a mathematical proof creates a new concept.—Every proof is as it were an avowal of a particular employment of signs.

But what is it an avowal of? Only of *this* employment of the rules of transition from formula to formula? Or is it also an avowal in some sense, of the 'axioms'?

Could I say: I avow $p \supset p$ as a tautology?

I accept '$p \supset p$' as a maxim, e.g. of inference.

The idea that proof creates a new concept might also be roughly put as follows: a proof is not its foundations plus the rules of inference, but a *new* building—although it is an example of such and such a style. A proof is a *new* paradigm.

The concept which the proof creates may for example be a new concept of inference, a new concept of correct inferring. But as for *why* I accept this as *correct* inferring, the reasons for that lie outside the proof.

The proof creates a new concept by creating or being a new sign. Or—by giving the proposition which is its result a new place. (For the proof is not a movement but a route.)

42.   It must not be *imaginable* for *this* substitution in *this* expression to yield anything else. Or: I must declare it unimaginable. (The result of an experiment, however, can turn out this way or that.)

Still, the case could be imagined in which a proof altered in appearance—engraved in rock, it is stated to be the same whatever the appearance says.

Are you really saying anything but: a proof is taken as *proof*?

Proof must be a procedure plain to view. Or again: the proof is the procedure that is *plain to view*.

It is not something behind the proof, but the proof, that proves.

43.   When I say: "it must first and foremost be evident that *this* substitution really yields *this* expression"—I might also say: "I must accept it as indubitable"—but then there must be good reasons for this: for example, that the same substitution practically always yields

the same result etc. . And isn't this exactly what surveyability consists in?

I should like to say that where surveyability is not present, i.e. where there is room for a doubt whether what we have really is the result of this substitution, the *proof* is destroyed. And not in some silly and unimportant way that has nothing to do with the *nature* of proof.

Or: logic as the foundation of all mathematics does not work, and to shew this it is enough that the cogency of logical proof stands and falls with its geometrical cogency.[1]

We incline to the belief that *logical* proof has a peculiar, absolute cogency, deriving from the unconditional certainty in logic of the fundamental laws and the laws of inference. Whereas propositions proved in this way can after all not be more certain than is the correctness of the way those laws of inference are *applied*.

That is to say: logical proof, e.g. of the Russellian kind, is cogent only so long as it also possesses geometrical cogency.[1] And an abbreviation of such a logical proof may have this cogency and so be a proof, when the Russellian construction, completely carried out, is not.

---

[1] But compare § 38. (Eds.)

The logical certainty of proofs—I want to say—does not extend beyond their geometrical certainty.

44. Now if a proof is a model, then the point must be what is to count as a correct reproduction of the proof.

If, for example, the sign '| | | | | | | | |' were to occur in a proof, it is not clear whether merely 'the same number' of strokes (or perhaps little crosses) should count as the reproduction of it, or whether some other, not too small, number does equally well. Etc.

But the question is what is to count as the criterion for the reproduction of a proof—for the identity of proofs. How are they to be compared to establish the identity? Are they the same if they look the same?

I should like, so to speak, to shew that we can get away from logical proofs in mathematics.

45. "By means of suitable definitions, we can prove '25 × 25 = 625' in Russell's logic."—And can I define the ordinary technique of proof by means of Russell's? But how can one technique of proof be *defined* by means of another? How can one explain the *essence* of another? For if the one is an 'abbreviation' of the other, it must surely be a *systematic*

abbreviation. Proof is surely required that I can systematically shorten the long proofs and thus once more get a system of proofs.

Long proofs at first always go along with the short ones and as it were tutor them. But in the end they can no longer follow the short ones and these shew their independence.

The consideration of *long* unsurveyable logical proofs is only a means of shewing how this technique—which is based on the geometry of proving—may collapse, and new techniques become necessary.

46. I should like to say: mathematics is a MOTLEY of techniques of proof.——And upon this is based its manifold applicability and its importance.

But that comes to the same thing as saying: if you had a system like that of Russell and produced systems like the differential calculus out of it by means of suitable definitions, you would be producing a new bit of mathematics.

Now surely one could simply say: if a man had invented calculating in the decimal system—that would have been a mathematical invention! —Even if he had already got Russell's *Principia Mathematica*.—

What is it to co-ordinate one system of proofs with another? It involves a translation rule by means of which proved propositions of the one can be translated into proved propositions of the other.

Now it is possible to imagine some—or all—of the proof systems of present-day mathematics as having been co-ordinated in such a way with one system, say that of Russell. So that all proofs could be carried out in this system, even though in a roundabout way. So would there then be only the single system—no longer the many?—But then it must surely be possible to shew of the *one* system that it can be resolved into the many.—*One* part of the system will possess the properties of trigonometry, another those of algebra, and so on. Thus one *can* say that different techniques are used in these parts.

I said: whoever invented calculation in the decimal notation surely made a mathematical discovery. But could he not have made this discovery all in Russellian symbols? He would, so to speak, have discovered a new *aspect*.

"But in that case the truth of true mathematical propositions can still be proved from those general foundations."—It seems to me there is a snag here. When do we say that a mathematical proposition is true?—

It seems to me as if we were introducing new concepts into the Russellian logic without knowing it.——For example, when we settle what signs of the form '$(\exists x, y, z \ldots)$' are to count as equivalent to one another, and what are not to count as equivalent.

Is it a matter of course that '$(\exists x, y, z)$' is not the same sign as '$(\exists x, y, z, n)$'?

But suppose I first introduce '$p \lor q$' and '$\sim p$' and use them to construct some tautologies—and then produce (say) the series $\sim p$, $\sim \sim p$, $\sim \sim \sim p$, etc. and introduce a notation like $\sim^1 p$, $\sim^2 p$, ... $\sim^{10} p$. ... I should like to say: we should perhaps originally never have thought of the *possibility* of such a sequence and we have now introduced a new concept into our calculation. Here is a 'new aspect'.

It is clear that I could have introduced the concept of number in this way, even though in a very primitive and inadequate fashion—but this example gives me all I need.

In what sense can it be correct to say that one would have introduced a new concept into logic with the series $\sim p$, $\sim \sim p$, $\sim \sim \sim p$, etc.? —Well, first of all one could be said to have done it with the '*etc.*'. For this '*etc.*' stands for a law of sign formation which is new to me. A characteristic mark of this is the fact that *recursive* definition is required for the explanation of the decimal notation.

A new *technique* is introduced.

It can also be put like this: having the concept of the Russellian formation of proofs and propositions does *not* mean you have the concept of every *series* of Russellian signs.

I should like to say: Russell's foundation of mathematics postpones the introduction of new techniques—until finally you believe that this is no longer necessary at all.

(It would perhaps be as if I were to philosophize about the concept of measurement of length for so long that people forgot that the actual fixing of a unit of length is necessary before you can measure length.)

47.   Can what I want to say be put like *this*: "If we had learnt from the beginning to do all mathematics in Russell's system, the differential calculus, for example, would not have been invented just by our having Russell's calculus. So if someone discovered this kind of calculation *in Russell's calculus*————."

Suppose I had Russellian proofs of the propositions

$$'p \equiv \sim \sim p'$$
$$'\sim p \equiv \sim \sim \sim p'$$
$$'p \equiv \sim \sim \sim \sim p'$$

and I were now to find a shortened way of proving the proposition

$$'p \equiv \sim {}^{10}p'.$$

It is as if I had discovered a new kind of calculation within the old calculus. What does its having been discovered consist in?

Tell me: have I discovered a new kind of calculation if, having once learnt to multiply, I am struck by multiplications with all the factors the same, as a special branch of these calculations, and so I introduce the notation '$a^n = \ldots$'?

Obviously the mere 'shortened', or *different*, notation—'16^2' instead of '16×16'—does not amount to that. What is important is that we now merely *count* the factors.

Is '16^{15}' merely another notation for '$16 \times 16 \times 16 \times 16 \times 16 \times 16 \times 16 \times 16 \times 16 \times 16 \times 16 \times 16 \times 16 \times 16 \times 16$'?

The proof that $16^{15} = \ldots$ does not simply consist in my multiplying 16 by itself fifteen times and getting this result—the proof must shew that I take the number as a factor 15 times.

When I ask "What is new about the 'new kind of calculation'—exponentiation"—that is difficult to say. The expression 'new aspect' is vague. It means that we now look at the matter differently—but the question is: what is the essential, the *important* manifestation of this 'looking at it differently'?

First of all I want to say: "It need never have *struck* anyone that in certain products all the factors are equal"—or: " 'Product of all equal factors' is a new concept"—or: "What is new consists in our classifying calculations differently". In exponentiation the essential thing is evidently that we look at the *number* of the factors. But who says we ever attended to the number of factors? It *need* not have struck us that there are products with 2, 3, 4 factors etc. although we have often worked out such products. A new aspect—but once more: what is *important* about it? For what purpose do I use what has struck me?—Well, first of all perhaps I put it down in a notation. Thus I write e.g. 'a^2' instead of '$a \times a$'. By this means I refer to the series of numbers (allude to it), which did not happen before. So I am surely setting up a new connexion!—A connexion—between what objects? Between the technique of counting factors and the technique of multiplying.

But in that way every proof, each individual calculation makes new connexions!

But the *same* proof as shews that $a \times a \times a \times a \ldots = b$, surely also shews that $a^n = b$; it is only that we have to make the transition according to the definition of 'a^n'.—

But this transition is exactly what is new. But if it is only a transition to the old proof, how can it be important?

'It is only a different notation.' Where does it stop being—just a different notation?

Isn't it where only the one notation and not the other can be used in such-and-such a way?

It might be called "finding a new aspect", if someone writes '$a(f)$' instead of '$f(a)$'; one might say: "He *looks at* the function as an argument of its argument". Or if someone wrote '$\times(a)$' instead of '$a \times a$' one could say: "he looks at what was previously regarded as a special case of a function with two argument places as a function with *one* argument place".

If anyone does this he has certainly altered the aspect in a sense, he has for example classified *this* expression with others, compared it with others, with which it was not compared before.—But now, is that an *important* change of aspect? *No*, not so long as it does not have certain consequences.

It is true enough that I changed the aspect of the logical calculation by introducing the concept of the *number* of negations: "I never looked at it like that"—one might say. But this alteration only becomes important when it connects with the application of the sign.

Conceiving one foot as *12 inches* would indeed mean changing the aspect of 'a foot', but this change would only become important if one now also *measured* lengths in inches.

If you introduce the counting of negation signs, you bring in a new way of reproducing signs.

For arithmetic, which does talk about the equality of numbers, it is indeed a matter of complete indifference how equality of number of two classes is established—but for its inferences it is not indifferent how its signs are compared with one another, and so e.g. what is the method of establishing whether the number of figures in two numerical signs is the same.

It is not the introduction of numerical signs as abbreviations that is important, but the *method* of counting.

48.   I want to give an account of the motley of mathematics.

49. "I can carry out the proof that $127 : 18 = 7 \cdot 0\dot{5}$ in Russell's system too." Why not.—But must the same result be reached in the

Russellian proof as in ordinary division? The two are of course connected by means of a type of *calculation* (by rules of translation, say—); but still, is it not risky to work out the division by the new technique, —since the truth of the result is now dependent on the geometry of the rendering?

But now suppose someone says: "Nonsense—such considerations play no part in mathematics".—

—But the question is not one of uncertainty, for we *are* certain of our conclusions, but of whether we are still doing (Russellian) logic when we e.g. divide.

50.   Trigonometry has its original importance in connexion with measurements of lengths and angles: it is a bit of mathematics adapted to employment on measurements of lengths and angles.
Applicability to this field might also be called an 'aspect' of trigonometry.

When I divide a circle into equal sectors and determine the cosine of one of these sectors by measurement—is that a calculation or an experiment?

If a calculation—is it SURVEYABLE?
Is calculation with a slide-rule *surveyable*?

If the cosine of an angle has to be determined by measurement, is a proposition of the form 'cos α = n' a *mathematical* proposition? What is the criterion for this decision? Does the proposition say something external about our rulers etc.; or something internal about our concepts?—How is this to be decided?

Do the figures (drawings) in trigonometry belong to pure mathematics, or are they only examples of a possible *application*?

51.   If there is something true about what I am trying to say, then—e.g.—calculating in the decimal notation must have its own life.—One can of course represent any decimal number in the form:

and hence carry out the four species of calculation in this notation. But the life of the decimal notation would have to be independent of calculating with unit strokes.

52.   In this connexion the following point constantly occurs to me: while indeed a proposition '*a* : *b* = *c*' can be *proved* in Russell's logic, still that logic does not teach us to construct a correct sentence of this form, i.e. does not teach us to *divide*. The procedure of dividing would correspond e.g. to that of a *systematic testing* of Russellian proofs with a view, say, to getting the proof of a proposition of the form '37 × 15 = *x*'. "But the technique of such a systematic testing is in its turn founded on logic. It can surely be logically proved in turn that

this technique must lead to the goal." So it is like proving in Euclid that such-and-such can be constructed in such-and-such a way.

53.   If someone tries to shew that mathematics is not logic, what is he trying to shew? He is surely trying to say something like:—If tables, chairs, cupboards, etc. are swathed in enough paper, certainly they will look spherical in the end.

He is not trying to shew that it is impossible that, for every mathematical proof, a Russellian proof can be constructed which (somehow) 'corresponds' to it, but rather that the acceptance of such a correspondence does not lean on logic.

"But surely we can always go back to the primitive logical method!" Well, assuming that we can—how is it that we don't *have* to? Or are we hasty, reckless, if we do not?

But how do we get back to the primitive expression? Do we e.g. take the route through the secondary proof and back from the end of it into the primary system, and then look to see where we have got; or do we go forward in both systems and then connect the end points? And how do we know that we reach the same result in the primary system in the two cases?

Does not proceeding in the secondary system carry the power of conviction with it?

"But at every step in the secondary system, we can imagine that it could be taken in the primary one too!"—That is just it: *we can imagine that it could be done*—without doing it.

And why do we accept the one in place of the other? On grounds of *logic*?

"But can't one prove logically that both transformations must lead to the same result?"—But what is in question here is surely the result of transformations of signs! How can logic decide this?

54.   How can the proof in the stroke system prove that the proof in the decimal system is a proof?

Well—isn't it the same for the proof in the decimal system, as it is for a *construction* in Euclid of which it is proved that it really is the construction of such-and-such a figure?

Can I put it like this: "The translation of the stroke system into the decimal system presupposes a recursive definition. This definition, however, does not introduce the abbreviation of *one* expression to another. Yet of course inductive proof in the decimal system does not contain the whole set of those signs which would have to be translated by means of the recursive definition into stroke signs. Therefore this general proof cannot be translated by recursive definition into a proof in the stroke system."?

Recursive definition introduces a new sign-technique.—It must therefore make the transition to a new 'geometry'. We are taught a new method of recognizing signs. A new criterion for the identity of signs is introduced.

55.   A proof shews us what OUGHT to come out.—And since every reproduction of the proof must demonstrate the same thing, while on the one hand it must reproduce the result automatically, on the other hand it must also reproduce the *compulsion* to get it.

That is: we reproduce not merely the *conditions* which once yielded this result (as in an experiment), but the result itself. And yet the proof is not a stacked game, inasmuch as it must always be capable of guiding us.

On the one hand we must be able to reproduce the proof *in toto* automatically, and on the other hand this reproduction must once more be *proof* of the result.

"Proof must be surveyable": this aims at drawing our attention to the difference between the concepts of 'repeating a proof', and 'repeating an experiment'. To repeat a proof means, not to reproduce the conditions under which a particular result was once obtained, but to repeat every step *and the result*. And although this shews that proof is something that must be capable of being reproduced *in toto* automatically, still every such reproduction must contain the force of proof, which compels acceptance of the result.

56.   When do we say that one calculus 'corresponds' to another, is only an abbreviated form of the first?—"Well, when the results of the latter can be translated by means of suitable definitions into the results of the former." But has it been said how one is to calculate with these definitions? What makes us accept this translation? Is it a stacked game in the end? It is, if we are decided on only accepting the translation that leads to the accustomed result.

Why do we call a part of the Russellian calculus the part corresponding to the differential calculus?—Because the propositions of the differential calculus are proved in it.—But, ultimately, after the event. —But does that matter? Sufficient that proofs of these propositions can be found in the Russellian system! But aren't they proofs of these propositions only when their results can be translated only into *these* propositions? But is that true even in the case of multiplying in the stroke system with numbered strokes?

57.   Now it must be clearly stated that calculations in the stroke notation will normally always agree with those in the decimal notation. Perhaps, in order to make sure of agreement, we shall at some point have to take to getting the stroke-calculation worked over by *several* people. And we shall do the same for calculations with still higher numbers in the decimal system.

But that of course is enough to shew that it is not the proofs in the stroke notation that make the proofs in the decimal system cogent.

"Still, if we did not have the latter, we could use the former to prove the same thing."—The same thing? What is the same thing?— Well, the stroke proof will convince me of the same thing, though not in the same way.—Suppose I were to say: "The place to which a proof leads us cannot be determined independently of this proof."—Did a proof in the stroke system demonstrate to me that the proved proposition possesses the applicability given it by the proof in the decimal system—was it e.g. proved in the stroke system that the proposition is also provable in the decimal system?

58.   Of course it would be nonsense to say that *one* proposition cannot have two proofs—for we do say just that. But can we not say: *this* proof shews that . . . results when we do *this*; the other proof shews that this expression results when we do something else?

For is e.g. the mathematical fact that 129 is divisible by 3 independent of the fact that *this* is the result in *this* calculation? I mean: is the fact of this divisibility independent of the *calculus* in which it is a result; or is it a fact of this calculus?

Suppose it were said: "By calculating we get acquainted with the properties of numbers".

But do the properties of numbers *exist* outside the calculating?

"Two proofs prove the same when what they convince me of is the same."—And when is what they convince me of the same?—How do I know that what they convince me of is the same? Not of course by introspection.

I can be brought to accept this rule by a variety of paths.

59.   "Each proof proves not merely the truth of the proposition proved, but also that it can be proved *in this way*."—But this latter can also be proved in another way.—"Yes, but the proof proves this in a particular way and in doing so proves that it can be demonstrated in this way."—But even *that* could be shewn by means of a different proof.—"Yes, but then not in this way."—

But this means e.g.: this proof is a mathematical entity that cannot be replaced by any other; one can say that it can convince us of something that nothing else can, and this can be given expression by our assigning to it a proposition that we do not assign to any other proof.

60.   But am I not making a crude mistake? For just this is essential to the propositions of arithmetic and to the propositions of the Russellian logic: various proofs lead to them. Even: infinitely many proofs lead to any one of them.

Is it correct to say that every proof demonstrates something to us which it alone can demonstrate? Would not—so to speak—the proved proposition then be superfluous, and the proof itself also be the thing proved?

Is it only the proved proposition that the proof convinces me of?

What is meant by: "A proof is a mathematical entity which cannot be replaced by any other"? It surely means that every single proof has a usefulness which no other one has. It might be said: "—that every proof, even of a proposition which has already been proved, is a contribution to mathematics". But why is it a contribution if its only point was to prove the proposition? Well, one can say: "the new proof shews (or *makes*) a new connexion". (But in that case is there not a mathematical proposition saying that this connexion exists?)

What do we *learn* when we see the new proof—apart from the proposition, which we already know anyhow? Do we learn something that cannot be expressed in a mathematical proposition?

61. How far does the application of a mathematical proposition depend on what is allowed to count as a proof of it and what is not?

I can surely say: if the proposition '137 × 373 = 46792' is true in the ordinary sense, *then there must be a multiplication-sum*, at the ends of which stand the two sides of this equation. And a multiplication-sum is a pattern satisfying certain rules.

I want to say: if I did not accept the multiplication-sum as *one* proof of the proposition, then that would mean that the application of the proposition to multiplication-sums would be gone.

62. Let us remember that it is not enough that two proofs meet in the same propositional sign. For how do we know that this sign

says the same thing both times? *That* must proceed from other connexions.

63.   The *exact* correspondence of a correct (convincing) transition in music and in mathematics.

64.   Suppose I were to set someone the problem: "Find a proof of the proposition . . ."—The answer would surely be to shew me certain signs. Very well: *what* condition must these signs satisfy? They must be a proof of that proposition—but is that, say, a *geometrical* condition? Or a psychological one? Sometimes it could be called a geometrical condition; where the means of proof are already prescribed and all that is being looked for is a particular arrangement.

65.   Are the propositions of mathematics anthropological propositions saying how we men infer and calculate?—Is a statute book a work of anthropology telling how the people of this nation deal with a thief etc.?——Could it be said: "The judge looks up a book about anthropology and thereupon sentences the thief to a term of imprisonment"? Well, the judge does not USE the statute book as a manual of anthropology.

66.   The prophecy does *not* run, that a man will get *this* result when he follows this rule in making a transformation—but that he will get this result, when we *say* that he is following the rule.

What if we said that mathematical propositions were prophecies in *this* sense: they predict what result members of a society who have learnt this technique will get in agreement with other members of the society? '25 × 25 = 625' would thus mean that men, if we judge them to obey the rules of multiplication, will reach the result 625 when they multiply 25 × 25.—That this is a correct prediction is beyond doubt; and also that calculating is in essence founded on such predictions. That is to say, we should not call something 'calculating' if we could not make such a prophecy with certainty. This really means: calculating is a technique. And what we have said pertains to the essence of a technique.

67.   This consensus belongs to the essence of *calculation*, so much is certain. I.e.: this consensus is part of the phenomenon of our calculating.

In a technique of *calculating* prophecies must be possible.
And that makes the technique of calculating similar to the technique of a *game*, like chess.

But what about this consensus—doesn't it mean that *one* human being by himself could not calculate? Well, *one* human being could at any rate not calculate just *once* in his life.

It might be said: all *possible* positions in chess can be conceived as propositions saying that they (themselves) are *possible* positions, or again as prophecies that people will be able to reach these positions by moves which they agree in saying are in accordance with the rules. A position *reached* in this way is then a proved proposition of this kind.

"A calculation is an experiment."——A calculation can be an experiment. The teacher makes the pupil do a calculation in order to see whether he can calculate; that is an experiment.

When the stove is lit in the morning, is that an experiment? But it could be one.

And in the same way moves in chess are *not* proofs either, and chess positions are not propositions. And mathematical propositions are not positions in a game. And in *this* way they are not prophecies either.

68.   If a calculation is an experiment, then what is a mistake in calculation? A mistake in the experiment? Surely not; it would have been a mistake in the experiment, if I had not observed the *conditions* of the experiment—if, e.g., I had made someone calculate when a terrible noise was going on.

But why should I not say: while a mistake in calculating is not a *mistake* in the experiment, still, it is a *miscarriage* of the experiment—sometimes explicable, sometimes inexplicable?

69.   "A calculation, for example a multiplication, is an experiment: *we do not know what will result* and we learn it once the multiplication is done."

—Certainly; nor do we know when we go for a walk where exactly we shall be in five minutes' time—but does that make going for a walk into an experiment?—Very well; but in the calculation I surely wanted from the beginning to know what the result was going to be; *that* was what I was interested in. I am, after all, curious about the result. Not, however, as what I am *going* to say, but as what I *ought* to say.

But isn't this just what interests you about this multiplication—how the generality of men will calculate? No—at least not usually—even if I am running to a common meeting point with everybody else.

But surely this is just what the calculation shews me experimentally —where this meeting point is. I as it were let myself unwind and see where I get. And the correct multiplication is the pattern of the way we all work, when we are wound up like *this*.

Experience teaches that we all find this calculation correct.

We let ourselves unwind and get the result of the calculation. But now—I want to say—we aren't interested in having—under such and such conditions say—actually produced this result, but in the pattern of our working; it interests us as a convincing, harmonious, pattern— not, however, as the result of an experiment, but as a *path*.

We say, not: "So *that's* how we go!", but: "So *that's* how it goes!"

70.   In what we accept we all work the same way, but we do not make use of this identity merely to predict what people will accept. Just as we do not *use* the proposition "this notebook is red" only to predict that most people will call it 'red'.

"And that's what we *call* 'the same'." If there did not exist an agreement in what we call 'red', etc. etc., language would stop. But what about the agreement in what we call 'agreement'?

We can describe the phenomenon of a confusion of language; but what are our tokens of confusion of language? Not necessarily tumult and muddle in action.   But rather that, e.g. I am lost when people talk, I cannot react in agreement with them.

"For me this is not a language-game."   But in this case I might also say: though they accompany their actions with spoken sounds and I cannot call their actions 'confused', still they haven't a *language*.—But perhaps their actions would become confused if they were prevented from emitting those sounds.

71.   It could be said: a proof helps communication.   An experiment presupposes it.

Or even: a mathematical proof moulds our language.

But it surely remains the case that we can use a mathematical proof to make scientific predictions about the proving done by other people.—

If someone asks me: "What colour is this book?" and I reply: "It's green"—might I as well have given the answer: "The generality of English-speaking people call that 'green' "?

Might he not ask: "And what do *you* call it?" For he wanted to get my reaction.

'*The limits of empiricism.*'[1]

72.   But there is such a thing as a science of conditioned calculating reflexes;—is that mathematics? That science will rely on experiments: and these experiments will be *calculations*. But suppose this science became quite exact and in the end even a 'mathematical' science?

Now is the result of these experiments that human beings agree in their calculations, or that they agree in what they call "agreeing"? And it goes on like that.

It could be said: that science would not function if we did not agree regarding the idea of agreement.

It is clear that we can make use of a mathematical work for a study in anthropology. But then one thing is not clear:—whether we

[1] Probably refers to Bertrand Russell's article *The Limits of Empiricism*. *Proceedings of the Aristotelian Society*, 1935–1936. (Eds.)

ought to say: "This writing shews us how operating with signs was done among these people", or: "This writing shews us what parts of mathematics these people had mastered".

73.   Can I say, on reaching the end of a multiplication: "So *this* is what I agree with!—"?—But can I say it at a single *step* of the multiplication? E.g. at the step '2 × 3 = 6'? Any more than I can say: "So this is what I call '*white*'!", looking at this paper?

It seems to me it would be a similar case if someone were to say: "When I call to mind what I have done to-day, I am making an experiment (starting myself off), and the memory that then comes serves to shew me what other people, who saw me, will reply to the question what I did".

What would happen if we rather often had this: we do a calculation and find it correct; then we do it again and find it isn't right; we believe we overlooked something before—then when we go over it again our second calculation doesn't seem right, and so on.

Now should I call this calculating or not?—At any rate he cannot use this calculation to predict that he will land there again next time.— But could I say that he calculated *wrong* this time, because the next time he did not calculate again the same way? I might say: where *this* uncertainty existed there would be no calculating.

But on the other hand I say again: 'Calculating is right—as it is done'. There *can* be no mistake of calculation in '12 × 12 = 144'. Why? This proposition has assumed a place among the rules.

But is '12 × 12 = 144' the assertion that it is natural to all men to work out 12 × 12 in such a way that the answer is 144?

74. If I go over a calculation several times so as to be sure of having done it right, and if I then accept it as correct,—haven't I repeated an experiment so as to be sure that I shall tick the same way the next time?—But why should going over the calculation three times convince me that I shall tick the same way the fourth time?—I'd say: I went over the calculation 'so as to be sure of not having overlooked anything'.

The danger here, I believe, is one of giving a justification of our procedure where there is no such thing as a justification and we ought simply to have said: *that's how we do it.*

When somebody makes an experiment repeatedly 'always with the same result', has he at the same time made an experiment which tells him *what* he will call 'the same result', i.e. how he uses the word "the same"? If you measure a table with a yardstick, are you also measuring the yardstick? If you are measuring the yardstick, then you cannot be measuring the table at the same time.

Suppose I were to say: "When someone measures the table with a yardstick he is making an experiment which tells him the results of measuring this table with *all other* yardsticks"? It is after all beyond doubt that a measurement with one yardstick can be used to predict the results of measurement with others. And, further, that if it could not—our whole system of measuring would collapse.

No yardstick, it might be said, would be correct, if in general they did not agree.—But when I say that, I do not mean that then they would all be *false*.

75. Calculating would lose its point, if *confusion* supervened. Just as the use of the words "green" and "blue" would lose its point. And yet it seems to be nonsense to say—that a proposition of arithmetic *asserts* that there will not be confusion.—Is the solution simply that the arithmetical proposition would not be *false* but useless, if confusion supervened?

Just as the proposition that this room is 16 foot long would not become *false*, if rulers and measuring fell into confusion. Its sense, not its truth, is founded on the regular working of measurements. (But don't be dogmatic here. There are transitional cases which complicate the discussion.)

Suppose I were to say: an arithmetical proposition expresses confidence that confusion will not supervene.

Then the use of all words expresses confidence that confusion will not supervene.

We cannot say, however, that use of the word "green" signifies that confusion will not supervene—because then the use of the word "confusion" would have in its turn to assert just the same thing about *this* word.

If '25 × 25 = 625' expresses the confidence that we shall always find it easy to agree on taking the road that ends with this proposition—

then why doesn't this last clause express confidence in something different, viz. that we should always be able to agree about *its* use?

We do not play the same language-game with the two propositions.

Or can one equally well be confident that one will see the same colour over there as here—and also: that one will be inclined to call the colour the same, if it is the same?

What I want to say is: mathematics as such is always measure, not thing measured.

76.   The concept of calculating excludes *confusion*.—Suppose someone were to get different results at different times when he did a multiplication, and *saw* this, but found it all right?—But then surely he could not use the multiplication for the same purposes as we!—Why not? Nor is there anything to say that he would necessarily fare ill if he did.

The conception of calculation as an experiment tends to strike us as the only *realistic* one.

Everything else, we think, is moonshine. In an experiment we have something tangible. It is almost as if one were to say: "When a poet composes he is making a psychological experiment; that is the only way of explaining how a poem can have value". We mistake the nature of '*experiment*',—believing that whenever we are keen on knowing the end of a process, it is what we call an "experiment".

It looks like obscurantism to say that a calculation is not an experiment. And in the same way so does the statement that mathematics does not *treat* of signs, or that pain is not a form of behaviour. But only because people believe that one is asserting the existence of an intangible, i.e. a shadowy, object side by side with what we all can grasp. Whereas we are only pointing to different modes of employment of words.

It is almost as if one were to say: 'Blue' has to stand for a blue object——otherwise we could not see what the word was for.

77. I have invented a game—realize that whoever begins must always win: so it isn't a game. I alter it; now it is all right.

Did I make an experiment, whose result was that whoever begins must always win? Or that we are inclined to play in such a way that this happens? No.——But the result was not what you would have expected! Of course not; but that does not make the game into an experiment.

But what does it mean not to know *why* it always has to work out like that? Well, it is because of the rules.—I want to know how I must alter the rules in order to get a proper game.—But you can e.g. alter them *entirely*—and so give a quite different game in place of this one.—But that is not what I want. I want to keep the general outline of the rules and only eliminate a mistake.—But that is vague. It is now simply *not clear* what is to be considered as the mistake.

It is almost like when one says: What is the mistake in this piece of music? It doesn't sound well on the instruments.—Now the mistake is not necessarily to be looked for in the instrumentation; it *could* be looked for in the themes.

Let us suppose, however, that the game is such that whoever begins can always win by a particular simple trick. But this has not been realized;—so it is a game. Now someone draws our attention to it; —and it stops being a game.

What turn can I give this, to make it clear to myself?—For I want to say: "and it stops being a game"—not: "and we now see that it wasn't a game".

That means, I want to say, it can also be taken like this: the other man did not *draw our attention* to anything; he taught us a different game in place of our own.——But how can the new game have made the old one obsolete?—We now see something different, and can no longer naïvely go on playing.

On the one hand the game consisted in our actions (our play) on the board; and these actions I could perform as well now as before. But on the other hand it was essential to the game that I blindly tried to win; and now I can no longer do that.

78.   Let us suppose that people originally practised the four kinds of calculation in the usual way. Then they began to calculate with bracketed expressions, including ones of the form $(a - a)$. Then they noticed that multiplications, for example, were becoming ambiguous. Would this have to throw them into confusion? Would they have to say: "Now the solid ground of arithmetic seems to wobble"?

And if they now demand a proof of consistency, because otherwise they would be in danger of falling into the bog at every step——what are they demanding? Well, they are demanding a kind of *order*. But was there *no* order before?—Well, they are asking for an order which appeases them now.—But are they like small children, that merely have to be lulled asleep?

Well, multiplication would surely become unusable in practice because of its ambiguity—that is for the former normal purposes. Predictions based on multiplications would no longer hit the mark.— (If I tried to predict the length of the line of soldiers that can be formed from a square 50 × 50, I should keep on arriving at wrong results.)

Is this kind of calculation wrong, then?—Well, it is unusable for *these* purposes. (Perhaps usable for other ones.) Isn't it as if I were once to divide instead of multiplying? (As can actually happen.)

What is meant by: "You have to *multiply* here; not divide!"—

Now is ordinary multiplication a *proper* game; is it *impossible* to trip up? And is the calculation with $(a - a)$ not a proper game—is it impossible *not* to trip up?

(What we want is to *describe*, not to explain.)

Now, what is it for us not to know our way about in our calculus?

We went sleepwalking along the road between abysses.—But even if we now say: "Now we are awake",—can we be certain that we shall not wake up one day? (And then say:—so we were asleep again.)

Can we be certain that there are not abysses now that we do not see? But suppose I were to say: The abysses in a calculus are not there if I don't see them!

Is no demon deceiving us at present? Well, if he is, it doesn't matter. What the eye doesn't see the heart doesn't grieve over.

Suppose I were to divide by 3 sometimes like this:

sometimes like this

without noticing it.—Then someone draws my attention to it.

To a mistake? Is it necessarily a mistake? And in what circumstances do we call it one?

79. $\left.\begin{array}{c} \sim f(f) = \phi\,(f)\,\text{Def.} \\ \therefore \\ \phi(\phi) = \sim \phi(\phi) \end{array}\right\}$

The propositions '$\phi(\phi)$' and '$\sim \phi(\phi)$' sometimes seem to say the same thing and sometimes opposite things. *According as we look at it* the proposition '$\phi(\phi)$' sometimes seems to say $\sim \phi(\phi)$, sometimes the opposite. And we sometimes see it as the product of the substitution:

$$\phi(f)\,\Big|^{f}_{\phi}$$

At other times as:

$$f(f)\,\Big|^{f}_{\phi}$$

We should like to say: " 'Heterological' is not heterological; so by definition it can be called 'heterological'." And it sounds all right, goes quite smoothly, and the contradiction need not strike us at all. If we become aware of the contradiction, we should at first like to say that we do not mean the same thing by the assertion, ξ is heterological, in the two cases. The one time it is the unabbreviated assertion, the other time the assertion abbreviated according to the definition.

We should then like to get out of the thing by saying: '$\sim \phi(\phi) = \phi_1(\phi)$'. But why should we lie to ourselves like this? Here two *contrary* routes really do lead—to the *same* thing.

Or again:—*it is equally natural* in this case to say '$\sim \phi(\phi)$' and '$\phi(\phi)$'.

According to the rule it is an equally natural expression to say that C lies to the right of the point A and that it lies to the left.

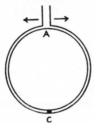

According to this rule—which says that a place lies in the direction of the arrow if the street that begins in that direction leads to it.

Let us look at it from the point of view of the language-games.—
Originally we played the game only with straight streets.———

80. Could it perhaps be imagined that where I see *blue*, this means that the object that I see is *not* blue—that the colour that appears to me always counts as the one that is *excluded*? I might for example believe that God always shews me a colour in order to say: *not* this.

Or does this work: the colour that I see merely tells me that this colour plays a part in the description of the object. It corresponds, not to a proposition, but merely to the word "blue". And the description of the object can then equally well run: "it is blue", and "it is not blue". Then one says: the eye only shows me blue, but not the role of this blue.—We compare seeing the colour with hearing the word "blue" when we have not heard the rest of the sentence.

I should like to shew that we could be led to want to describe something's being blue, both by saying it was blue, and by saying it was not blue.

And so that it is in our hands to make such a shift in the method of projection that '*p*' and '∼*p*' get the same sense. By which, however, they lose it, if I do not introduce something new as negation.

Now a language-game can lose its sense through a contradiction, can lose the character of a language-game.

And here it is important to say that this character is not described by saying that the sounds must have a certain *effect*. For our language-game (2)[1] would lose the character of a language-game if the builders kept on uttering different sounds instead of the 4 orders; even if it could be shewn, say physiologically, that it was always these noises that moved the assistant to bring the stones that he did bring.

Even here it could be said that of course the examination of language-games gets its importance from the fact that language-games continue to function. And so that it gets its importance from the fact that human beings can be trained to such a reaction to sounds.

---

[1] *Philosophical Investigations*, § 2 quoted here *infra*, VI § 40n. (Eds.)

It seems to me that there is a connexion between this and the question whether a calculation is an experiment made with a view to predicting the course of calculations. For suppose that one did a calculation and —correctly—predicted that one would calculate differently the next time, since the circumstances have changed then precisely by one's already having done the calculation *so-and-so* many times.

Calculating is a phenomenon which we know from calculating. As language is a phenomenon which we know from our language.

Can we say: 'Contradiction is harmless if it can be sealed off'? But what prevents us from sealing it off? That we do not know our way about in the calculus. Then *that* is the harm. And this is what one means when one says: the contradiction indicates that there is something wrong about our calculus. It is merely the (local) *symptom* of a sickness of the whole body. But the body is only sick if we do not know our way about.

The calculus has a secret sickness, means: what we have got is, as it is, not a calculus, and *we do not know our way about*—i.e. cannot give a calculus which corresponds 'in essentials' to this simulacrum of a calculus, and only excludes what is wrong in it.

But how is it possible not to know one's way about in a calculus: isn't it there, open to view?

Let us imagine having been taught Frege's calculus, contradiction and all. But the contradiction is not presented as a disease. It is, rather, an accepted part of the calculus, and we calculate with it. (The calculations do not serve the usual purpose of logical calculations.)—Now we are set the task of changing this calculus, of which the contradiction is an entirely respectable part, into another one, in which this contradiction is not to exist, as the new calculus is wanted for purposes which make a contradiction undesirable.—What sort of problem is this? And what sort of inability is it, if we say: "We have not yet found a calculus satisfying this condition"?

When I say: "I don't know my way about in the calculus"—I do not mean a mental state, but an inability to *do* something.

It is often useful, in order to help clarify a philosophical problem, to imagine the historical development, e.g. in mathematics, as quite different from what it actually was. If it had been different no one would have had the idea of saying what is actually said.

I should like to ask something like: "Is it usefulness you are out for in your calculus?—In that case you do not get any contradiction. And if you aren't out for usefulness—then it doesn't matter if you do get one."

81.   Our task is, not to discover calculi, but to describe the *present* situation.

The idea of the predicate which is true of itself etc. does of course lean on *examples*—but these examples were *stupidities*, for they were not thought out at all. But that is not to say that such predicates could not be applied, and that the contradiction would not then have its application!

I mean: if one really fixes one's eye on the application, it does not occur to one at all to write '$f(f)$'. On the other hand, if one is using the signs in the calculus, *without presuppositions* so to speak, one may also write '$f(f)$', and must then draw the consequences and not forget that one has not yet an *inkling* of a possible practical application of this calculus.

Is the question this: "Where did we forsake the region of usability?"?—

For might we not possibly have *wanted* to produce a contradiction? Have said—with pride in a mathematical discovery: "Look, this is how we produce a contradiction"? Might not e.g. a lot of people possibly have tried to produce a contradiction in the domain of logic, and then at last *one* person succeeded?

But why should people have tried to do *this*? Perhaps I cannot at present suggest the most plausible purpose. But why not e.g. in order to show that everything in this world is uncertain?

These people would then never actually employ expressions of the form $f(f)$, but still would be glad to lead their lives in the *neighbourhood* of a contradiction.

"Can I see an *order* which prevents me from unwittingly arriving at a contradiction?" That is like saying: shew me an order in my calculus to convince me that I can never in this way arrive at a number which. . . . Then I shew him e.g. a recursive proof.

But is it wrong to say: "Well, I shall go on. If I *see* a contradiction, then will be the time to do something about it."?—Is that: not really doing mathematics? Why should that *not* be calculating? I travel this road untroubled; if I should come to a precipice I shall try to turn round. Is that not 'travelling'?

Let us imagine the following case: the people of a certain tribe only know oral calculation. They have no acquaintance with writing. They teach their children to count in the decimal system. Among them mistakes in counting are very frequent, digits get repeated or left out without their noticing. Now a traveller makes a gramophone record of their counting. He teaches them writing and written calculation, and then shews them how often they make mistakes when they calculate just by word of mouth.—Would these people now have to admit that they had not really calculated before? That they had merely been groping about, whereas now they walk? Might they not perhaps even say: our affairs went better before, our intuition was not burdened with the dead stuff of writing? You cannot lay hold of the spirit with a machine. They say perhaps: "If we repeated a digit then, as your machine asserts—well, that will have been right".

We may trust 'mechanical' means of calculating or counting more than our memories. Why?—Need it be like this? I may have miscounted, but the machine, once constructed by us in such-and-such a way, cannot have miscounted. Must I adopt this point of view?— "Well, experience has taught us that calculating by machine is more trustworthy than by memory. It has taught us that our life goes smoother when we calculate with machines." But must smoothness necessarily be our ideal (must it be our ideal to have everything wrapped in cellophane)?

Might I not even trust memory and not trust the machine? And might I not mistrust the *experience* which 'gives me the illusion' that the machine is more trustworthy?

82.   Earlier I was not certain that, among the kinds of multiplication corresponding to *this* description, there was none yielding a result different from the accepted one. But say my uncertainty is such as only to arise at a certain distance from calculation of the normal kind; and suppose that we said: there it does no harm; for if I calculate in a very abnormal way, then I must just reconsider everything. Wouldn't this be all right?

I want to ask: *must* a proof of consistency (or of non-ambiguity) necessarily give me greater certainty than I have without it? And, if I am really out for adventures, *may* I not go out for ones where this proof no longer offers me any certainty?

My aim is to alter the *attitude* to contradiction and to consistency proofs. (*Not* to shew that this proof shews something unimportant. How *could* that be so?)

If for example I were anxious to produce contradictions, say for aesthetic purposes, then I should now unhesitatingly accept the inductive proof of consistency and say: it is hopeless to try and produce a contradiction in this calculus; the proof shews that it won't work. (Proof in theory of harmony.)————

83. It is a good way of putting things to say: "this order (this method) is unknown to this calculus, but not to that one".

What if one said: "A calculus to which this order is unknown is really not a calculus"?

(An office system to which this order is unknown is not really an office system.)

It is—I should like to say—for practical, not for theoretical purposes, that the disorder is avoided.

A kind of order is introduced because one has fared ill without it—or again, it is introduced, like streamlining in perambulators and lamps, because it has perhaps proved its value somewhere else and in this way has become the style or fashion.

The misuse of the idea of *mechanical* insurance against contradiction. But what if the parts of the mechanism fuse together, break or bend?

84.   "Only the proof of consistency shews me that I can rely on the calculus."

What sort of proposition is it, that only *then* can you rely on the calculus?   But what if you do rely on it *without* that proof! What sort of mistake have you made?

I introduce order; I say: "There are only *these* possibilities: . . .". It is like determining the set of possible permutations of *A*, *B*, *C*: before the order was there, I had perhaps only a foggy idea of this set.—Am I now quite certain that I have overlooked nothing? The order is a method for not overlooking anything. But—for not overlooking any possibility in the calculus, or: for not overlooking any possibility in reality?—Is it now certain that people will never want to calculate differently? That people will never look at our calculus as we look at the counting of aborigines whose numbers only go up to 5?—that we shall never want to look at reality differently? But *that* is not at all the certainty that this order is supposed to give us. It is not the eternal correctness of the calculus that is supposed to be assured, but only, so to speak, the temporal.

'But these are the possibilities that you *mean*!—Or do you mean other ones?'

The order convinces me that I have overlooked nothing when I have these 6 possibilities. But does it also convince me that nothing is going to be able to upset my present conception of such possibilities?

85. Could I imagine our fearing a possibility of constructing the heptagon, like the construction of a contradiction; and that the proof that the construction of the heptagon is impossible should have a settling effect, like a consistency proof?

How does it come about that we are at all tempted (or at any rate come near it) to divide through by $(3-3)$ in $(3-3) \times 2 = (3-3) \times 5$? How does it come about that by the rules this step looks plausible, and that even so it is still unusable?

When one tries to describe this situation it is enormously easy to make a mistake in the description. (So it is very difficult to describe.) The descriptions which immediately suggest themselves are all misleading—that is how our language in this field is arranged.

And there will be constant lapses from description into explanation here.

It was, or appears to be, *roughly* like this: we have a calculus, let us say, with the beads of an abacus; we then replace it by a calculus with written signs; this calculus suggests to us an extension of the method of calculating which the first calculus did not suggest—or perhaps better: the second calculus *obliterates* a distinction which was not to be overlooked in the first one. Now if it was the point of the first calculus that this distinction was made, and it is not made in the second one then the latter thereby lost its usability as an equivalent of the former. And now—it seems—the problem might arise: *where* did we depart from the original calculus, what frontiers in the new one correspond to the natural frontiers of the old?

I formed a system of rules of calculation which were modelled on those of another calculus. I took the latter as a model. But exceeded its limits. This was even an advantage; but now the new calculus became unusable in certain parts (at least for the former purposes). I therefore seek to alter it: that is, to replace it by one that is *to some extent* different. And by one that has the advantages without the disadvantages of the new one. But is that a clearly *defined* task?

Is there such a thing—it might also be asked—as *the right* logical calculus, only without the contradictions?

Could it be said, e.g., that while Russell's Theory of Types avoids the contradiction, still Russell's calculus is not THE universal logical calculus but perhaps an artificially restricted, mutilated one? Could it be said that the *pure, universal* logical calculus has yet to be found?

I was playing a game and in doing so I followed certain rules: but as for *how* I followed them, that depended on circumstances and the way it so depended was not laid down in black and white. (This is to some extent a misleading account.) Now I wanted to play this game in such a way as to follow rules 'mechanically' and I 'formalized' the game. But in doing this I reached positions where the game lost *all* point; I therefore wanted to avoid these positions 'mechanically'.— The formalization of logic did not work out satisfactorily. But what was the attempt made for at all? (What was it useful for?) Did not this need, and the idea that it must be capable of satisfaction, arise from a lack of clarity in another place?

The question "what was it useful for?" was a quite *essential* question. For the calculus was not invented for some practical purpose, but in order 'to give arithmetic a foundation'. But who says that arithmetic is logic, or what has to be done with logic to make it in some sense into a substructure for arithmetic? If we had e.g. been led to attempt this by aesthetic considerations, who says that it can succeed? (Who says that this English poem can be translated into German to our satisfaction?!)

(Even *if* it is clear that there is in *some* sense a translation of any English sentence into German.)

Philosophical dissatisfaction disappears by our seeing *more*.

By my allowing the cancelling of (3 — 3) this type of calculation loses its point. But suppose that, for example, I were to introduce a new sign of equality which was supposed to express: 'equal after *this* operation'? Would it, however, make sense to say: "Won in *this* sense", if in this sense I should win *every* game?

At certain places the calculus led me to its own abrogation. Now I want a calculus that does not do this and that excludes these places.— Does this mean, however, that any calculus in which such an exclusion does not occur is an uncertain one? "Well, the discovery of these places was a warning to us."—But did you not *misunderstand* this 'warning'?

86.   Can one prove that one has not overlooked anything?—Certainly. And must one not perhaps admit later: "Yes, I did overlook something; but not in the field for which my proof held"?

The proof of consistency must give us reasons for a prediction; and that is its *practical purpose*. That does not mean that this proof is a proof from the physics of our technique of calculation—and so a proof from applied mathematics—but it does mean that that prediction is the application that first suggests itself to us, and the one for whose sake we have this proof at heart. The prediction is not: "No disorder will arise *in this way*" (for that would not be a prediction: it is the mathematical proposition) but: "no disorder will arise".

I wanted to say: the consistency-proof can only set our minds at rest, if it is a cogent reason for this prediction.

87.   Where it is enough for me to get a proof that a contradiction or a trisection of the angle cannot be constructed in *this* way, the recursive proof achieves what is required of it. But if I had to fear that something somehow might at some time be interpreted as the construction of a contradiction, then no proof can take this indefinite fear from me.

The fence that I put round contradiction is not a super-fence.
How can a proof have put the calculus right in principle?

How can it have failed to be a proper calculus until this proof was found?

"This calculus is purely mechanical; a machine could carry it out."
What sort of machine? One constructed of the usual materials—or a
super-machine? Are you not confusing the hardness of a rule with the
hardness of a material?

We shall see contradiction in a quite different light if we look at its
occurrence and its consequences as it were anthropologically—and
when we look at it with a mathematician's exasperation. That is to
say, we shall look at it differently, if we try merely to *describe* how the
contradiction influences language-games, and if we look at it from the
point of view of the mathematical law-giver.

88.   But wait—isn't it clear that no one wants to reach a contradiction? And so that if you shew someone the possibility of a contradiction, he will do everything to make such a thing impossible?
(And so that if someone does not do this, he is a sleepyhead.)

But suppose he replied: "I can't imagine a contradiction in my calculus.—You have indeed shewn me a contradiction in another, but not in *this* one. In this *there is none*, nor can I see the possibility of one."

"If my conception of the calculus should sometime alter; if its aspect should alter because of some context that I cannot see now—then we'll talk some more about it."

"I do *not* see the possibility of a contradiction. Any more than you—as it seems—see the possibility of there being one in your consistency-proof."

Do I know whether, if I ever should see a contradiction where at present I can see no possibility of such a thing, it will then look dangerous to me?

89. "What does a proof teach me, apart from its result?"—What does a new tune teach me? Am I not under a temptation to say it teaches me something?—

90. I have not yet made the role of miscalculating clear. The role of the proposition: "I must have miscalculated". It is really the key to an understanding of the 'foundations' of mathematics.

PART IV

1942–1944

1. "The axioms of a mathematical axiom-system ought to be self-evident." How are they self-evident, then?

What if I were to say: *this* is how I find it easiest to imagine.

And here imagining is not a particular mental process during which one usually shuts one's eyes or covers them with one's hands.

2. What do we say when we are presented with such an axiom, e.g. the parallel axiom? Has experience shewn us that this is how it is? Well perhaps; but *what* experience? I mean: experience plays a part; but not the one that one would *immediately expect*. For we haven't made experiments and found that in reality only *one* straight line through a given point fails to cut another. And yet the proposition is evident.— Suppose I now say: it is quite indifferent why it is evident. It is enough that we accept it. All that is important is how we use it.

The proposition describes a picture. Namely:

We find this picture acceptable. As we find it acceptable to indicate our rough knowledge of a number by rounding it off at a multiple of 10.

'We accept this proposition.' But as *what* do we accept it?

3.   I want to say: when the words of e.g. the parallel-axiom are given (and we understand the language) the kind of use this proposition has and hence its sense are as yet quite undetermined. And when we say that it is evident, this means that we have already chosen a definite kind of employment for the proposition without realizing it. The proposition is not a mathematical axiom if we do not employ it precisely *for this purpose*.

The fact, that is, that here we do not make experiments, but accept the self-evidence, is enough to fix the employment. For we are not so naïf as to make the self-evidence count in place of experiment.

It is not our finding the proposition self-evidently true, but our making the self-evidence count, that makes it into a mathematical proposition.

4.   Does experience tell us that a straight line is possible between any two points? Or that two different colours cannot be at the same place?
It might be said: *imagination* tells us it. And the germ of truth is here; only one must understand it right.

Before the proposition the concept is still pliable.

But might not experience determine us to reject the axiom?! Yes. And nevertheless it does not play the part of an empirical proposition.

Why are the Newtonian laws not axioms of mathematics? Because we could quite well imagine things being otherwise. But—I want to say—this only assigns a certain role to those propositions in contrast to another one. I.e.: to say of a proposition: 'This could be imagined otherwise' or 'We can imagine the opposite too', ascribes the role of an empirical proposition to it.

A proposition which it is supposed to be impossible to imagine as other than true has a different *function* from one for which this does not hold.

5. The functioning of the axioms of mathematics is such that, if experience moved us to give up an axiom, that would not make its opposite into an axiom.

$$\text{'2} \times \text{2} \neq \text{5'} \text{ does not mean:}$$
$$\text{'2} \times \text{2} = \text{5'} \text{ has not worked.}$$

One might, so to speak, preface axioms with a special assertion sign.

Something is an axiom, *not* because we accept it as extremely probable, nay certain, but because we assign it a particular function, and one that conflicts with that of an empirical proposition.

We give an axiom a different kind of acknowledgment from an empirical proposition. And by this I do not mean that the 'mental act of acknowledgment' is a different one.

An axiom, I should like to say, is a different part of speech.

6. When one hears the mathematical axiom that such and such is possible, one assumes offhand that one knows what 'being possible' means here; because this form of sentence is naturally familiar to us.

We are not made aware how various the employment of the assertion "... is possible" is! And that is why it does not occur to us to ask about the special employment in this case.

Lacking the slightest survey of the whole use, we are here quite unable to doubt that we understand the proposition.

Does the proposition that there is no such thing as action at a distance belong to the family of mathematical propositions? Here again one would like to say: the proposition is not designed to express any experience, but rather to express the impossibility of imagining anything different.

To say that between two points a straight line is—geometrically—always possible means: the proposition "The points ... lie on a straight line" is an assertion about the position of the points only if more than 2 points are involved.

Just as one does not ask oneself, either, what is the meaning of a proposition of the form "There is no . . ." (e.g. "there is no proof of this proposition") in a particular case. Asked what it means, one replies both to someone else and to oneself with an example of non-existence.

7.   A mathematical proposition stands on four feet, not on three; it is over-determined.

8.   When we describe what a man does, e.g., by means of a rule, we want the person to whom we give the description to know, by applying the rule, what happens in the particular case. Now do I give him an *indirect* description by means of the rule?

There is of course such a thing as a proposition saying: if anyone tries to multiply the numbers . . . according to such and such rules, he gets. . . .

One application of a mathematical proposition must always be the calculating itself. That determines the relation of the activity of calculating to the sense of mathematical propositions.

We judge identity and agreement by the results of our calculating; that is why we cannot use agreement to explain calculating.

We describe by means of the rule. What for? Why? That is another question.

'The rule, applied to these numbers, yields those' might mean: the expression of the rule, applied to a human being, makes him produce those numbers from these.

One feels, quite rightly, that that would *not* be a mathematical proposition.

The mathematical proposition determines a path, lays down a path for us.

It is no contradiction of this that it is a rule, and not simply stipulated but produced according to rules.

If you use a rule to give a description, you yourself do not know more than you say. I.e. you yourself do not foresee the application that you will make of the rule in a particular case. If you say "and so on", you yourself do not know more than "and so on".

9. How could one explain to anybody what you have to do if you are to follow a rule?

One is tempted to explain: first and foremost do the *simplest* thing (if the rule e.g. is always to repeat the same thing). And there is of course something in this. It is significant that we can say that it is simpler to write down a sequence of numbers in which each number is the same as its predecessor than a sequence in which each number is greater by 1 than its predecessor. And again that this is a simpler law than that of alternately adding 1 and 2.

10. Isn't it over-hasty to apply a proposition that one has tested on sticks and stones, to wavelengths of light? I mean: that $2 \times 5000 = 10,000$.

Does one actually count on it that what has proved true in so many cases must hold for these too? Or is it not rather that with the arithmetical assumption we have not committed ourselves *at all*?

11. Arithmetic as the natural history (mineralogy) of numbers. But *who* talks like this about it? Our whole thinking is penetrated with this idea.

The numbers (I don't mean the numerals) are shapes, and arithmetic tells us the properties of these shapes. But the difficulty here is that these properties of the shapes are *possibilities*, not the properties in respect to shape of the things of this shape. And these possibilities in turn emerge as physical, or psychological possibilities (of separation, arrangement, etc.). But the role of the shapes is merely that of pictures which are used in such-and-such a way. What we give is not properties of shapes, but transformations of shapes, set up as paradigms of some kind or other.

12. We do not judge the pictures, we judge by means of the pictures.

We do not investigate them, we use them to investigate something else.

You get him to decide on accepting this picture. And you do so by means of the proof, i.e. by exhibiting a series of pictures, or simply by shewing him the picture. What moves him to decide does not matter here. The main thing is that it is a question of accepting a picture.

The picture of combining is not a combining; the picture of separating is not a separating; the picture of something's fitting not a case of fitting. And yet these pictures are of the greatest significance. *That is what it is like*, if a combination is made; if a separation; and so on.

13. What would it be for animals or crystals to have as beautiful properties as numbers? There would then be e.g. a series of forms, each bigger than another by a unit.

I should like to be able to describe how it comes about that mathematics appears to us now as the natural history of the domain of numbers, now again as a collection of rules.

But could one not study transformations of (e.g.) the forms of animals? But *how* 'study'? I mean: might it not be useful to pass transformations of animal shapes in review? And yet this would not be a branch of zoology.

It would then be a mathematical proposition (e.g.), that this shape is derived from *this* one by way of *this* transformation. (The shapes and transformations being recognizable.)

14. We must remember, however, that by its transformations a mathematical proof proves not only propositions of sign-geometry, but propositions of the most various *content*.

In this way the transformation in a Russellian proof proves that this logical proposition can be formed from the fundamental laws by the use of these rules. But the proof is looked at as a proof of the truth of the conclusion, or as a proof that the conclusion says *nothing*.

Now this is possible only through a relation of the proposition to something outside itself; I mean, e.g., through its relation to other propositions and to their application.

"A tautology (e.g. '$p \vee \sim p$') says nothing" is a proposition referring to the language-game in which the proposition p has application. (E.g. "It is raining or it is not raining" tells us nothing about the weather.)

Russellian logic says nothing about kinds of *propositions*—I don't mean *logical* propositions—and their employment: and yet logic gets its whole sense simply from its presumed application to propositions.

15.   People can be imagined to have an applied mathematics without any pure mathematics. They can e.g.—let us suppose—calculate the path described by certain moving bodies and predict their place at a given time. For this purpose they make use of a system of co-ordinates, of the equations of curves (*a form of description of actual movement*) and of the technique of calculating in the decimal system.   The idea of a proposition of pure mathematics may be quite foreign to them.

Thus these people have rules in accordance with which they transform the appropriate signs (in particular, e.g., numerals) with a view to predicting the occurrence of certain events.

But when they now multiply, for example, will they not arrive at a proposition saying that the result of the multiplication is the same, however the factors are shifted round? That will not be a primary rule of notation, nor yet a proposition of their physics.

They do not *need* to obtain any such proposition—even if they allow the shift of factors.

I am imagining the matter as if this mathematics were done entirely in the form of orders. "You must do *such-and-such*"—so as to get the answer, that is, to the question 'where will this body be at such-and-such a time?' (It does not matter at all how these people have arrived at this method of prediction.)

The centre of gravity of their mathematics lies for these people *entirely* in *doing*.

16. But is this possible? Is it possible that they should not pronounce the commutative law (e.g.) to be a *proposition?*

But I want to say: these people are not supposed to arrive at the conception of making mathematical discoveries—but *only* of making physical discoveries.

Question: Must they make mathematical discoveries as discoveries? What do they miss if they make none? Could they (for example) use the proof of the commutative law, but without the conception of its culminating in a *proposition*, and so having a result which is in some way comparable with their physical propositions?

17. The mere picture

```
o   o   o   o   o

o   o   o   o   o

o   o   o   o   o

o   o   o   o   o
```

regarded now as four rows of five dots, now as five columns of four dots, might convince someone of the commutative law. And he might thereupon carry out multiplications, now in the one direction, now in the other.

One look at the pattern and pieces convinces him that he will be able to make them into that shape, i.e. he thereupon *undertakes* to do so.

"Yes, but only if the pieces don't change."—If they don't change, and we don't make some unintelligible mistake, or pieces disappear or get added without our noticing it.

"But it is surely essential that the pieces can as a matter of fact always be made into that shape! What would happen if they could not?"—Perhaps we should think that something had put us out. But—what then?—Perhaps we should even accept the thing as it was. And then Frege might say: "Here we have a new kind of insanity!"[1]

18. It is clear that mathematics as a technique for transforming signs for the purpose of prediction has nothing to do with grammar.

19. The people whose mathematics was only such a technique, are now also supposed to accept proofs convincing them of the replaceability of one sign-technique by another. That is to say, they find transformations, series of pictures, on the strength of which they can venture to use one technique in place of another.

20. If calculating looks to us like the action of a machine, it is *the human being* doing the calculation that is the machine.

In that case the calculation would be as it were a diagram drawn by a part of the machine.

---

[1] Cf. *Grundgesetze der Arithmetik*, Vol. I, Preface p. XVI. Compare also above, p. 95. (Eds.)

21. And that brings me to the fact that a picture may very well convince us that a particular part of a mechanism will move in such-and-such a way when the mechanism is set in motion.

The effect of such a picture (or series of pictures) is like that of a proof. In this way I might e.g. make a construction for how the point X of the mechanism

will move.

Is it not *queer* that it is not instantly clear *how* the picture of the period in division convinces us of the recurrence of that row of digits?

(I find it so difficult to separate the inner from the outer—and the picture from the prediction.)

The twofold character of the mathematical proposition—as *law* and as *rule*.

22. Suppose that one were to say "guessing right" instead of "intuition"? This would shew the value of an intuition in a quite

different light. For the phenomenon of guessing is a psychological one, but not that of guessing right.

23. Our having learned a technique brings it about that we now alter it in such and such a way after seeing this picture.

'We decide on a new language-game.'
'We decide *spontaneously*' (I should like to say) 'on a new language-game.'

24. True;—it looks as though, if our memory functioned differently, we could not calculate as we do. But in that case could we give definitions as we do; talk and write as we do?
But how can we describe the foundation of our language by means of empirical propositions?

25. Suppose that when we worked out a division it did not lead to the same result as the copying of its period. That might arise e.g. from our altering our tables, without being aware of it. (Though it might also arise from our copying in a different way.)

26. What is the difference between *not* calculating and calculating *wrong*?—Or: is there a sharp dividing line between *not* measuring time and measuring it *wrong*? Not knowing any measurement of time and knowing a wrong one?

27. Pay attention to the patter by means of which we convince someone of the truth of a mathematical proposition. It tells us something about the function of this conviction. I mean the patter by which intuition is awakened.

By which, that is, the machine of a calculating technique is set in motion.

28. Can it be said that if you learn a technique, that convinces you of the uniformity of its results?

29. The limit of the empirical[1]—is *concept-formation*.

What is the transition that I make from "It will be like this" to "it *must* be like this"? I form a different concept. One involving something that was not there before. When I say: "If these derivations are the same, then it *must* be that . . .", I am making something into a criterion of identity. So I am recasting my concept of identity.

But what if someone now says: "I am not aware of these *two* processes, I am only aware of the empirical, not of a formation and transformation of concepts which is independent of it; everything seems to me to be in the service of the empirical"?

In other words: we do not seem to become now more, now less, rational, or to alter the form of our thinking, so as to alter *what we call "thinking"*. We only seem always to be fitting our thinking to experience.

---

[1] See note, p. 197. (Eds.)

So much is clear: when someone says: "If you follow the *rule*, it *must* be like this", he has not any *clear* concept of what experience would correspond to the opposite.

Or again: he has not any clear concept of what it would be like for it to be otherwise. And this is very important.

30. What compels us *so* to form the concept of identity as to say, e.g., "If you really do the same thing both times, then the result must be the same too"?—What compels us to proceed according to a rule, to conceive something as a rule? What compels us to talk to ourselves in the forms of the languages we have learnt?

For the word "must" surely expresses our inability to depart from *this* concept. (Or ought I to say "refusal"?)

And even if I have made the transition from one concept-formation to another, the old concept is still there in the background.

Can I say: "A proof induces us to make a certain decision, namely that of accepting a particular concept-formation"?

Do not look at the proof as a procedure that *compels* you, but as one that *guides* you.—And what it guides is your *conception* of a (particular) situation.

But how does it come about that it guides *each one* of us in such a way that we agree in the influence it has on us? Well, how does it come about that we agree in *counting*? "That is just how we are trained" one may say, "and the agreement produced in this way is carried further by the proofs."

In the course of this proof we formed our way of looking at the trisection of the angle, which excludes a construction with ruler and compass.

By accepting a proposition as self evident, we also release it from all responsibility in face of experience.

In the course of the proof our way of seeing is changed—and it does not detract from this that it is connected with experience.

Our way of seeing is remodelled.

31. It must be like this, does not mean: it will be like this. On the contrary: 'it will be like this' chooses between one possibility and another. 'It must be like this' sees only *one* possibility.

The proof as it were guides our experience into definite channels. Someone who has tried again and again to do such-and-such gives the attempt up after the proof.

Someone tries to arrange pieces to make a particular pattern. Now he sees a model in which one *part* of that pattern is seen to be composed of all his pieces, and he gives up his attempt. The model was the *proof* that his proposal is impossible.

That model too, like the one that shews that he will be able to make a pattern of these pieces, changes his *concept*. For, one might say, he never looked at the task of making the pattern of these pieces in this way before.

Is it obvious that if anyone sees that part of the pattern can be made with these pieces, he realizes that there is no way of making the whole pattern with them? May it not be that he goes on trying and trying whether after all some arrangement of the pieces does not achieve this end? And may he not achieve it? (Use of one piece twice over, e.g.)

Must we not distinguish here between thinking and the practical success of the thinking?

32.   "... who do not have immediate knowledge of certain truths, as we do, but perhaps are reduced to the roundabout path of induc-

tion", says Frege.[1] But what interests me is this immediate insight, whether it is of a truth or of a falsehood. I am asking: what is the characteristic demeanour of human beings who 'have insight into' something 'immediately', whatever the practical result of this insight is?

What interests me is not having immediate insight into a truth, but the phenomenon of immediate insight. Not indeed as a special mental phenomenon, but as one of human action.

33. Yes: it is as if the formation of a concept guided our experience into particular channels, so that one experience is now seen together with another one in a new way. (As an optical instrument makes light come from various sources in a particular way to form a pattern.)

Imagine that a proof was a work of fiction, a stage play. Cannot watching a play lead me to something?

I did not know how it would go,—but I saw a picture and became convinced that it would go as it does in the picture.

The picture helped me to make a prediction. Not as an experiment ——it was only midwife to the prediction.

---

[1] *Grundgesetze der Arithmetik*, Vorwort, p. XVI.

For, whatever my experience is or has been, I surely still have to *make* the prediction. (Experience does not make it for me.)

No great wonder, then, that proof helps us to *predict*. Without this picture I should not have been able to say how it will be, but when I see it I seize on it with a view to prediction.

I cannot predict the colour of a chemical compound by means of a picture exhibiting the substances in the test-tube and the reaction. If the picture shewed frothing, and finally red crystals, I should not be able to say: "Yes, *that* is how it has to be" or "No, it cannot be like that". It is otherwise, however, when I see the picture of a mechanism in motion; that can tell me how a part actually will move. Though if the picture represented a mechanism whose parts were composed of a very soft material (dough, say), and hence bent about in various ways in the picture, then this picture might not help me to make a prediction either.

Can we say that a concept is so formed as to be adapted to a certain prediction, i.e. it enables it to be made in the simplest terms—?

34.   The philosophical problem is: how can we tell the truth and *pacify* these strong prejudices in doing so?

It makes a difference whether I think of something as a deception of my senses or an external event, whether I take this object as a measure of that or the other way round, whether I resolve to make two criteria decide or only one.

35. If the calculation has been done right, then this must be the result. Must *this always* be the result, in that case? Of course.

By being educated in a technique, we are also educated to have a way of looking at the matter which is just as firmly rooted as that technique.

Mathematical propositions seem to treat neither of signs nor of human beings, and therefore they *do* not.

They shew *those* connexions that we regard as rigid. But to a certain extent we look away from these connexions and at something else. We turn our back upon them, so to speak. Or: we rest, or lean, on them.

Once more: we do not look at the mathematical proposition as a proposition dealing with signs, and hence it *is* not that.

We acknowledge it *by* turning our back on it.

What about e.g. the fundamental laws of mechanics? If you understand them you must know how experience supports them. It is
otherwise with the propositions of pure mathematics.

36. A proposition may describe a picture and this picture be
variously anchored in our way of looking at things, and so in our way
of living and acting.

Is not the proof too flimsy a reason for entirely giving up the search
for a construction of the trisection? You have only gone through the
sequence of signs once or twice; will you decide on the strength of
that? Just because you have seen this one transformation, will you
give up the search?

The effect of proof is, I believe, that we plunge into the new rule.

Hitherto we have calculated according to such and such a rule; now
someone shews us the proof that it can also be done in another way,
and we switch to the other technique—not because we tell ourselves
that it will work this way too, but because we feel the new technique as
identical with the old one, because we have to give it the same sense,
because we recognize it as the same just as we recognize this colour as
green.

That is to say: insight into mathematical relations has a role similar to
that of seeing an identity. It might almost be said to be a more complicated kind of identity.

It might be said: the reasons why we now shift to a different technique are of the same kind as those which make us carry out a new multiplication as we do; we accept the technique as the *same* as we have applied in doing other multiplications.

37.   A human being is *imprisoned* in a room, if the door is unlocked but opens inwards; he, however, never gets the idea of *pulling* instead of pushing against it.

38.   When white turns black some people say "Essentially it is still the same"; and others, when the colour turns a shade darker: "It is *completely* different".

39.   The proposition '$a = a$', '$p \supset p$', "The word 'Bismarck' has 8 letters", "There is no such thing as reddish-green", are all obvious and are propositions about essence: what have they in common? They are evidently each of a different kind and differently used. The last but one is the most like an empirical proposition. And it can understandably be called a synthetic *a priori* proposition.

It can be said: unless you put the series of numbers and the series of letters side by side, you cannot know how many letters the word has.

40.   One pattern derived from another according to a rule. (Say the reversal of a theme.)

Then the result put as equivalent to the operation.

41. When I wrote "proof must be perspicuous" that meant: *causality* plays no part in the proof.

Or again: a proof must be capable of being reproduced by mere copying.

42. That, if you go on dividing 1 : 3, you must keep on getting 3 in the result is not known by intuition, any more than that the multiplication 25 × 25 yields the same product every time it is repeated.

43. It might perhaps be said that the synthetic character of the propositions of mathematics appears most obviously in the unpredictable occurrence of the prime numbers.

But their being synthetic (in this sense) does not make them any the less *a priori*. They could be said, I want to say, not to be got out of their concepts by means of some kind of analysis, but really to determine a concept by synthesis, e.g. as crossing prisms can be made to determine a body.

The distribution of primes would be an ideal example of what could be called synthetic *a priori*, for one can say that it is at any rate not discoverable by an analysis of the concept of a prime number.

44. Might one not really talk of intuition in mathematics? Though it would not be a *mathematical* truth that was grasped intuitively, but a physical or psychological one. In this way I know with *great* certainty that if I multiply 25 by 25 ten times I shall get 625 every time. That is to say I know the psychological fact that this calculation will keep on seeming correct to me; as I know that if I write down the series of numbers from 1 to 20 ten times my lists will prove identical on collation.—Now is that an empirical fact? Of course—and yet it would be difficult to mention experiments that would convince me of it. Such a thing might be called an intuitively known *empirical* fact.

45. You want to say that every new proof alters the concept of proof in one way or another.

But then by what principle is something recognized as a new proof? Or rather there is certainly no 'principle' here.

46. Now ought I to say: "we are convinced that the same result will always come out"? No, that is not enough. We are convinced that the same *calculation* will always come out, be calculated. Now is *that* a mathematical conviction? No—for if it were not always the same that was calculated, we could not conclude that the calculation yields at one time one result and at another time another.

We are *of course* also convinced that when we repeat a calculation we shall repeat the pattern of the calculation.—

47.   Might I not say: if you do a multiplication, in any case you do not find the mathematical fact, but you do find the mathematical proposition? For what you *find* is the non-mathematical fact, and in this way the mathematical proposition. For a mathematical proposition is the determination of a concept following upon a discovery.

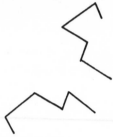

You *find* a new physiognomy. Now you can e.g. memorize or copy it.

A *new* form has been found, constructed. But it is used to give a new concept together with the old one.

The concept is altered so that this *had* to be the result.

I find, not the result, but that I reach it.

And it is not this route's beginning here and ending here that is an empirical fact, but my having gone this road, or some road to this end.

48.   But might it not be said that the *rules* lead this way, even if no one went it?

For that is what one would like to say—and here we see the mathematical machine, which, driven by the rules themselves, obeys only mathematical laws and not physical ones.

I want to say: the working of the mathematical machine is only the *picture* of the working of a machine.

The rule does not do work, for whatever happens according to the rule is an interpretation of the rule.

49.   Let us suppose that I have the stages of the movement of

in a picture in front of me; then this enables me to form a proposition, which I as it were read off from this picture. The proposition contains the word "roughly" and is a proposition of geometry.

It is queer that I should be able to read off a proposition from a *picture*.

The proposition, however, does not treat of the picture that I see. It does not say that such-and-such can be seen in this picture. But nor does it say what the actual mechanism will do, although it suggests it.

But could I draw the movement of the mechanism in other ways too, if its parts do not alter? That is to say, am I not *compelled*, *under these conditions*, to accept just this as the picture of the movement?

Let us imagine the construction of the phases of the mechanism carried out with lines of changing colour. Let the lines be partly black on a white ground, partly white on a black ground. Imagine the constructions in Euclid carried out in this way; they will lose all obviousness.

50.   A word in reverse has a *new* face.

What if it were said: If you reverse the sequence 123, you *learn* about it that it yields 321 when reversed? And what you learn is not a property of these ink-marks, but of the sequence of *forms*. You learn a *formal* property of forms. The proposition asserting this formal property is proved by experience, which shews you the one form arising in this way out of the other.

Now, if you learn this, do you have *two* impressions? One of the fact that the sequence is *reversed*, the other of the fact that 321 arises? And could you not have the experience, the impression, of 123's being reversed and yet not of 321's arising? Perhaps it will be said: "Only by a queer illusion".—

The reason why one really cannot say that one learns that formal proposition from experience is—that one only calls it this experience when this process leads to this result. The experience meant consists as such of this process with this result.

That is why it is more than the experience: seeing a pattern.

Can one row of letters have two reverses?

Say one acoustic, and another, optical, reverse. Suppose I explain to someone what the reverse of a word on paper is, what we call that. And now it turns out that he has an acoustic reverse of the word, i.e., something that he would like to call that, but it does not quite agree with the written reverse. So that one can say: he hears *this* as the reverse of the word. As if, as it were, the word got distorted for him in being turned round. And this might perhaps occur if he pronounced the word and its reverse fluently, as opposed to the case of spelling it out. Or the reverse might seem different when he spoke the word forwards and backwards in a single utterance.

It might be that the exact mirror-image of a profile, seen immediately after it, was never pronounced to be the same thing, merely turned in the other direction; but that in order to give the impression of exact reversal, the profile had to be altered a little in its measurements.

But I want to say that we have no right to say: though we may indeed be in doubt about the correct reverse of, for example, a long word, still we *know* that the word has only *one* reverse.

"Yes, but if it is supposed to be a reverse in *this* sense there can be only one." Does 'in this sense' here mean: by these rules, or: with this physiognomy? In the first case the proposition would be tautological, in the second it need not be true.

51.   Think of a machine which 'is so constructed' that it reverses a row of letters. And now of the proposition that in the case of

O V E R

the result is   R E V O.—

The rule, as it is actually meant, seems to be a driving power which reverses an ideal sequence like *this*,—whatever a human being may do with an actual sequence.

This is the mechanism which is the yardstick, the ideal, for the actual mechanism.

And that is *intelligible*. For if the result of the reversal becomes the criterion for the row's really having been reversed, and if we express this as our imitating an ideal machine, then this machine must produce this result *infallibly*.

52.   Now can it be said that the concepts which mathematics produces are a convenience, that essentially we could do without them?

First and foremost the adoption of these concepts expresses the *sure* expectation of certain experiences.

We do not accept e.g. a multiplication's not yielding the same result every time.

And what we expect with certainty is essential to our whole life.

53.   Why, then, should I not say that mathematical propositions just express those special expectations, i.e., therefore, that they express matters of experience? Only because they just do not. Perhaps I should not take the measure of adopting a certain concept if I did not quite definitely expect the occurrence of certain facts; but for that reason laying down this measure and expressing the expectations are not equivalent.

54. It is difficult to put the body of fact right side up: to regard the given as given. It is difficult to place the body differently from the way one is accustomed to see it. A table in a lumber room may always lie upside down, in order to save space perhaps. Thus I have always seen the body of fact placed like *this*, for reasons of various kinds; and now I am supposed to see something else as its beginning and something else as its end. That is difficult. It as it were will not stand like that, unless one supports it in this position by means of other contrivances.

55. It is one thing to use a mathematical technique consisting in the avoidance of contradiction, and another to philosophize against contradiction in mathematics.

56. Contradiction. Why just this *one* bogy? That is surely very suspicious.

Why should not a calculation made for a practical purpose, with a contradictory result, tell me: "Do as you please, I, the calculation, do not decide the matter"?

The contradiction might be conceived as a hint from the gods that I am to act and *not* consider.

57. "Why should contradiction be disallowed in mathematics?" Well, why is it not allowed in our simple language-games? (There is

certainly a connexion here.) Is this then a fundamental law governing all thinkable language-games?

Let us suppose that a contradiction in an order, e.g. produces astonishment and indecision—and now we say: that is just the purpose of contradiction in this language-game.

58.   Someone comes to people and says: "I always lie". They answer: "Well, in that case we can trust you!"—But could *he* mean what he said? Is there not a feeling of being incapable of saying something really true; let it be what it may?—

"I always lie!"—Well, and what about *that?*—"It was a lie too!"— But in that case you don't always lie!—"No, it's all lies!"

Perhaps we should say of this man that he doesn't mean the same thing as we do by "true" and by "lying". He means perhaps something like: What he says flickers; or nothing really comes from his heart.

It might also be said: his "I always lie" was not really an *assertion*. It was rather an exclamation.

And so it can be said: "If he was saying that sentence, not thought-lessly—then he must have meant the words in such-and-such a way, he *cannot* have meant them in the usual way"?

59.   Why should Russell's contradiction not be conceived as something supra-propositional, something that towers above the propositions and looks in both directions like a Janus head? N.B. the proposition $F(F)$—in which $F(\xi) = {\sim}\xi(\xi)$—contains no variables and so might hold as something supra-logical, as something unassailable, whose negation itself in turn only *asserts* it. Might one not even begin logic with this contradiction? And as it were descend from it to propositions.

The proposition that contradicts itself would stand like a monument (with a Janus head) over the propositions of logic.

60.   The pernicious thing is not: to produce a contradiction in the region in which neither the consistent nor the contradictory proposition has any kind of work to accomplish; no, what *is* pernicious is: not to know how one reached the place where contradiction no longer does any harm.

PART V

1942-1944

1. It is of course clear that the mathematician, in so far as he really is 'playing a game' *does not infer*. For here 'playing' must mean: *acting in accordance with certain rules*. And it would already be something outside the mere game for him to infer that he could act in this way according to the general rule.

2. Does a calculating machine *calculate*?

Imagine that a calculating machine had come into existence by accident; now someone accidentally presses its knobs (or an animal walks over it) and it calculates the product 25×20.

I want to say: it is essential to mathematics that its signs are also employed in *mufti*.

It is the use outside mathematics, and so the *meaning* of the signs, that makes the sign-game into mathematics.

Just as it is not logical inference either, for me to make a change from one formation to another (say from one arrangement of chairs to another) if these arrangements have not a linguistic function apart from this transformation.

3. But is it not true that someone with no idea of the meaning

of Russell's symbols could *work over* Russell's proofs? And so could in an important sense test whether they were right or wrong?

A human calculating machine might be trained so that when the rules of inference were shewn it and perhaps exemplified, it read through the proofs of a mathematical system (say that of Russell), and nodded its head after every correctly drawn conclusion, but shook its head at a mistake and stopped calculating. One could imagine this creature as otherwise perfectly imbecile.

We call a proof something that can be worked over, but can also be copied.

4. If mathematics is a game, then playing some game is doing mathematics, and in that case why isn't dancing mathematics too?

Imagine that calculating machines occurred in nature, but that people could not pierce their cases. And now suppose that these people use these appliances, say as we use calculation, though of that they know nothing. Thus e.g. they make predictions with the aid of calculating machines, but for them manipulating these queer objects is experimenting.

These people lack concepts which we have; but what takes their place?

Think of the mechanism whose movement we saw as a geometrical (kinematic) proof: clearly it would not normally be said of someone turning the wheel that he was proving something. Isn't it the same with someone who makes and changes arrangements of signs as a game; even when what he produces could be seen as a proof?

To say mathematics is a game is supposed to mean: in proving, we need never appeal to the meaning of the signs, that is to their extra-mathematical application. But then what does appealing to this mean at all? How can such an appeal be of any avail?

Does it mean passing out of mathematics and returning to it again, or does it mean passing from *one* method of mathematical inference to another?

What does it mean to obtain a new concept of the surface of a sphere? How is it then a concept of the surface of a *sphere*? Only in so far as it can be applied to real spheres.

How far does one need to have a concept of 'proposition', in order to understand Russellian mathematical logic?

5. If the intended application of mathematics is essential, how about parts of mathematics whose application—or at least *what*

mathematicians take for their application—is quite fantastic? So that, as in set theory, one is doing a branch of mathematics of whose application one forms an entirely false idea. Now, isn't one doing mathematics *none the less*?

If the operations of arithmetic only served to construct a cipher, its application would of course be fundamentally different from that of our arithmetic. But would these operations then be mathematical operations at all?

Can someone who is applying a decoding rule be said to be performing mathematical operations? And yet his transformations can be so conceived. For he could surely say that he was calculating what had to come out in decoding the symbols . . . with such-and-such a key. And the proposition: the signs . . ., decoded according to this rule, yield . . . is a mathematical one. As is the proposition that you can get to this position from *that* one in chess.

Imagine the geometry of four-dimensional space done with a view to learning about the living conditions of spirits. Does that mean that it is not mathematics? And can I now say that it determines concepts?

Would it not sound queer to say that a child could already do thousands and thousands of multiplications—by which is supposed to be meant that it can already calculate in the unlimited number domain. And indeed this might be reckoned an extremely modest way of putting it, as it says only 'thousands and thousands' instead of 'infinitely many'.

Could people be imagined, who in their ordinary lives only calculated up to 1000 and kept calculations with higher numbers for mathematical investigations about the world of spirits?

"Whether or not this holds of the surface of a *real* sphere—it does hold for the mathematical one"—this makes it look as if the special difference between the mathematical and an empirical proposition was that, while the truth of the empirical proposition is rough and oscillating, the mathematical proposition describes *its* object precisely and absolutely. As if, in fact, the 'mathematical sphere' were a sphere. And it might e.g. be asked whether there was only *one* such sphere, or several (a Fregean question).

Does a misunderstanding about the possible application constitute an objection to the calculation as a part of mathematics?

And apart from misunderstanding,—what about mere lack of clarity?

Imagine someone who believes that mathematicians have discovered a queer thing, $\sqrt{-1}$, which when squared does yield -1, can't he nevertheless calculate quite well with complex numbers, and apply such calculations in physics? And does this make them any the less *calculations*?

In *one* respect of course his understanding has a weak foundation; but he will draw his conclusions with certainty, and his calculus will have a *solid* foundation.

Now would it not be ridiculous to say this man wasn't doing mathematics?

Someone makes an addition to mathematics, gives new definitions and discovers new theorems——and in a *certain* respect he can be said not to know what he is doing.—He has a vague imagination of having *discovered* something like a space (at which point he thinks of a room), of having opened up a kingdom, and when asked about it he would talk a great deal of nonsense.

Let us imagine the primitive case of someone carrying out enormous multiplications in order, as he says, to conquer gigantic new provinces of the domain of numbers.

Imagine calculating with $\sqrt{-1}$ invented by a madman, who, attracted merely by the paradox of the idea, does the calculation as a kind of service, or temple ritual, of the absurd. He imagines that he is writing down the impossible and operating with it.

In other words: if someone believes in mathematical *objects* and their queer properties—can't he nevertheless do mathematics? Or—isn't he also doing mathematics?

'Ideal object.' "The symbol '*a*' stands for an ideal object" is evidently supposed to assert something about the meaning, and so about the use, of '*a*'. And it means of course that this use is in a certain respect

similar to that of a sign that has an object, and that it does not stand
for any object. But it is interesting what the expression 'ideal object'
makes of this fact.

6. In certain circumstances we might speak of an endless row of
marbles.—Let us imagine such an endless straight row of marbles at
equal distances from one another; we calculate the force exerted by all
these marbles on a certain body according to a certain law of attraction.
We regard the number yielded by this calculation as the ideal of
exactness for certain measurements.

The feeling of something *queer* here comes from a misunderstanding.
The kind of misunderstanding that is produced by a thumb-catching of
the intellect—to which I want to call a halt.

The objection that 'the finite cannot grasp the infinite' is *really*
directed against the idea of a psychological act of grasping or understanding.

Or imagine that we simply say: "This force corresponds to the
attraction of an endless row of marbles which we have arranged in
such-and-such a way and which attract the body according to such-
and-such a law of attraction". Or again: "Calculate the force which
an endless row of marbles of such-and-such a kind exerts on the body".
—It certainly makes sense to give such an order. It describes a particular calculation.

What about the following question: "Calculate the weight of a pillar composed of as many slabs lying on top of one another as there are cardinal numbers; the undermost slab weighs 1 kg., and every higher one weighs half of the one just below it".

The difficulty is *not* that we can't form an image. It is easy enough to form some kind of image of an endless row, for example. The question is what use the image is to us.

Imagine infinite numbers used in a fairy tale. The dwarves have piled up as many gold pieces as there are cardinal numbers—etc. What can occur in this fairy tale must surely make sense.—

7.   Imagine set theory's having been invented by a satirist as a kind of parody on mathematics.—Later a reasonable meaning was seen in it and it was incorporated into mathematics. (For if one person[1] can see it as a paradise of mathematicians, why should not another see it as a joke?)

The question is: even as a joke isn't it evidently mathematics?—

[1] D. Hilbert. *Über das Unendliche.* Mathematische Annalen 95 (1926) (Translated in: Putnam and Bennaceraf, *Philosophy of Mathematics*; also in Heijenoort, *From Frege to Gödel.*) Eds.

And why is it evidently mathematics?—Because it is a game with signs according to rules?

But isn't it evident that there are concepts formed here—even if we are not clear about their application?

But how is it possible to have a concept and not be clear about its application?

8.   Take the construction of the polygon of forces: isn't that a bit of applied mathematics? And where is the proposition of *pure* mathematics which is invoked in connexion with this graphical calculation? Is this case not like that of the tribe which has a technique of calculating in order to make certain predictions, but no propositions of pure mathematics?

Calculation that belongs to the performance of a ceremony. For example, let the number of words in a form of blessing that is to be applied to a home be derived by a particular technique from the ages of the father and mother and the number of their children. We could imagine procedures of calculating described in such a law as the Mosaic law. And couldn't we imagine that the nation with these ceremonial prescriptions for calculating never calculated in practical life?

This would indeed be a case of *applied* calculation, but it would not serve the purpose of a prediction.

Would it be any wonder if the technique of calculating had a family of applications?

9. We only see how queer the question is whether the pattern ϕ (a particular arrangement of digits e.g. '770') will occur in the infinite expansion of π, when we try to formulate the question in a quite common or garden way: men have been trained to put down signs according to certain rules. Now they proceed according to this training and we say that it is a problem whether they will *ever* write down the pattern ϕ in following the given rule.

But what are you saying if you say that one thing is clear: either one will come on ϕ in the infinite expansion, or one will not?

It seems to me that in saying this you are yourself setting up a rule or postulate.

What if someone were to reply to a question: 'So far there is no such thing as an answer to this question'?

So, e.g., the poet might reply when asked whether the hero of his poem has a sister or not—when, that is, he has not yet decided anything about it.

The question—I want to say—changes its status, when it becomes decidable. For a connexion is made then, which formerly *was not there*.

Of someone who is trained we can ask 'How *will* he interpret the rule for this case?', or again 'How *ought* he to interpret the rule for this case?'—but what if no decision about this question has been made?—Well, then the answer is, not: 'he ought to interpret it in such a way that ϕ occurs in the expansion' or: 'he ought to interpret it in such a way that it does not occur', but: 'nothing has so far been decided about this'.

However queer it sounds, the further expansion of an irrational number is a further expansion of mathematics.

We do mathematics with concepts.—And with certain concepts more than with other ones.

I want to say: it *looks* as if a ground for the decision were already there; and it has yet to be invented.

Would this come to the same thing as saying: in thinking about the technique of expansion, which we have learnt, we use the false picture of a completed expansion (of what is ordinarily called a "row") and this forces us to ask unanswerable questions?

For after all in the end every question about the expansion of $\sqrt{2}$ must be capable of formulation as a practical question concerning the technique of expansion.

And what is in question here is of course not merely the case of the expansion of a real number, or in general the production of mathematical signs, but every analogous process, whether it is a game, a dance, etc., etc..

10.   When someone hammers away at us with the law of excluded middle as something which cannot be gainsaid, it is clear that there is something wrong with his question.

When someone sets up the law of excluded middle, he is as it were putting two pictures before us to choose from, and saying that one must correspond to the fact. But what if it is questionable whether the pictures can be applied here?

And if you say that the infinite expansion must contain the pattern ϕ or not contain it, you are so to speak shewing us the picture of an unsurveyable series reaching into the distance.

But what if the picture began to flicker in the far distance?

11.   To say of an unending series that it does *not* contain a particular

pattern makes sense only under quite special conditions.

That is to say: this proposition has been given a sense for certain cases.

Roughly, for those where it is in the *rule* for this series, not to contain the pattern. . . .

Further: when I calculate the expansion further, I am deriving new rules which the series obeys.

"Good,—then we can say: 'It must either reside in the rule for this series that the pattern occurs, or the opposite'." But is it like that?— "Well, doesn't the rule of expansion *determine* the series completely? And if it does so, if it allows of no ambiguity, then it must implicitly determine *all* questions about the structure of the series."—Here you are thinking of finite series.

"But surely all members of the series from the 1st up to 1,000th, up to the 10^{10}-th and so on, are determined; so surely *all* the members are determined." That is correct if it is supposed to mean that it is not the case that e.g. the so-and-so-many'th is *not* determined. But you can see that *that* gives you no information about whether a particular pattern is going to appear in the series (if it has not appeared so far). *And so we can see* that we are using a misleading *picture*.

If you want to know more about the series, you have, so to speak, to get into another dimension (as it were from the line into a surrounding plane).—But then isn't the plane *there*, just like the line, and merely something to be *explored*, if one wants to know what the facts are?

No, the mathematics of this further dimension has to be invented just as much as any mathematics.

In an arithmetic in which one does not count further than 5 the question what 4 + 3 makes doesn't yet make sense. On the other hand the problem may very well exist of giving this question a sense. That is to say: the question makes *no more* sense than does the law of excluded middle in application to it.

12.   In the law of excluded middle we think that we have already got something solid, something that at any rate cannot be called in doubt. Whereas in truth this tautology has just as shaky a sense (if I may put it like that), as the question whether p or $\sim p$ is the case.

Suppose I were to ask: what is meant by saying "the pattern . . . occurs in this expansion"? The reply would be: "you surely *know* what it means. It occurs as the pattern . . . in fact occurs in the expansion." —So *that* is the way it occurs?—But '*what way* is that?

Imagine it were said: "Either it occurs in that way, or it does not occur in that way"!

"But don't you really understand what is meant?"—But may I not believe I understand it, and be wrong?—

For how do I know what it means to say: the pattern . . . occurs in the expansion? Surely by way of examples—which shew me what it is like for. . . . But these examples do not shew me what it is like for this pattern to occur in the expansion!

Might one not say: if I really had a right to say that these examples tell me what it is like for the pattern to occur in the expansion, then they would also have to shew me what the opposite means.

13.   The general proposition that that pattern does not occur in the expansion can only be a *commandment*.

Suppose we look at mathematical propositions as commandments, and even utter them as such? "Let 25^2 be 625."
Well—a commandment has an internal and an external negation.

The symbols "$(x).\phi x$" and "$(\exists x).\phi x$" are certainly useful in mathematics so long as one is acquainted with the technique of the proofs of the existence or non-existence to which the Russellian signs *here* refer. If however this is left open, then these concepts of the old logic are extremely misleading.

If someone says: "But you surely know what 'this pattern occurs in the expansion' means, namely *this*"—and points to a case of occurring, —then I can only reply that what he shews me is capable of illustrating a *variety* of facts. For that reason I can't be said to know what the proposition means just from knowing that he will certainly use it in this case.

The opposite of "there exists a law that p" is not: "there exists a law that $\sim p$". But if one expresses the first by means of P, and the second by means of $\sim P$, one will get into difficulties.

14.   Suppose children are taught that the earth is an infinite flat surface; or that God created an infinite number of stars; or that a star keeps on moving uniformly in a straight line, without ever stopping.

Queer: when one takes something of this sort as a matter of course, as it were in one's stride, it loses its whole paradoxical aspect. It is as if I were to be told: Don't worry, this series, or movement, goes on without ever stopping. We are as it were excused the labour of thinking of an end.

'We won't bother about an end.'

It might also be said: 'for us the series is infinite'.

'We won't worry about an end to this series; for us it is always beyond our ken.'

15.   The rational numbers cannot be *enumerated*, because they cannot be counted—but one can count with them, as with the cardinal numbers. That squint-eyed way of putting things goes with the whole system of pretence, namely that by using the new apparatus we deal with

infinite sets with the same certainty as hitherto we had in dealing with finite ones.

It should not have been called 'denumerable', but on the other hand it would have made sense to say 'numberable'. And this expression also informs us of an application of the concept. For one cannot set out to enumerate the rational numbers, but one can perfectly well set out to assign numbers to them.

But where is the problem here? Why should I not say that what we call mathematics is a family of activities with a family of purposes?

People might for example use calculating as a kind of competitive activity. As children do sometimes have races in doing sums; only this use of sums plays a quite subordinate role among us.

Or multiplication might strike us as much more difficult than it does —if e.g. we only calculated orally, and in order to take note of, and so to grasp, a multiplication it were necessary to bring it into the form of rhyming verse. When someone succeeded in doing this he would have the feeling of having discovered a wonderful great truth.

Every new multiplication would require a new individual piece of work.

If these people believed that numbers were spirits and that they were exploring the domain of spirits by means of their calculations, or compelling the spirits to manifest themselves—would this now be arithmetic? Again—would it be arithmetic even in the case where these people used the calculations for nothing else?

16. The comparison with alchemy seems natural. We might speak of a kind of alchemy in mathematics.

Is it already mathematical alchemy, that mathematical propositions are regarded as statements about mathematical objects,—and mathematics as the exploration of these objects?

In a certain sense it is not possible to appeal to the meaning of the signs in mathematics, just because it is only mathematics that gives them their meaning.

What is typical of the phenomenon I am talking about is that a *mysteriousness* about some mathematical concept is not *straight away* interpreted as an erroneous conception, as a mistake of ideas; but rather as something that is at any rate not to be despised, is perhaps even rather to be respected.

All that I can do, is to shew an easy escape from this obscurity and this glitter of the concepts.

Strangely, it can be said that there is so to speak a solid core to all these glistening concept-formations. And I should like to say that that is what makes them into mathematical productions.

It might be said: what you see does of course look more like a gleaming Fata Morgana; but look at it from another quarter and you can see the solid body, which only looks like a gleam without a corporeal substrate when seen from that other direction.

17. 'The pattern is in the series or it is not in the series' means: either the thing looks like *this* or it does not look like this.

How does one know what is meant by the opposite of the proposition "ϕ occurs in the series", or even of the proposition "ϕ does not occur in the series"? This question sounds like nonsense, but does make sense all the same.

Namely: how do I know that I understand the proposition "ϕ occurs in this series"?

True, I can give examples illustrating the use of such statements, and also of the opposite ones. And they are examples of there being a rule prescribing the occurrence in a definite region or series of regions, or determining that such an occurrence is excluded.

If "you do it" means: you must do it, and "you do not do it" means: you must not do it—then "Either you do it, or you do not" is not the law of excluded middle.

Everyone feels uncomfortable at the thought that a proposition can state that such-and-such does not occur in an infinite series—while on the other hand there is nothing startling about a command's saying that this must not occur in this series however far it is continued.

But what is the source of this distinction between: "however far you go you will never find this"—and "however far you go you must never do this"?

On hearing the proposition one can ask: "how can we know anything like that?" but nothing analogous holds for the command.

The statement seems to overreach itself, the command not at all.

Can we imagine all mathematical propositions expressed in the imperative? For example: "Let 10 × 10 be 100".

And if you now say: "Let it be like this, or. let it not be like this", you are not pronouncing the law of excluded middle—but you are pronouncing a *rule*. (As I have already said above.)

18.   But is this really a way out of the difficulty? For how about all

the other mathematical propositions, say '$25^2 = 625$'; isn't the law of excluded middle valid for these *inside* mathematics?

How is the law of excluded middle applied?

"Either there is a rule that prescribes it, or one that forbids it."

Assuming that there is no rule forbidding the occurrence,—why is there then supposed to be one that prescribes it?

Does it make sense to say: "While there isn't any rule forbidding the occurrence, as a matter of fact the pattern does not occur"?—And if this does not make sense, how can the opposite make sense, namely, that the pattern does occur?

Well, when I say it occurs, a picture of the series from its beginning up to the pattern floats before my mind—but if I say that the pattern does *not* occur, then no such picture is of any use to me, and my supply of pictures gives out.

What if the rule should bend in use without my noticing it? What I mean is, that I might speak of different spaces in which I use it.

The opposite of "it must not occur" is "it can occur". For a finite segment of the series, however, the opposite of "it must not occur in it" seems to be: "it must occur in it".

The queer thing about the alternative "ϕ occurs in the infinite series or it does not", is that we have to imagine the two possibilities individually, that we look for a distinct idea of each, and that *one* is not adequate for the negative and for the positive case, as it is elsewhere.

19.   How do I know that the general proposition "There is . . ." makes sense here? Well, if it can be used to tell something about the technique of expansion in a language game.

In *one* case what we are told is: "it must not occur"—i.e.: if it occurs you calculated wrong.

In one case what we are told is: "it can occur", i.e., no such interdict exists. In another: "it must occur in such-and-such a region (always in this place in these regions)". But the opposite of this seems to be: "it must not occur in such-and-such places"—instead of "it *need* not occur there".

But what if the rule were given that, e.g., everywhere where the formation rule for π yields 4, any arbitrary digit other than 4 can be put in its place?

Consider also the rule which forbids one digit in certain places, but otherwise leaves the choice open.

Isn't it like this? The concepts of infinite decimals in mathematical propositions are not concepts of series, but of the unlimited technique of expansion of series.

We learn an endless technique: that is to say, something is done for us first, and then we do it; we are told rules and we do exercises in following them; perhaps some expression like "and so on *ad inf.*" is also used, but what is in question here is not some gigantic extension.

These are the facts. And now what does it mean to say: "ϕ either occurs in the expansion, or does not occur"?

20.　But does this mean that there is no such problem as: "Does the pattern ϕ occur in this expansion?"?—To ask this is to ask for a rule regarding the occurrence of ϕ. And the alternative of the existence or non-existence of such a rule is at any rate not a mathematical one.

Only within a mathematical structure which has yet to be erected does the question allow of a *mathematical* decision, and at the same time become a demand for such a decision.

21.　Then is infinity not actual—can I not say: "these two edges of the slab meet at infinity"?

Say, not: "the circle has this property because it passes through the two points at infinity . . ."; but: "the properties of the circle can be regarded in this (extraordinary) perspective".

It is essentially a perspective, and a far-fetched one. (Which does not express any reproach.) But it must always be quite clear *how far*-fetched this way of looking at it is. For otherwise its real *significance* is dark.

22.   What does it mean to say: "the mathematician does not know what he is doing", or: "he knows what he is doing"?

23.   Can one make infinite predictions?—Well, why should one not for example call the law of inertia one? Or the proposition that a comet describes a parabola?

In a certain sense of course the infinity of the prediction is not taken very seriously.

Now what about a *prediction* that if you expand π, however far you go, you will never come across the pattern ϕ?—Well, we could say that this is either a *non-mathematical* prediction, or alternatively a mathematical rule.

Someone who has learned to expand $\sqrt{2}$ goes to a fortune-teller, and she tells him that however far he may expand $\sqrt{2}$ he will never arrive at the pattern. . . .—Is her soothsaying a mathematical proposition? No.—Unless she says: "If you always expand correctly you will never reach it". But is that still a prediction?

Now it looks as if such a *prediction* of the correct expansion were imaginable and were distinct from a mathematical law that it *must* be thus and thus. So that in the mathematical expansion there would be a distinction between what as a matter of fact comes out like this—as it were accidentally—and what must come out.

How is it to be decided whether an infinite prediction makes sense? At any rate not by one's saying: "I am certain I *mean* something when I say . . .".

Besides, the question is not so much whether the prediction makes some kind of sense, as: what kind of sense it makes. (That is, in what language games it occurs.)

24.   "The disastrous invasion" of mathematics by logic.

In a field that has been prepared in this way *this* is a proof of existence.

The harmful thing about logical technique is that it makes us forget the special mathematical technique. Whereas logical technique is only an auxiliary technique in mathematics. For example it sets up certain connexions between different techniques.

It is almost as if one tried to say that cabinet-making consisted in glueing.

25. A proof convinces you that there is a root of an equation (without giving you any idea *where*)——how do you know that you understand the proposition that there is a root? How do you know that you are really convinced of anything? You may be convinced that the application of the proved proposition will turn up. But you do not understand the proposition so long as you have not found the application.

When a proof proves in a general way that *there is* a root, then everything depends on the form in which it proves this. On what it is that here leads to this verbal expression, which is a mere shadow, and keeps mum about *essentials*. Whereas to logicians it seems to keep mum only about incidentals.

Generality in mathematics does not stand to particularity in mathematics in the same way as the general to the particular elsewhere.

Everything that I say really amounts to this, that one can know a proof thoroughly and follow it step by step, and yet at the same time not *understand* what it was that was proved.

And this in turn is connected with the fact that one can form a mathematical proposition in a grammatically correct way without understanding its meaning.

Now when does one understand it?—I believe: when one can apply it.

It might perhaps be said: when one has a clear picture of its application. For this, however, it is not enough to connect a clear picture with it. It would rather have been better to say: when one commands a clear view of its application. And even that is bad, for the matter is simply one of not imagining that the application is where it is not; of not being deceived by the verbal form of the proposition.

But how does it come about that one can fail to understand, or can misunderstand, a proposition or proof in this way? And what is then necessary in order to produce understanding?

There are here, I believe, cases in which someone can indeed apply the proposition (or proof), but is unable to give a clear account of the kind of application. And the case in which he is even unable to apply the proposition. (Multiplicative axiom.)[1]

How is it as regards $o \times o = o$?

---

[1] I.e. Axiom of choice. (Eds.)

One would like to say that the understanding of a mathematical proposition is not guaranteed by its verbal form, as is the case with most non-mathematical propositions. This means—so it appears—that the words don't determine the *language-game* in which the proposition functions.

The logical notation swallows the structure.

26. In order to see how something can be called an 'existence-proof', though it does not permit a construction of what exists, think of the different meanings of the word "where". (For example the topological and the metrical.)

For it is not merely that the existence-proof can leave the place of the 'existent' undetermined: there need not be any question of such a place.

That is to say: when the proved proposition runs: "there is a number for which . . ." then it need not make sense to ask "and which number is it?", or to say "and this number is . . .".

27. A proof that 777 occurs in the expansion of π, without shewing where, would have to look at this expansion from a totally new point of view, so that it shewed e.g. properties of regions of the expansion about which we only knew that they lay very far out. Only the picture floats before one's mind of having to assume as it were a dark zone of indeterminate length very far on in π, where we can no longer rely on our devices for calculating; and then still further out a zone where in a *different* way we can once more see something.

28. We can always imagine proof by *reductio ad absurdum* used in argument with someone who puts forward a non-mathematical assertion (e.g. that he has seen a checkmate with such-and-such pieces) which can be mathematically refuted.

The difficulty which is felt in connexion with *reductio ad absurdum* in mathematics is this: what goes on in this proof? Something mathematically absurd, and hence unmathematical? How—one would like to ask—can one so much as assume the mathematically absurd at all? That I can assume what is physically false and reduce it *ad absurdum* gives me no difficulty. But how to think the—so to speak—unthinkable?

What an indirect proof says, however, is: "If you want *this* then you cannot assume *that*: for only the opposite of what you do not want to abandon would be combinable with *that*".

29. The geometrical illustration of Analysis is indeed inessential; not, however, the geometrical application. Originally the geometrical illustrations were *applications of Analysis*. Where they cease to be this they can be wholly misleading.

What we have then is the imaginary application. The fanciful application.

The idea of a 'cut' is one such dangerous illustration.

Only in so far as the illustrations are also applications do they avoid producing that special feeling of dizziness which the illustration produces in the moment at which it ceases to be a possible application; when, that is, it becomes stupid.

30.   Dedekind's theorem could be derived, if what we call irrational numbers were *quite unknown,* but if there were a technique of deciding the places of decimals by throwing dice. And this theorem would then have its application even if the mathematics of irrational numbers did not exist. It is not as if Dedekind's expansions already foresaw all the special real numbers. It merely *looks* like that as soon as Dedekind's calculus is joined to the calculi of the special real numbers.

31.   It might be asked: what is there about the proof of Dedekind's theorem that a child 10 years old could *not* understand?—For isn't this proof far simpler than all the calculations which the child has to master?—And if now someone were to say: it can't understand the deeper content of the proposition—then I ask: how does this proposition come to have a deep content?

32.   The picture of the number line is an absolutely natural one up to a certain point; that is to say so long as it is not used for a general theory of real numbers.

33.   If you want to divide the *real* numbers into an upper and lower class, then do it first crudely by means of

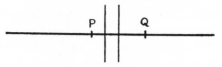

two rational points P and Q. Then halve PQ and decide in which half (if not at the point of division) the cut is supposed to lie; if for example in the lower one, halve this and make a more exact decision and so on.

If you have a principle for unlimited repetition of this procedure then you can say that this principle executes a cut, as it decides for each number whether it lies to the right or to the left.—Now the question is whether I can go all the way by means of such a principle of division, or whether some other way of deciding is still needed; and again, whether this would be *after* finishing the use of the principle, or *before*. Now in any case, not before the completion; for so long as the question still is, in which finite bit of the straight line the point is supposed to lie, further division may decide the matter.—But *after* the decision by a principle is there still room for a further decision?

It is the same with Dedekind's theorem as with the law of excluded middle: it seems to exclude a third possibility, whereas a third possibility is not in question here.

The proof of Dedekind's theorem works with a picture which cannot justify *it*; which ought rather to be justified by the theorem.

You readily see a principle of division as an unendingly repeated division, for at any rate it does not correspond to any finite division and seems to lead you on and on.

34. Couldn't we make a more *extensional preparation* for the theory of limits, functions, real numbers, than we do? Even if this preparatory calculus should seem *very* trivial and in itself useless?

The difficulty of looking at the matter now in an intensional, now again in an extensional way, is already there with the concept of a 'cut'. That every rational number can be called a principle of division of the rational numbers is perfectly clear. Now we discover something else that we can call a principle of division, e.g. what corresponds to $\sqrt{2}$. Then other similar ones—and now we are already quite familiar with the possibility of such divisions, and see them under the aspect of a cut made somewhere along the straight line, *hence extensionally*. For if I *cut*, I can of course choose where I want to cut.

But if a *principle* of division is a cut, it surely is so only because it is possible to say of any arbitrary rational number that it is on one side or the other of the cut. Can the idea of a cut now be said to have led us from the rational to the irrational numbers? Are we for example led to $\sqrt{2}$ by way of the concept of a cut?

Now what is a cut of the real numbers? Well, a principle of division into an upper and a lower class. Thus such a principle yields every rational and irrational number. For even if we have no system of irrational numbers, still those *that we have* divide into upper and lower by reference to the cut (so far, that is, as they are comparable with it).

But now Dedekind's idea is that the division into an upper and lower class (under the known conditions) is the real number.

The cut is an extensional *image*.

It is of course true that, if I have a mathematical criterion for establishing, for any arbitrary rational number, whether it belongs to the upper or the lower class, then it is easy for me systematically to approximate as close as I like to the place where the two classes meet.

In Dedekind we do not make a cut by cutting, i.e. pointing to the place, but—as in finding $\sqrt{2}$—by approaching the adjacent ends of the upper and the lower class.

The thing now is to prove that no other numbers except the real numbers can perform such a cut.

Let us not forget that the division of the rational numbers into two classes did not *originally* have any meaning, until we drew attention to a particular thing that could be so described. The concept *is taken over from the everyday use of language* and that is why it immediately looks as if it had to have a meaning for numbers too.

When the idea of a cut of the *real* numbers is now introduced by saying that we simply have to extend the concept of a cut of the rational numbers to the real numbers—all that we need is a property dividing the real numbers into two classes (etc.)—then *first of all* it is not clear what is meant by such a property, which thus divides *all* real numbers. Now our attention can be drawn to the fact that any real number can serve this purpose. But that gets us only so far and no further.

35. The extensional definitions of functions, of real numbers etc. pass over—although they presuppose—everything intensional, and refer to the ever-recurring outward form.

36. Our difficulty really already begins with the infinite straight line; although we learn even as children that a straight line has no end, and I do not know that this idea has ever given anyone any difficulty. Suppose a finitist were to try to replace this concept by that of a straight segment of definite length?!

But the straight line is a *law* for producing further.

The concept of the limit and of continuity, as they are introduced nowadays, depend, without its being said, on the concept of *proof*. For we say

$$\lim_{x \to \infty} F(x) = 1 \quad \text{when it can be proved that} \ldots$$

This means we use concepts which are infinitely harder to grasp than those that we make explicit.

37. The misleading thing about Dedekind's conception is the idea that the real numbers are there spread out in the number line. They may be known or not; that does not matter. And in this way all that one needs to do is to cut or divide into classes, and one has dealt with them all.

It is by *combining calculation and construction* that one gets the idea that there must be a point left out on the straight line, namely P,

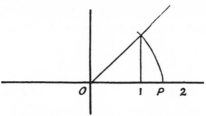

if one does not admit $\sqrt{2}$ as a measure of distance from O. 'For, if I were to construct really accurately, then the circle would have to cut the straight line *between* its points.'

This is a frightfully confusing picture.

The irrational numbers are—so to speak—special cases.

What is the *application* of the concept of a straight line in which a point is missing?! The application must be 'common or garden'. The expression "straight line with a point missing" is a fearfully misleading picture. The yawning gulf between illustration and application.

38.　The generality of functions is so to speak an *unordered* generality. And our mathematics is built up on such an unordered generality.

39.　If one imagines the general calculus of functions without the existence of examples, then the vague explanations by means of value-tables and diagrams, such as are found in the textbooks, are in place as *indications* of how e.g. a sense might sometime be given to this calculus.

Imagine someone's saying: "I want to hear a composition which goes like this":

Would that necessarily be senseless? Couldn't there be a composition whose correspondence to this line, in some important sense, could be shewn?

Or suppose one looked at continuity as a property of the sign '$x^2 + y^2 = z^2$'—of course only if this equation and others were *ordinarily* subjected to a known method of testing. '*This* is the relation of this rule (equation) to this particular test.' A test, which goes with a sidelong glance at a kind of extension.

In this test of the equation something is undertaken which is connected with certain extensions. Though not as if what were in question here were an extension which would be somehow equivalent to the equation itself. It is just that certain extensions are, so to speak, alluded to.—The real thing here is not the extension, which is only *faute de mieux* described intensionally; rather is the *intension* described—or presented—by means of certain extensions, which are yielded by it then and there.

The range of certain extensions casts a *sidelight* on the algebraic property of the function. In this sense, then, the drawing of a hyperbola could be said to cast a sidelight on the equation of the hyperbola.

It is no contradiction of this for those extensions to be the most important application of the rule; for it is *one* thing to draw an ellipse, and another to construct it *by means of its equation.*—

Suppose I were to say: extensional considerations (for example the Heine-Borel theorem) shew: *This* is how to deal with intensions.

The theorem gives us the main features of a method of proceeding with intensions. It says e.g.: '*this* is what it will have to be like'.

And it will then be possible to attach a diagram as a particular illustration, e.g. to a procedure with particular intensions. The illustration is a sign, a description, which is particularly easy to take in, particularly memorable.

To give the illustration here will in fact be to give a procedure.

A theory of the placing of figures in a picture (a painting),—say on general aesthetic grounds—*apart from* whether these figures are engaged in fighting, or love-making etc..

The theory of functions as a schema, into which on the one hand a host of examples fits, and which on the other hand is there as a standard for the classification of cases.

The misleading thing about the usual account consists in its looking as if the *general* account could be quite understood even without examples, without a thought of intension*s* (in the plural), since really everything could be managed extensionally, if that were not impossible for external reasons.

Compare the two forms of definition:
"We say

$$\lim_{x \to \infty} \phi(x) = L \text{ when it can be shewn that } \dots \text{"}$$

and

$$\text{"} \lim_{n \to \infty} \phi(n) = L \text{ means: for every } \epsilon \text{ there is a } \delta \dots \text{"}$$

40. Dedekind gives a general pattern of expression; so to speak a logical form of reasoning.

A general formulation of a procedure. The effect is similar to that of introducing the word "correlation" with a view to the general definition of functions. A general way of talking is introduced, which is very useful for the characterization of a mathematical procedure (as in Aristotelian logic). But the danger is that one will think one is in possession of the complete explanation of the individual cases when one has this general way of talking (the same danger as in logic).

We determine the concept of *the rule* for the construction of a non-terminating decimal further and further.

But the content of the concept?!—Well, can we not complete the construction of the concept as a receptacle for whatever application may turn up? May I not complete the construction of the *form* (the form for which some content has supplied me with the *stimulus*) and as it were prepare a form of language for possible employment? For, so long as it remains empty, the form will contribute to determining the form of mathematics.

For isn't the subject-predicate form open in this way; and waiting for the most various new applications?

That is to say: is it true that the whole difficulty about the generality of the concept of a mathematical function is already to be found in Aristotelian logic, since we can no more survey the generality of propositions and of predicates than that of mathematical functions?

41. Concepts which occur in 'necessary' propositions must also occur and have a meaning in non-necessary ones.

42. Would one say that someone understood the proposition '563 + 437 = 1000' if he did not know how it can be proved? Can

one deny that it is a sign of understanding a proposition, if a man knows how it could be proved?

The problem of finding a mathematical decision of a theorem might with some justice be called the problem of giving mathematical sense to a formula.

An equation links two concepts; so that I can now pass from one to the other.

An equation constructs a conceptual path. But is a conceptual path a concept? And if not, is there a sharp distinction between them?

Imagine that you have taught someone a technique of multiplying. He uses it in a language-game. In order not to have to keep on multiplying afresh, he writes the multiplication in an abbreviated form as an equation, and he uses this where he multiplied before.

Now he says that the technique of multiplying establishes connexions between the concepts. He will also say the same thing about a multiplication as a picture of this transition. And finally he will say the same thing about the equation itself: for it is essential that the transition should be capable of being represented simply by the pattern of the equation. That is, that the transition should *not* always have to be made anew.

Now will he also be inclined to say that the process of multiplying is a concept?

It is surely a *movement*. It seems to be a movement between two stationary points; these are the concepts.

If I conceive a proof as my *movement* from one concept to another, then I shall not want also to say that it is a new concept. But can I not conceive the written multiplication as *one* picture, comparable to a number-sign, and may not its functioning include functioning as a concept-sign?

43.   I should like to say: when we employ now the one, now the other side of the equation, we are employing two sides of the same concept.

44.   Is the conceptual apparatus a concept?

45.   How does anyone shew that he understands a mathematical proposition? E.g. by applying it. So not also by proving it?

I should like to say: the proof shews me a new connexion, and hence it also gives me a new concept.

Is not the new concept the proof itself?

But a proof certainly does enable you to form a new judgment. For you can after all say of a particular pattern that it is or is not this proof.

Yes, but is the proof, regarded, interpreted, as a *proof*, a pattern? As a *proof*, I might say, it has to convince me of something. In consequence of it I will do or not do something. And in consequence of a new concept I don't do or not do anything. So I want to say: the proof is the pattern of proof employed in a particular way.

And what it convinces me of can be of very various kinds. (Think of the proofs of Russellian tautologies, or proofs in geometry and in algebra.)

A mechanism can convince me of something (can prove something). But under what circumstances—in the context of what activities and problems—shall I say that it convinces me of something?

"But a concept surely does not convince me of anything, for it does not shew me a fact."—But why should a concept not first and foremost convince me that I want to use *it*?

Why should not the new concept, once formed, immediately license my transition to a judgment?

46.   'Understanding a mathematical proposition'—that is a very vague concept.

But if you say "The point isn't understanding at all. Mathematical propositions are only positions in a game" that too is nonsense! 'Mathematics' is *not* a sharply delimited concept.

Hence the issue whether an existence-proof which is not a construction is a real proof of existence. That is, the question arises: Do I *understand* the proposition "There is . . ." when I have no possibility of finding where it exists? And here there are two points of view: as an English sentence for example I understand it, so far, that is, as I can explain it (and note how far my explanation goes). But what can I do with it? Well, not what I can do with a constructive proof. And in so far as what I can do with the proposition is the criterion of understanding it, thus far it is not clear *in advance* whether and to what extent I understand it.

The curse of the invasion of mathematics by mathematical logic is that now any proposition can be represented in a mathematical symbolism, and this makes us feel obliged to understand it. Although of course this method of writing is nothing but the translation of vague ordinary prose.

47. A concept is not essentially a predicate.[1] We do indeed sometimes say: "This thing is not a bottle" but it is certainly not essential to the language-game with the concept 'bottle' that such judgments occur in it. The thing is to pay attention to how a concept word ("slab", e.g.) is used in a language-game.

---

[1] Cf. Frege, *Die Grundlagen der Arithmetik*, § 65n; "Begriff ist für mich ein mögliches Prädikat . . ."; also: *Grundgesetze der Arithmetik* II, p. 69: "Eine Definition eines Begriffes (möglichen Pradikates) muss vollständig sein . . .". (Eds.)

There need not e.g. be such a sentence as "This is a slab" at all; but e.g. merely: "Here is a slab."

48.   'Mathematical logic' has completely deformed the thinking of mathematicians and of philosophers, by setting up a superficial interpretation of the forms of our everyday language as an analysis of the structures of facts. Of course in this it has only continued to build on the Aristotelian logic.

49.   It is quite true: the numerical sign belongs with a concept-sign, and only together with this is it, so to speak, a measure.

50.   If you look into this mouse's jaw you will see two long incisor teeth.—How do you know?—I know that all mice have them, so this one will too. (And one does not say: "And this thing is a mouse, so it too . . .") Why is this such an important move? Well, we investigate e.g. animals, plants etc. etc.; we form general judgments and apply them in particular cases.—But it surely is a truth that this mouse has the property, *if all* mice have it! That is a determination about the application of the word "all". The factual generality is to be found somewhere else. Namely, for example, in the general occurrence of that method of investigation and its application.

Or: "This man is a student of mathematics." How do you know?— "All the people in this room are mathematicians; only such people have been admitted."

The interesting case of generality is this: we often have a means of ascertaining the general proposition before considering particular cases: and we then use the general method to judge the particular case.

We gave the porter the order only to admit people with invitations and now we count upon it that this man, who has been admitted, has an invitation.

The interesting generality in the case of the logical proposition is not the fact that it appears to express, but the ever-recurring situation in which this transition is made.

51.   If it is said that the proof shews *how* (e.g.) 25 × 25 yield 625, that is of course a queer way of talking, since for this to be the arithmetical result is not a temporal process. But the proof does not shew any temporal process either.

Imagine a sequence of pictures. They shew how two people fence with rapiers according to such-and-such rules. A sequence of pictures can surely shew that. Here the picture refers to a reality. It cannot be said to shew *that* fencing is done like this, but *how* fencing is done. In another sense we can say that the pictures shew how one can get from this position into that in three movements. And now they also shew *that* one can get into that position in this way.

52.   The philosopher must twist and turn about so as to pass by the mathematical problems, and not run up against one,—which would have to be solved before he could go further.

His labour in philosophy is as it were an idleness in mathematics.

It is not that a new building has to be erected, or that a new bridge has to be built, but that the geography, *as it now is*, has to be described.

We certainly see bits of the concepts, but we don't clearly see the declivities by which one passes into others.

This is why it is of no use in the philosophy of mathematics to recast proofs in new forms. Although there is a strong temptation here.

Even 500 years ago a philosophy of mathematics was possible, a philosophy of what mathematics was then.

53. The philosopher is the man who has to cure himself of many sicknesses of the understanding before he can arrive at the notions of the sound human understanding.

PART VI
ca. 1943/1944

1. Proofs give propositions an order. They organize them.

2. The concept of a formal test presupposes the concept of a transformation-rule, and hence of a technique.

For only through a technique can we *grasp* a regularity.

The technique is external to the pattern of the proof. One might have a perfectly accurate view of the proof, yet not understand it as a transformation according to such-and-such rules.

One will certainly call adding up the numbers . . . to see whether they come to 1000, a formal test of the numerals. But all the same that is *only* when adding is a practised technique. For otherwise how could the procedure be called any kind of test?

It is only within a *technique* of transformation that the proof is a formal test.

When you ask what right you have to pronounce this rule, the proof is the answer to your question.

What right have you to say that? *What* right have you to say it?

How do you test a theme for a contrapuntal property? You transform it according to *this* rule, you put it together with another one in *this* way; and the like. In this way you get a definite result. You get it, as you would also get it by means of an experiment. So far what you are doing may even have been an experiment. The word "get" is here used temporally; you got the result at three o'clock.—In the mathematical proposition which I then frame the verb ("get", "yields" etc.) is used non-temporally.

The activity of testing produced such and such a result.

So up to now the testing was, so to speak, experimental. Now it is taken as a proof. And the proof is the *picture* of a test.

The proof, like the application, lies in the background of the proposition. And it hangs together with the application.

The proof is the route taken by the test.

The test is a formal one only in so far as we conceive the result as the result of a formal proposition.

3.   And if this picture justifies the prediction—that is to say, if you only have to see it and you are convinced that a procedure will take such-and-such a course—then naturally this picture also justifies the rule. In this case the proof stands behind the rule as a picture that justifies the rule.

For why does the picture of the movement of the mechanism justify the belief that this kind of mechanism will always move in *this* way?—It gives our belief a particular direction.

When the proposition seems not to be right in application, the proof must surely shew me why and how it *must* be right; that is, *how* I must reconcile it with experience.

Thus the proof is a blue-print for the employment of the rule.

4.   How does the proof justify the rule?—It shews how, and therefore why, the rule can be used.

The King's Bishop[1] shews us how 8 × 9 makes 72—but here the rule of counting is not acknowledged as a rule.
The King's Bishop shews us *that* 8 × 9 makes 72: Now we are acknowledging the rule.

---

[1] It is possible to devise a 'rule of counting' to fit the text—*e.g.* one of counting up the positions commanded from eight of the ten squares commanding nine (the colour of the bishop's diagonals being determinate). But we have not been able to find out what routine Wittgenstein did have in mind. (Eds.)

Or ought I to have said: the King's Bishop shews me how 8 × 9 *can* make 72; that is to say, it shews me *a* way?

The procedure shews me a How of '*making*'.

In so far as 8 × 9 = 72 is a rule, of course it means nothing to say that that shews me *how* 8 × 9 = 72; unless this were to mean: someone shews me a process through the contemplation of which one is led to this rule.

Now isn't going through any proof such a process?

Would it mean anything to say: "I want to shew you how 8 × 9 originally made 72"?

5.   What is really queer is that the picture, not the reality, should be able to prove a proposition! As if here the picture itself took over the role of reality.—But that's not how it is: for what I derive from the picture is only a rule. And this rule does not stand to the picture as an empirical proposition stands to reality.—The picture of course does not shew that such-and-such happens. It only shews that what does happen can be taken in *this* way.

The proof shews how one proceeds according to the rule without a hitch.

And so one may even say: the procedure, the proof, shews one how far $8 \times 9 = 72$.

The picture shews one, not, of course, anything that happens, but that what ever does happen will allow of being looked at like this.

We are brought to the point of using this technique in this case. I am brought to this—and *to that extent* I am convinced of something.

See, in this way 3 and 2 make 5. Note this procedure. "In doing so you at once notice the rule."

6.　The Euclidean proof of the infinity of prime numbers might be so conducted that the investigation of the numbers between p and $p! + 1$ was carried out on one or more examples, and in this way we learned a technique of investigation. The force of the proof would of course in that case not reside in the fact that a prime number $> p$ was found in *this* example. And at first sight this is queer.

It will now be said that the algebraic proof is stricter than the one by way of examples, because it is, so to speak, the extract of the effective principle of these examples. But after all, even the algebraic proof is not quite naked. Understanding—I might say—is needed for both!

The proof teaches us a technique of finding a prime number between p and $p! + 1$. And we become convinced that this technique must always lead to a prime number $> p$. Or that we have miscalculated if it doesn't.

Would one be inclined to say here that the proof shews us *how* there is an infinite series of prime numbers? Well, one might say so. And at any rate: "What there being an infinity of primes amounts to." For it could also be imagined that we had a proof that did indeed determine us to say that there were infinitely many primes, but did not teach us to find a prime number $> p$.

Now perhaps it would be said: "Nevertheless, these two proofs prove the same proposition, the same mathematical fact." There might be reason at hand for saying this, or again there might not.

7.   The spectator sees the whole impressive procedure. And he becomes convinced of something; that is the special impression that he gets. He goes away from the performance convinced of something. Convinced that (for example) he will end up the same way with other numbers. He will be ready to express what he is convinced of in such-and-such a way. Convinced of what? Of a psychological fact?—

He will say that he has drawn a conclusion from what he has seen.— *Not*, however as one does from an experiment. (Think of periodic division.)

Could he say: "What I have seen was very impressive. I have drawn a conclusion from it. In future I shall . . ."?

(E.g.: In future I shall always calculate like *this*.)
He tells us: "I saw that it must be like that."

"I realised that it must be like that"—that is his report.

He will now perhaps run through the proof procedure in his mind.

But he does not say: I realised that *this* happens. Rather: that it must be like that. This "must" shews what kind of lesson he has drawn from the scene.
The "must" shews that he has gone in a circle.

I decide to see things like *this*. And so, to act in such-and-such a way.

I imagine that whoever sees the process also draws a moral from it.

'It must be so' means that this outcome has been defined to be essential to this process.

8.   This *must* shews that he has adopted a concept.

This *must* signifies that he has gone in a circle.

He has read off from the process, not a proposition of natural science but, instead of that, the determination of a concept.

Let concept here mean method. In contrast to the application of the method.

9. See, 50 and 50 make 100 like *this*. One has, say, added 10 to 50 five times in succession. And one goes on with the increase of the number until it grows to 100. Here of course the observed process would be a process of calculating in some fashion (on the abacus, perhaps); a proof.

The meaning of that "like *this*" is of course not that the proposition "50 + 50 = 100" says: this takes place somewhere. So it is not as when I say: "See, a horse canters like this"—and shew him a picture.

One could however say: "See, *this* is *why* I say 50 + 50 = 100".

Or: See, *this* is how one gets 50 + 50 = 100.
But if I now say: See, *this* is how 3 + 2 make 5, laying 3 apples on the table and then 2 more, here I mean to say: 3 apples and 2 apples

make 5 apples, if none are added or taken away.—Or one might even tell someone: If you put 3 apples and then 2 more on the table (as I am doing), then what you see now almost always happens—and there are now 5 apples lying there.

I want perhaps to shew him that 3 apples and 2 apples don't make 5 apples in *such* a way as they might make 6 (because e.g. one makes a sudden appearance). This is really an explanation, a definition of the operation of adding. This is indeed how one might actually explain adding with the abacus.

"If we put 3 things by 2 things, that may yield various counts of things. But we see as a *norm* the procedure that 3 things and 2 things make 5 things. See, *this* is how it looks when they make 5."

Couldn't one say to a child: "Shew me how 3 and 2 make 5." And the child would then have to calculate 3 + 2 on the abacus.

When, in teaching the child to calculate, one asks, "How do 3 + 2 make 5?"—what is he supposed to shew? Well, obviously he is supposed to move three beads up to 2 beads and then to count the beads (or something like that).

Might one not say "Shew me how this theme makes a canon." And someone asked this would have to prove that it does make a canon.—One would ask someone "*how*" if one wanted to to get him to shew that he does grasp what is in question here.

And if the child now shews how 3 and 2 make 5, then he shews a procedure that can be regarded as a ground for the rule "2 + 3 = 5."

10.   But suppose one asks the pupil: "Shew me how there are infinitely many prime numbers."—Here the grammar is doubtful! But it would be appropriate to say: "Shew me in how far one may say that there are infinitely many prime numbers."

When one says "Shew me that it is . . .," then the question *whether it is* is already put and it remains only to answer "yes" or "no". But if one says "Shew me *how* it is that . . .", then here the language-game itself needs to be explained. At any rate, one has so far no *clear* concept of what one is supposed to be at with this assertion. (One is asking, so to speak; "How can such an assertion be justified at all?")

Now am I meant to give different answers to the question: "Shew me *how* . . ." and "Shew me that . . ."?

From the proof you derive a theory. If you derive a theory from the proof, then the sense of the theory must be independent of the proof; for otherwise the theory could never have been separated from the proof.

In the same way as I can remove auxiliary construction lines in a drawing and leave the rest.

Thus it is as if the proof did not determine the sense of the proposition proved; and yet as if it did determine it.

But isn't it like that with any verification of any proposition?

11.   I believe this: Only in a large context can it be said at all that there are infinitely many prime numbers. That is to say: For this to be possible there must already exist an extended technique of calculating with cardinal numbers. That proposition only makes sense within this technique. A proof of the proposition locates it in the whole system of calculations. And its position therein can now be described in more than one way, as of course the whole complicated system in its background is presupposed.

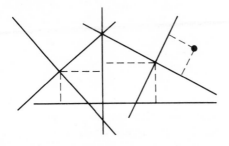

If for example 3 co-ordinate systems are given a definite mutual arrangement, I can determine the position of a point for all of them by giving it for any one.

The proof of a proposition certainly does not mention, certainly does not describe, the whole system of calculation that stands behind the proposition and gives it its sense.

Assume that an adult with intelligence and experience has learnt only the first elements of calculation, say the four fundamental operations with numbers up to 20. In doing so he has also learnt the word "prime number". And suppose someone said to him "I am going to prove to you that there are infinitely many prime numbers." Now, how can he prove it to him? He has got to *teach him to calculate*. That is here part of the proof. It takes that, so to speak, to give the question "Are there infinitely many prime numbers?" any sense.

12. Philosophy has to work things out in face of the temptations to misunderstand on *this* level of knowledge. (On another level there are again new temptations.) But that doesn't make philosophising any easier!

13. Now isn't it absurd to say that one doesn't understand the sense of Fermat's last theorem?—Well, one might reply: the mathematicians are not *completely* blank and helpless when they are confronted by this proposition. After all, they try certain methods of proving it; and, so far as they try methods, *so far* do they understand the proposition.—But is that correct? Don't they *understand* it just as completely as one can possibly understand it?

Now let us assume that, quite contrary to mathematicians' expectations, its contrary were proved. So now it is shewn that it *cannot* be so at all.

But, if I am to know what a proposition like Fermat's last theorem says, must I not know what the criterion is, for the proposition to be true? And I am of course acquainted with criteria for the truth of *similar* propositions, but not with any criterion for the truth of this proposition.

'Understanding' is a vague concept.

In the first place, there is such a thing as *belief* that one understands a proposition.

And if understanding is a psychical process—why should it interest us so much? Unless experience connects it with the capacity to make use of the proposition.

"Shew me how . . ." means: shew me the connexions in which you are using this proposition (this machine-part).

14. "I am going to shew you how there are infinitely many prime numbers" presupposes a condition in which the proposition that there are infinitely many prime numbers had no, or only the vaguest, meaning. It might have been merely a joke to him, or a paradox.

If this procedure convinces you of that, then it must be very impressive.—But is it?—Not particularly. Why is it not *more* so? I believe it would only be impressive if one were to explain it quite radically. If for example one did not merely write $p! + 1$, but first explained it and illustrated it with examples. If one did not presuppose the techniques as something obvious, but gave an account of them.

15.

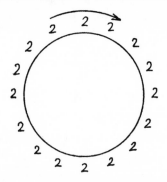

We keep on copying the last figure "2" going round to the right. If we copy correctly, the last figure is in turn a copy of the first one.

A language-game:

One person (A) predicts the result to another (B). The other follows the arrows with excitement, as it were curious how they will conduct him, and is pleased at the way they end by leading him to the predicted result. He reacts to it perhaps as one reacts to a joke.

A may have constructed the result before, or merely have guessed it. B knows nothing about it and it does not interest him.

Even if he was acquainted with the rule, still he had never followed it *thus*. He is *now* doing something new. But there is also such a thing as curiosity and surprise when one has already travelled this road. In this way one can read a story again and again, even know it by heart, and yet keep on being surprised at a particular turn that it takes.

Before I have followed the two arrows

like this ,

I don't know how the route or the result will look. I do not know
what face I shall see. Is it strange that I did not know it? How should I
have known it? I had never seen it! I knew the rule and had mastered
it and I saw the sheaf of arrows.

But why wasn't this a genuine prediction: "If you follow the rule,
you will produce this"? Whereas the following is certainly a genuine
prediction: "If you follow the rule as best you can, you will . . ." The
answer is: the first is not a prediction because I might also have said:
"If you follow the rule, you *must* produce this." It is not a prediction if
the concept of *following* the rule is so determined, that the result is the
criterion for whether the rule was followed.

A says: "If you follow the rule you will get *this*" or he says simply:
"You will get this." At the same time he draws the resulting arrow
there.

Now was what A said in this game a prediction? Well damn it,
Yes—in a certain sense. Does that not become particularly clear if we
make the suggestion that the prediction was *wrong*? It was only not a
prediction in the case where the *condition* turned the proposition into a
pleonasm.

A might have said: "If you are in agreement with each of your steps, then you will arrive *at this*."

Suppose that while B is deriving the polygon, the arrows of the sheaf were to alter their direction a little. B always draws an arrow parallel, as it is just at this moment. He is now just as surprised and excited as in the foregoing game, although here the result is not that of a calculation. So he had taken the first game in the same way as the second.

The reason why "If you follow the rule, this is where you'll get to" is not a prediction is that this proposition simply says: "The result of this calculation is . . ." and that is a true or false mathematical proposition: The allusion to the future and to yourself is mere clothing.

Now must A have a clear idea at all, of whether his prediction is meant mathematically or otherwise? He simply says "If you follow the rule . . . will result" and enjoys the game. If for example the predicted result does not come out, he does not investigate any further.

16.   . . . And this series is defined by a rule. Or again by the training in proceeding according to the rule. And the inexorable proposition is that according to this rule this number is the successor of this one.[1]

---

[1] An amendment of and addition to the fourth sentence of § 4, Part I, which runs: "And isn't *this* series just *defined* by this sequence?" (p. 37). In a revision belonging to about the same period as the present passage there then comes "Not by the sequence; but by a rule; or by the training in the use of a rule." (Eds.)

And this proposition is not an empirical one. But why not an empirical one? A rule is surely something that we go by, and we produce one numeral out of another. Is it not matter of experience, that this rule takes someone from here to there?

And if the rule + 1 carries him one time from 4 to 5, perhaps another time it carries him from 4 to 7. Why is that impossible?

The question arises, what we take as criterion of going according to the rule. Is it for example a feeling of satisfaction that accompanies the act of going according to the rule? Or an intuition (intimation) that tells me I have gone right? Or is it certain practical consequences of proceeding that determine whether I have really followed the rule?—In that case it would be possible that 4 + 1 sometimes made 5 and sometimes something else. It would be thinkable, that is to say, that an experimental investigation would shew whether 4 + 1 always makes 5.

If it is not supposed to be an empirical proposition that the rule leads from 4 to 5, then *this*, the result, must be taken as the criterion for one's having gone by the rule.

Thus the truth of the proposition that 4 + 1 makes 5 is, so to speak, *overdetermined*. Overdetermined by this, that the result of the operation is defined to be the criterion that this operation has been carried out.

The proposition rests on one too many feet to be an empirical proposition. It will be used as a determination of the concept 'applying the operation + 1 to 4'. For we now have a new way of judging whether someone has followed the rule.

Hence $4 + 1 = 5$ is now itself a rule, by which we judge proceedings.

This rule is the result of a proceeding that we assume as *decisive* for the judgment of other proceedings. The rule-grounding proceeding is the proof of the rule.

17.   How does one describe the process of learning a rule?—If A claps his hands, B is always supposed to do it too.

Remember that the description of a language-game is already a description.

I can train someone in a *uniform* activity. E.g. in drawing a line like this with a pencil on paper:

— . . — . . — . . — . . — . . — . .

Now I ask myself, what is it that I want him to do, then? The answer is: He is always to go on as I have shewn him. And what do I really mean by: he is always to go on in that way? The best answer to this that I can give myself, is an example like the one I have just given.

I would use this example in order to shew him, and *also* to shew myself, what I mean by uniform.

We talk and act. That is already presupposed in everything that I am saying.

I say to him "That's right," and this expression is the bearer of a tone of voice, a gesture. I leave him to it. Or I say "No!" and hold him back.

18. Does this mean that 'following a rule' is indefinable? No. I can surely define it in countless ways. Only definitions are no use to me in these considerations.

19. I might also teach him to understand an order of the form:

$$(- \cdot \cdot) \rightarrow \text{ or } (- \cdot \cdot \cdot -) \rightarrow$$

(Let the reader guess what I mean.)

Now what do I mean him to do? The best answer that I can give myself to this is to carry these orders on a bit further. Or do you believe that an algebraic expression of this rule presupposes less?

And now I train him to follow the rule

$$- \cdot - \cdot \cdot - \cdot \cdot \cdot \quad \text{etc.}$$

And again I don't myself know any more about what I want from him, than what the example itself shews. I can of course paraphrase the rule in all sorts of different forms, but that makes it more intelligible only for someone who can already follow these paraphrases.

20. This, then, is how I have taught someone to count and to multiply in the decimal system, for example.

"365 × 428" is an order and he complies with it by carrying out the multiplication.

Here we insist on this, that the same sum that is set always has the same multiplication-pattern in its train, and so the same result. Different patterns of multiplication for the same set sum we reject.

The situation will now arise, of a calculator making mistakes in calculation; and also of his correcting mistakes.

A further language-game is this: He gets asked "How much is '365 × 428'?" And he may act on this question in two different ways. Either he does the multiplication, or if he has already done it before, he reads off the previous result.

21. The application of the concept 'following a rule' presupposes a custom. Hence it would be nonsense to say: just once in the history of

the world someone followed a rule (or a signpost; played a game, uttered a sentence, or understood one; and so on).

Here there is nothing more difficult than to avoid pleonasms and only to say what really describes something.

For here there is an overwhelming temptation to say something more, when everything has already been described.

It is of the greatest importance that a dispute hardly ever arises between people about whether the colour of this object is the same as the colour of that, the length of this rod the same as the length of that, etc. This peaceful agreement is the characteristic surrounding of the use of the word "same".

And one must say something analogous about proceeding according to a rule.

No dispute breaks out over the question whether a proceeding was according to the rule or not. It doesn't come to blows, for example.

This belongs to the framework, out of which our language works (for example, gives a description).

22.   Now someone says that in the series of cardinal numbers that obeys the rule + 1, the technique of which was taught to us in such-and-such a way, 450 succeeds 449. That is not the empirical proposition that we come from 449 to 450 when it strikes us that we have applied the operation + 1 to 449. Rather is it a stipulation that only when the result is 450 have we applied this operation.

It is as if we had hardened the empirical proposition into a rule. And now we have, not an hypothesis that gets tested by experience, but a paradigm with which experience is compared and judged. And so a new kind of judgment.

For one judgment is: "He worked out 25 × 25, was attentive and conscientious in doing so and made it 615"; and another: "He worked out 25 × 25 and got 615 out instead of 625."
But don't the two judgments come to the same thing in the end?

The arithmetical proposition is not the empirical proposition: "When I do *this*, I get *this*"—where the criterion for my doing *this* is not supposed to be what results from it.

23.   Might we not imagine that the main point in multiplying was the concentration of the mind in a definite way, and that indeed one didn't always work out the same sums the same way, but for the particular practical problems that we want to solve, just these differences of result were advantageous?

Is the main thing not this: that in *calculating* the main weight would be placed on whether one has calculated right or wrong, quite prescinding from the psychical condition etc. of the person who is doing the calculation?

The justification of the proposition $25 \times 25 = 625$ is, naturally, that if anyone has been trained in such-and-such a way, then under normal circumstances he gets 625 as the result of multiplying 25 by 25. But the arithmetical proposition does not assert *that*. It is so to speak an empirical proposition hardened into a rule. It stipulates that the rule has been followed only when that is the result of the multiplication. It is thus withdrawn from being checked by experience, but now serves as a paradigm for judging experience.

If we want to make practical use of a calculation, we convince ourselves that it has been "worked out right", that the *correct* result has been obtained. And there can be only *one* correct result of (e.g.) the multiplication; it doesn't depend on what you get when you *apply* the calculation. Thus we judge the facts by the aid of the calculation and quite differently from the way in which we should do so, if we did not regard the result of the calculation as something determined once for all.

Not empiricism and yet realism in philosophy, that is the hardest thing. (Against Ramsey.)

You do not yourself understand any more of the rule than you can explain.

24.   "I have a particular concept of the rule. If in this sense one
follows it, then from that number one can only arrive at this one". That
is a spontaneous decision.

But why do I say "I *must*", if it is my decision? Well, may it not be
that I must decide?

Doesn't its being a spontaneous decision merely mean: that's how I
act; ask for no reason!

You say you must; but cannot say what compels you.

I have a definite concept of the rule. I know what I have to do in
any particular case. I know, that is I am in no doubt: it is obvious to
me. I say "Of course". I can give no reason.

When I say "I decide spontaneously", naturally that does not mean:
I consider which number would really be the best one here and then
plump for . . .

We say: "First the calculations must be done right, and then it will
be possible to pass some judgment on the facts of nature."

25.   Someone has learned the rule of counting in the decimal system. Now he takes pleasure in writing down number after number in the "natural" number series.

Or he follows the rule in the language-game "Write down the successor of the number .... in the series ....."—How can I explain this language-game to anyone? Well, I can describe an example (or examples).—In order to see whether he has understood the language-game, I may make him work out examples.

Suppose someone were to verify the multiplication tables, the logarithm tables etc., because he did not trust them. If he reaches a different result, he trusts it, and says that his mind had been so concentrated on the rule that the result it gets must count as the right one. If someone points out a mistake to him he says that he would rather doubt the trustworthiness of his own understanding and his own meaning *now* than then when he first made the calculation.

We can take agreement for granted in all questions of calculation. But now, does it make any difference whether we utter the proposition used in calculating as an empirical proposition or as a rule?

26.   Should we acknowledge the rule $25^2 = 625$, if we did not all arrive at this result? Well, why then should we not be able to make use of the empirical proposition instead of the rule?—Is the answer to that: Because the contrary of the empirical proposition does not correspond to the contrary of the rule?

When I write down a bit of a series for you, that you then see *this* regularity in it may be called an empirical fact, a psychological fact. But, *if* you have seen this law in it, that you then continue the series in *this* way—that is no longer an empirical fact.

But how is it not an empirical fact?—for "seeing *this* in it" was presumably not the *same* as: continuing it like this.

One can only say that it is not an empirical proposition, by *defining* the step on this level as the one that corresponds to the expression of the rule.

Thus you say: "By the rule that *I* see in this sequence, it goes on in *this* way." Not: according to experience! Rather: that just is the meaning of this rule.

I understand: You say "that is not according to experience"—but still *isn't* it according to experience?

"By this rule it goes like *this*": i.e., you *give* this rule an extension. But why can't I give it this extension today, that one tomorrow?

Well, so I can. I might for example alternately give one of two interpretations.

27.   If I have once grasped a rule I am bound in what I do further. But of course that only means that I am bound in my *judgment* about

what is in accord with the rule and what not.

If I now see a rule in the sequence that is given me—can that simply consist in, for example, my seeing an algebraic expression before me? Must it not belong to a language?

Someone writes up a sequence of numbers. At length I say: "Now I understand it; I must always . . ." And this *is* the expression of a rule. *But*, only within a language!

For when do I say that I see the rule—or a rule—in this sequence? When, for example, I can talk to myself about this sequence in a particular way. But surely also when I simply can continue it? No, I give myself or someone else a general explanation of how it is to be continued. But might I not give this explanation purely in the mind, and so without any real language?

28.   Someone asks me: What is the colour of this flower? I answer: "red".—Are you absolutely sure? Yes, absolutely sure! But may I not have been deceived and called the wrong colour "red"? No. The certainty with which I call the colour "red" is the rigidity of my measuring-rod, it is the rigidity from which I start. When I give descriptions, *that* is not to be brought into doubt. This simply characterizes what we call describing.

(I may of course even here assume a slip of the tongue, but nothing else.)

Following according to the rule is FUNDAMENTAL to our language-game. It characterizes what we call description.

This is the similarity of my treatment with relativity-theory, that it is so to speak a consideration about the clocks with which we compare events.

Is $25^2 = 625$ a fact of experience? You'd like to say: "No".—Why isn't it?—"Because, by the rules, it can't be otherwise."—And why so?—Because *that* is the meaning of the rules. Because that is the procedure on which we build all judging.

29. When we carry out a multiplication, we give a law. But what is the difference between the law and the empirical proposition that we give this law?

When I have been taught the rule of repeating the ornament

and now I have been told "Go on like that": how do I know what I have to do the next time?—Well, I do it with certainty, I shall also know how to defend what I do——that is, up to a certain point. If that does not count as a defence then there is none.

"As I understand the rule, *this* comes next."

Following a rule is a human activity.

I give the rule an extension.

Might I say: See here, if I follow the order I draw this line? Well in certain cases I shall say that. When for example I have constructed a curve according to an equation.

"See here! if I follow the order I do *this*!" That is naturally not supposed to mean: if I follow the order I follow the order. So I must have a different identification for the "this".

"So *that's* what following this order looks like!"

Can I say: "Experience teaches me: if I take the rule like *this* then *this* is how I must go on?"

Not if I make 'taking it so' one and the same with 'continuing so'.

Following a rule of transformation is not more problematic than following the rule: "keep on writing the same". For the transformation is a kind of identity.

30. It might however be asked: if all humans that are educated like this also calculate like *this*, or at least agree to *this* calculation as the right one; then what does one need the *law* for?

"$25^2 = 625$" cannot be the empirical proposition that people calculate like that, because $25^2 \neq 626$ would in that case not be the proposition that people get not this but another result; and also it could be true if people did not calculate at all.

The agreement of people in calculation is not an agreement in opinions or convictions.

Could it be said: "In calculating, the rules strike you as inexorable; you feel that you can only do that and nothing else if you want to follow the rule"?

"As I see the rule, *this* is what it requires." It does not depend on whether I am disposed this way or that.

I feel that I have given the rule an interpretation before I have followed it; and that this interpretation is enough to *determine* what I have to do in order to follow it in the particular case.

If I take the rule as I have taken it, then only doing *this* will correspond to it.

"Have you understood the rule?"—Yes, I have understood—"Then apply it now to the numbers . . . . ." If I want to follow the rule, have I now any choice left?

Assuming that he orders me to follow the rule and that I am frightened not to obey him: am I now not compelled?

But that is surely so too if he orders me: "Bring me this stone." Am I compelled less by *these* words?

31.   To what extent can the function of language be described? If someone is not master of a language, I may bring him to a mastery of it by training. Someone who is master of it, I may remind of the kind of training, or I may describe it; for a particular purpose; thus already using a technique of the language.

To what extent can the function of a rule be described? Someone who is master of none, I can only train. But how can I explain the nature of a rule to myself?

The difficult thing here is not, to dig down to the ground; no, it is to recognize the ground that lies before us as the ground.

For the ground keeps on giving us the illusory image of a greater depth, and when we seek to reach this, we keep on finding ourselves on the old level.

Our disease is one of wanting to explain.

"Once you have got hold of the rule, you have the route traced for you."

32. What sort of public must there be if a game is to exist, if a game can be invented?

What surrounding is needed for someone to be able to invent, say, chess?

Of course I might invent a board-game today, which would never actually be played. I should simply describe it. But that is possible only because there already exist similar games, that is because such games *are played*.

One might also ask: is regularity possible *without* repetition?

I may give a new rule today, which has never been applied, and yet is understood. But would that be possible, if no rule had *ever* actually been applied?

And if it is now said: "Isn't it enough for there to be an imaginary application?" the answer is: No. (Possibility of a private language.)

A game, a language, a rule is an institution.

"But how often must a rule have actually been applied, in order for one to have the right to speak of a rule?" How often must a human being have added, multiplied, divided, before we can say that he has

mastered the technique of these kinds of calculation? And by that I
don't mean: how often must he have calculated right in order to
convince *others* that he can calculate? No, I mean: in order to prove it to
himself.

33. But couldn't we imagine that someone without any training
should see a sum that was set to do, and straightway find himself in the
mental state that in the normal course of things is only produced by
training and practice? So that he knew he could calculate although he
had never calculated. (One might, then, it seems, say; The training
would merely be history, and merely as a matter of empirical fact
would it be necessary for the production of knowledge.)—But suppose
now he is in that state of certainty and he calculates wrong? What is he
supposed to say himself? And suppose he then multiplied sometimes
right, sometimes again quite wrong.—The training may of course be
overlooked as mere history, if he now *always* calculates right. But
that he *can* calculate he shews, to himself as well as to others only by
this, that he *calculates* correctly.

What, in a complicated surrounding, we call "following a rule" we
should certainly not call that if it stood in isolation.

34. Language, I should like to say, relates to a *way* of living.

In order to describe the phenomenon of language, one must describe
a practice, not something that happens once, *no matter of what kind.*

It is very hard to realize this.

Let us imagine a god creating a country instantaneously in the middle of the wilderness, which exists for two minutes and is an exact reproduction of a part of England, with everything that is going on there in two minutes. Just like those in England, the people are pursuing a variety of occupations. Children are in school. Some people are doing mathematics. Now let us contemplate the activity of some human being during these two minutes. One of these people is doing exactly what a mathematician in England is doing, who is just doing a calculation.—Ought we to say that this two-minute-man is calculating? Could we for example not imagine a past and a continuation of these two minutes, which would make us call the processes something quite different?

Suppose that these beings did not speak English but apparently communicated with one another in a language that we are not acquainted with. What reason should we have to say that they were speaking a language? And yet *could* one not conceive what they were doing as that?

And suppose that they were doing something that we were inclined to call "calculating"; perhaps because its outward appearance was similar.—But *is* it calculating; and do (say) the people who are doing it know, though we do not?

35.   How do I know that the colour that I am now seeing is called "green"? Well, to confirm it I might ask other people; but if they did not agree with me, I should become totally confused and should perhaps

take them or myself for crazy. That is to say: I should either no longer trust myself to judge, or no longer react to what they say as to a judgement.

If I am drowning and I shout "Help!", how do I know what the word Help means? Well, that's how I react in this situation.—Now *that* is how I know what "green" means as well and also know how I have to follow the rule in the particular case.

Is it *imaginable* that the polygon of forces of

looks, not like this:

but otherwise? Well, is it imaginable that the parallel to *a* should not look to have the direction of *a'* but a different direction? That is to say: is it imaginable that I should regard not *a'* but a differently directed arrow as parallel to *a*? Well, I might for example imagine that I was somehow seeing the parallel lines in perspective and so I call ↗ ↑ parallel arrows, and that it never occurs to me that I have been using a different way of looking at them. Thus, then, it *is* imaginable that I should draw a different polygon of forces corresponding to the arrows.

36.   What sort of proposition is this: "There are four sounds in the word *OBEN*"?
Is it an empirical proposition?

Before we have counted the letters, we don't know it.

Someone who counts the letters in the word 'OBEN' in order to find out how many sounds there are in a sequence that sounds like that, does just the same thing as someone who counts in order to find out how many letters there are in the word that is written in such-and-such a place. So the former is doing something that might also be an experiment. And that might be reason to call the proposition that 'OBEN' has four letters synthetic *a priori*.

The word "Plato" has as many sounds in it as the pentacle has corners.
Is that a proposition of logic?—Is it an empirical proposition?

Is counting an experiment? It *may* be one.

Imagine a language-game in which someone has to count the sounds in a word. Now it might be that a word apparently always had the same sound, but that when we count its sounds we come to different numbers on different occasions. It might be, for example, that a word did seem to us to sound the same in different contexts (as it were by an acoustical illusion) but the difference emerged when we counted the sounds. In such a case we shall perhaps keep on counting the sounds of a word on different occasions, and this will perhaps be a kind of experiment.

On the other hand it may be that we count the sounds in words once for all, make a calculation, and make use of the result of this counting.

The resulting proposition will in the first case be a temporal one, in the second it will be non-temporal.

When I count the sounds in the word "Daedalus" I can regard the result in two different ways: (1) The word that is written there (or looks like this or was just now pronounced or etc.) has 7 sounds. (2) The sound-pattern "Dædalus" has 7 sounds.

The second proposition is timeless.

The employment of the two propositions must be different.

The *counting* is the same in the two cases. Only, what we reach by means of it is different.

The timelessness of the second proposition is not e.g. a result of the counting, but of the decision to employ the result of counting in a particular way.

In English the word Dædalus has 7 sounds. That is surely an empirical proposition.

Imagine that someone counted the sounds in words in order to find or test a linguistic law, say a law of development of language. He says: "'Dædalus' has 7 sounds". That's an empirical proposition. Consider here the *identity* of the word. The same word may here have now this, now that number of sounds.

Now I tell someone: "Count the sounds in these words and write down the number by each word."

I should like to say: "Through counting the sounds one may get an empirical proposition—but also one may get a rule."

To say: "The word .... has .... sounds—in the timeless sense" is a determination about the identity of the concept 'The word ....'. Hence the timelessness.

Instead of "The word .... has .... sounds—in the timeless sense," one might also say: "The word .... has *essentially* .... sounds."

37.

$$p/p \cdot | \cdot q/q = p \cdot q$$
$$p/q \cdot | \cdot p/q = p \vee q$$
$$x/y \cdot | \cdot z/u \overset{\text{Def}}{=} // (x, y, z, u)$$

Definitions would not at all need to be abbreviations; they might make new connexions in another way. Say by means of brackets or the use of different colours for the signs.

I may for example prove a proposition by using colours to indicate that it has the form of one of my axioms, lengthened by a certain substitution.

38. "I know how I have to go" means: I am in no doubt how I have to go.

"How can one follow a rule?" That is what I should like to ask.

But how does it come about that I want to ask that, when after all I find no kind of difficulty in following a rule?

Here we obviously misunderstand the facts that lie before our eyes.

How can the word "Slab" indicate what I have to do, when after all I can bring any action into accord with any interpretation?

How can I follow a rule, when after all whatever I do can be interpreted as following it?

What must I know, in order to be able to obey the order? Is there some *knowledge*, which makes the rule followable only in *this* way?

Sometimes I must *know* something, *sometimes* I must *interpret* the rule before I apply it.

Now, *how* was it possible for the rule to have been given an interpretation during instruction, an interpretation which reaches as far as to any arbitrary step?

And if this step was not named in the explanation, how then *can* we agree about what has to happen at this step, since after all whatever happens can be brought into accord with the rule and the examples?

Thus, you say, nothing definite has been said about these steps.

Interpretation comes to an end.

39. It is true that *anything* can be somehow justified. But the phenomenon of language is based on regularity, on agreement in action.

Here it is of the greatest importance that all or the enormous majority of us agree in certain things. I can, e.g., be quite sure that the colour of this object will be called 'green' by far the most of the human beings who see it.

It would be imaginable that humans of different stocks possessed languages that all had the same vocabulary, but the meanings of the words were different. The word that meant green among one tribe, meant same among another, table for a third and so on. We could even imagine that the same sentences were used by the tribes, only with entirely different senses.

Now in this case I should not say that they spoke the same language.

We say that, in order to communicate, people must agree with one another about the meanings of words. But the criterion for this agreement is not just agreement with reference to definitions, e.g., ostensive definitions—but *also* an agreement in judgments. It is essential for communication that we agree in a large number of judgments.

40.   Language-game (2),[1] how can I explain it to someone, or to myself? Whenever A shouts "Slab" B brings *this* kind of object.—I might also ask: how can *I* understand it? Well, *only* as far as I can explain it.

But there is here a queer temptation which expresses itself in my inclination to say: I cannot understand it, because the interpretation of the explanation is still vague.

---

[1] §2 of *Philosophical Investigations*. An imaginary language 'is supposed to serve for communication between a builder A and an assistant B. A is constructing a building out of building stones; there are cubes, pillars, slabs and beams available. B has to pass him the blocks, and in the order that A needs them in. To this end they make use of a language consisting of the words "cube", "pillar", "slab" and "beam". A calls them out;—B brings the block that he has learnt to bring at this call. Conceive this as a complete primitive language.' (Eds.)

That is to say, both to you and to myself I can only give examples of the application.

41. The word "agreement" and the word "rule" are *related*, they are cousins. The phenomena of agreement and of acting according to a rule hang together.

There might be a cave-man who produced *regular* sequences of marks for himself. He amused himself, e.g., by drawing on the wall of the cave:

— . — — . — — . — — .

or

— . — . . — . . . — . . . . —

But he is not following the general expression of a rule. And when we say that he acts in a regular way that is not because we can form such and expression.

But suppose he now developed π! (I mean without a general expression of the rule.)

Only in the practice of a language can a word have meaning.

Certainly I can give myself a rule and then follow it. But is it not a rule only for this reason, that it is analogous to what is called 'rule' in human dealings?

When a thrush always repeats the same phrase several times in its song, do we say that perhaps it gives itself a rule each time, and then follows the rule?

42.   Let us consider very simple rules. Let the expression be a figure, say this one:

$$| - - |$$

and one follows the rule by drawing a straight sequence of such figures (perhaps as an ornament).

$$| - - || - - || - - || - - || - - |$$

Under what circumstances should we say: someone gives a rule by writing down such a figure? Under what circumstances: someone is following this rule when he draws that sequence? It is difficult to describe this.

If one of a pair of chimpanzees once scratched the figure $| - - |$ in the earth and thereupon the other the series $| - - || - - |$ etc., the first would not have given a rule nor would the other be following it, whatever else went on at the same time in the mind of the two of them.

If however there were observed, e.g., the phenomenon of a kind of instruction, of shewing how and of imitation, of lucky and misfiring attempts, of reward and punishment and the like; if at length the one who had been so trained put figures which he had never seen before one after another in sequence as in the first example, then we should probably say that the one chimpanzee was writing rules down, and the other was following them.

43.   But suppose that already the first time the one chimpanzee had *purposed* to repeat this procedure? Only in a particular technique of

acting, speaking, thinking, can someone purpose something. (This 'can' is the grammatical 'can'.)

It is possible for me to invent a card-game today, which however never gets played. But it means nothing to say: in the history of mankind just once was a game invented, and that game was never played by anyone. That means nothing. Not because it contradicts psychological laws. Only in a quite definite surrounding do the words "invent a game" "play a game" make sense.

In the same way it cannot be said either that just once in the history of mankind did someone follow a sign-post. Whereas it can be said that just once in the history of mankind did some walk parallel with a board. And that first impossibility is again not a psychological one.

The words "language", "proposition", "order", "rule", "calculation", "experiment", "following a rule" relate to a technique, a custom.

A preliminary step towards acting according to a rule would be, say, pleasure in simple regularities such as the tapping out of simple rhythms or drawing or looking at simple ornaments. So one might train someone to obey the order: "draw something regular", "tap regularly". And here again one must imagine a particular technique.

You must ask yourself: under what special circumstances do we say that someone has "made a mere slip of the pen" or "he could perfectly well have gone on, but on purpose did not do so" or "he had meant to repeat the figure that he drew, but he happened not to do it".

The concept "regular tapping", "regular figure", is taught us in the same way as 'light-coloured' or 'dirty' or 'gaudy'.

44.   But aren't we guided by the rule? And how can it guide us, when its expression can after all be interpreted by us both thus and otherwise? I.e. when after all various regularities correspond to it. Well, we are inclined to say that an expression of the rule guides us, i.e., we are inclined to use this metaphor.

Now what is the difference between the proceeding according to a rule (say an algebraic expression) in which one derives number after number according to the series, and the following proceeding: When we shew someone a certain sign, e.g. ✑, a numeral occurs to him; if he looks at the numeral and the sign, another numeral occurs to him and so on. And each time we engage in this experiment the same series of numerals occurs to him. Is the difference between this proceeding and that of going on according to the rule the psychological one that in the second case we have something occurring to him? Might I not say: When he was following the rule "| – –|", then "| – – |" kept on occurring to him?

Well in our own case we surely have intuition, and people say that intuition underlies acting according to a rule.

So let us assume that that, so to speak, magical sign produces the series 123123123 etc.: is the sign *then* not the expression of a rule? No.

Acting according to a rule presupposes the recognition of a *uniformity* and the sign "123123123 etc." was the natural expression of a uniformity.

Now perhaps it will be said that | 22 || 22 || 22 | is indeed a uniform sequence of marks but surely

$$| 2 || 22 || 222 || 2222 |$$

is not.

Well, I might call this another kind of uniformity.

45. Suppose however there were a tribe whose people apparently had an understanding of a kind of regularity which I do not grasp. That is they would also have learning and instruction, quite analogous to that in § 42. If one watches them one would say that they follow rules, learn to follow rules. The instruction effects, e.g., agreement in actions on the part of pupil and teacher. But if we look at one of their series of figures we can see no regularity of any kind.

What should we say now? We *might* say: "They appear to be following a rule which escapes us," but also "Here we have a phenomenon of behaviour on the part of human beings, which we don't understand".

Instruction in acting according to the rule can be described without employing "and so on".

What can be described in this description is a gesture, a tone of voice, a sign which the teacher uses in a particular way in giving instruction, and which the pupils imitate. The effect of these expressions can also be described, again without calling 'and so on' to our aid, i.e. finitely. The effect of "and so on" will be to produce agreement going beyond what is done in the lessons, with the result that we all or nearly all count the same and calculate the same.

It would be possible, though, to imagine the very instruction without any "and so on" in it. But on leaving school the people would still all calculate the same beyond the examples in the instruction they had had.

Suppose one day instruction no longer produced agreement?

Could there be arithmetic without agreement on the part of calculators?

Could there be only one human being that calculated? Could there be only one that followed a rule?

Are these questions like, say, this one: "Can one man alone engage in commerce?"

It only makes sense to say "and so on" when "and so on" is *understood*. I.e., when the other is as capable of going on as I am, i.e., does go on just as I do.

Could two people engage in trade with one another?

46.   When I say: "If you follow the rule, this *must* come out," that doesn't mean: it must, because it always has. Rather, that it comes out is one of my *foundations*.

What *must* come out is a foundation of judgment, which I do not touch.

On what occasion will it be said: "If you follow the rule this *must* come out"?

This may be a mathematical definition given in the train of a proof that a particular route branches. It may also be that one says it to someone in order to impress the nature of a rule upon him, in order to tell him something like: "You are *not* making an experiment here".

47.   "But at every step I know absolutely what I have to do; what the rule demands of me." The rule, as I conceive it. I don't reason. The picture of the rule makes it clear how the picture of the series is to be continued.

"But I know at every step what I have to do. I see it quite clear before me. It may be boring, but there is no doubt what I have to do."

Whence this certainty? But why do I ask that question? Is it not enough that this certainty exists? What for should I look for a source of it? (And I can indeed give *causes* of it.)

When someone, whom we fear to disobey, orders us to follow the rule ... which we understand, we shall write down number after number without any hesitation. And that is a typical kind of reaction to a rule.

"You already know how it is"; "You already know how it goes on."

I can now determine to follow the rule (–·–) →.

Like this: – · – – · – – · – – · –

But it is remarkable that I don't lose the meaning of the rule as I do it. For how do I hold it fast?

But—how do I know that I do hold it fast, that I do not lose it?! It makes no sense at all to say I have held it fast unless there is such a thing as an outward mark of this. (If I were falling through space I might hold something, but not hold it still.)

Language just is a phenomenon of human life.

48.   One person makes a bidding gesture, as if he meant to say "Go!" The other slinks off with a frightened expression. Might I not call this procedure "order and obedience", even if it happened only once?

What is this supposed to mean: "Might I not call the proceeding ——"? Against any such naming the objection could naturally be made, that among human beings other than ourselves a quite different gesture corresponds to "Go away!" and that perhaps our gesture for this order has among them the significance of our extending the hand in token of friendship. And whatever interpretation one has to give to a gesture depends on other actions, which precede and follow the gesture.

As we employ the word "order" and "obey", gestures no less than words are intertwined in a net of multifarious relationships. If I am now construing a simplified case, it is not clear whether I ought still to call the phenomenon "ordering" and "obeying".

We come to an alien tribe whose language we do not understand. Under what circumstances shall we say that they have a chief? What will occasion us to say that this man is the chief even if he is more poorly clad than others? The one whom the others obey—is he without question the chief?

What is the difference between inferring wrong and not inferring? between adding wrong and not adding? Consider this.

49.   What you say seems to amount to this, that logic belongs to the natural history of man. And that is not combinable with the hardness of the logical "must".

But the logical "must" is a component part of the propositions of
logic, and these are not propositions of human natural history. If
what a proposition of logic said was: Human beings agree with one
another in such and such ways (and that would be the form of the
natural-historical proposition), then its contradictory would say that
there is here a *lack* of agreement. Not, that there is an agreement of
another kind.

The agreement of humans that is a presupposition of logic is not an
agreement in *opinions*, much less in opinions on questions of logic.

PART VII

1941 and 1944

1. The role of propositions which deal with measures and are not 'empirical propositions'.—Someone tells me: "this stretch is two hundred and forty inches long". I say: "that's twenty foot, so it's roughly seven paces" and now I have got an idea of the length.—The transformation is founded on arithmetical propositions and on the proposition that 12 inches = 1 foot.

No one will ordinarily see this last proposition as an empirical proposition. It is said to express a convention. But measuring would entirely lose *its ordinary character* if, for example, putting 12 bits each one inch long end to end didn't ordinarily yield a length which can in its turn be preserved in a special way.

Does this mean that I have to say that the proposition '12 inches = 1 foot' asserts all those things which give measuring its present point?
No. The proposition *is grounded in* a technique. And, if you like, also in the physical and psychological facts that make the technique *possible*. But it doesn't follow that its sense is to express these conditions. The opposite of that proposition, 'twelve inches = one foot' does not say that rulers are not rigid enough or that we don't all count and calculate in the same way.

2. The proposition has the typical (but that doesn't mean *simple*) role of a rule.

I can use the proposition '12 inches = 1 foot' to make a prediction; namely that twelve inch-long pieces of wood laid end to end will turn out to be of the same length as one piece measured in a different way. Thus the point of that rule is, e.g., that it can be used to make certain predictions. Does it lose the character of a *rule* on that account?

Why can one make those predictions? Well,—all rulers are made alike; they don't alter much in length; nor do pieces of wood cut up into inch lengths; our memory is good enough for us not to take numbers twice in counting up to '12', and not to leave any out; and so on.

But then can the rule not be replaced by an empirical proposition saying that rulers are made in such and such ways, that people do *this* with them? One might give an ethnological account of this human institution.

Now it is evident that this account could take over the function of a rule.

If you know a mathematical proposition, that's not to say you yet know anything. If there is confusion in our operations, if everyone calculates differently, and each one differently at different times, then there isn't any calculating yet; if we agree, then we have only set our watches, but not yet measured any time.

If you know a mathematical proposition, that's not to say you yet know *anything*.

I.e., the mathematical proposition is only supposed to supply a framework for a description.

3. How can the mere transformation of an expression be of practical consequence?

The fact that I have 25 × 25 nuts can be verified by my counting 625 nuts, but it can also be discovered in another way which is closer to the form of expression '25 × 25'. And of course it is in the linking of these two ways *of determining* a number that one point of multiplying lies.

A rule *qua* rule is detached, it stands as it were alone in its glory; although what gives it importance is the facts of daily experience.

What I have to do is something like describing the office of a king;— in doing which I must never fall into the error of explaining the kingly dignity by the king's usefulness, but I must leave neither his usefulness nor his dignity out of account.

I am guided in practical work by the result of transforming an expression.

But in that case how can I still say that it means the same thing whether I say "here are 625 nuts", or "here are 25 × 25 nuts"?

If you verify the proposition "here are 625 ..." then in doing that you are also verifying "here are 25 × 25 ..."; etc. But the one form is closer to one kind of verification, the other closer to another.

How can you say that "... 625 ..." and "... 25 × 25 ..." say the same thing?—Only through our arithmetic do they *become one*.

I can at one time arrive at the one, and at another time at the other kind of description, e.g. by counting. That is to say, I can arrive at either of these forms in either way; but by different routes.

It might now be asked: if the proposition "... 625 ..." was verified at one time in this way and at another time in a different way, then did it mean the same thing both times?

Or: what happens if one method of verification gives '625', but the other not '25 × 25'?—Is "... 625 ..." true and "... 25 times 25 ..." false? No.—To doubt the one means to doubt the other: that is the grammar given to these signs by our arithmetic.

If both ways of counting are supposed to justify *giving a number* then giving *one* number, even though in different forms, is all that is *provided for*. On the other hand there is no contradiction in saying: "By one method of counting I get 25 × 25 (and so 625), by the other not 625 (and so not 25 × 25)". Arithmetic has no objection to this.

For arithmetic to equate the two expressions is, one might say, a grammatical trick.

In this way arithmetic bars a particular kind of description and conducts description into other channels. (And it goes without saying that this is connected with the facts of experience.)

4. Suppose I have taught somebody to multiply; not, however, by using an explicit general rule, but only by his seeing how I work out examples for him. I can then set him a *new* question and say: "Do the same with *these* two numbers as I did with the previous ones". But I can also say: "If you do with these two what I did with the others, then you will arrive at the number . . .". What kind of proposition is that?

"You will write such-and-such" is a prediction. 'If you write such-and-such, then you will have done it as I shewed you' determines what he calls "following his example".

'The solution to this problem is . . .'.—If I read this before I have worked out the sum,—what sort of proposition is it?

"If you do with these numbers what I did with the others, you will get . . ."—that surely means: "The result of this calculation is . . ."— and that is not a prediction but a mathematical proposition. But it is none the less a prediction too—A prediction of a special kind. Just as someone who at the end finds that he really does get such-and-such when he adds up the column may be really surprised; for example may exclaim: Good Lord, it does come out!

Just think of this procedure of prediction and confirmation as a special language-game—I mean: isolated from the rest of arithmetic and its application.

What is so singular about this game of prediction? What strikes me as singular would disappear if the prediction ran: "If you believe that you have gone by my example, then you will have produced *this*" or: "If everything seems correct to you, *this* will be the result". This game could be imagined in connexion with the administration of a particular poison and the prediction would be that the injection affects our faculties, our memory for example, in such-and-such a way.—But if we can imagine the game with the administration of a poison, then why not with the administration of a medicine? But even then the weight of the prediction may still always rest on the fact that the *healthy* man sees *this* as the result. Or perhaps: that *this* satisfies the healthy man.

"Do as I do, and this is what you will get" doesn't of course mean: "If you do as I do then you will do as I do"—nor: "Calculate like *this*, and you will calculate like *this*".—But what does "Do as I do" mean? In the language game—it can simply be an order: "Now do as I do!"

What is the difference between these predictions: "If you calculate correctly you will get *this* result"—and: "If you believe you are calculating correctly you will get *this* result"?

Now who says that the prediction in my language-game above does not mean the latter? It seems not to——but what *shews* this? Ask yourself *in what circumstances* the prediction would seem to predict the one thing and in what circumstances the other. For it is clear that it all depends on the rest of the circumstances.

If you predict that I shall get *this*, are you not simply predicting that I shall take this result as correct?—"But"—perhaps you say—"only because it really *is* correct!"—But what does it mean to say: "I take the calculation as correct because it is correct"?

And yet we can say: the person who is calculating in my language-game does not think of it as a peculiarity of *his* nature that he gets *this*; the fact does not appear to him as a psychological one.

I am imagining him as under the impression that he has only followed a thread that is already there, and accepting the How of the following as something that is a matter of course; and only knowing *one* explanation of his action, namely: how the thread runs.

He does just let himself go on when he follows the rule or the examples; however, he does not regard what he does as a peculiarity of *his* course; he says, not: "so *that's* how I went", but: "so *that's* how it goes".

But now, suppose someone did say at the end of the calculation in our language-game: "so *that's* how I went"—or: "so *this* course satisfies me"—can I say he has misunderstood the whole language-game? Certainly not! So long as he does not make some further unwelcome application of it.

5. Isn't it the *application* that elicits that conception: that it is not we, but the calculation, that takes a certain course?

The different 'conceptions' must correspond to different applications.

For there is indeed a distinction between these two things: being surprised that the figures on the paper seem to behave like *this*; and being surprised that *this* is what comes out as the result. In each case, however, I see the calculation in a different context.

I think of the feeling of its 'coming out' when for instance we add up a rather long column of numbers of various patterns, and a round number of 1,000,000 comes out, as we had been told it would before, "Yes, by Jove, another nought—" we say.
"One wouldn't guess it from looking at the numbers", I might say.

How would it be if we said—instead of '6 × 6 gives 36':—'The number 36's being given by 6 × 6'?—Replacing the *proposition* by a substantival expression. (The proof shews *the being given*.)

Why do you always want to look at mathematics under the aspect of finding and not of doing?

It must have a great influence, that we use the words "right" and "true" and "wrong" and the form of statement, in calculating. (Head-shaking and nodding.)

Why should I say that the knowledge that *this* is the way in which all human beings who have learned to calculate do calculate isn't *mathematical* knowledge? Because it seems to point in the direction of a different context.

Then is working out what someone will get out by a calculation already applied mathematics?—and hence also: working out what I myself get out?

6. There is no doubt at all that *in certain language-games* mathematical propositions play the part of rules of description, as opposed to descriptive propositions.

But that is not to say that this contrast does not shade off in all directions. And *that* in turn is not to say that the contrast is not of the greatest importance.

We feel that mathematics stands on a pedestal—this pedestal it has because of a particular role that its propositions play in our language games.

What is proved by a mathematical proof is set up as an internal relation and withdrawn from doubt.

7. What is common to a mathematical proposition and a mathematical proof, that they are both called "mathematical"?

Not, that the mathematical proposition has to be proved mathematically; not, that the mathematical proof has to prove a mathematical proposition.

What is mathematical about an unproved proposition (an axiom)? what has it in common with a mathematical *proof*?

Should I answer: "The inference rules of mathematical proof are always mathematical propositions"? Or: "Mathematical propositions and proofs are used in inference"? That would be getting closer to the truth.

8. Proof must shew an internal relation, not an external one. For we might also imagine a process of transforming a sentence by *experiment*, and a transformation which would be used to predict what would be asserted by the transformed sentence. One might imagine, e.g., signs getting shifted through adding other signs to them, in such fashion that they form a true prediction on the basis of the conditions expressed in their initial position. And if you like, you may regard the calculating human being as an apparatus for such an experiment.

For, that a human being *works out* the result, in the sense that he doesn't write down the result at once, but only after he has written down various other things—doesn't make him any the less a physical-chemical means of producing one sequence of signs from another.

Thus I should have to say: The proved proposition is not: that sequence of signs which the man who has received such-and-such schooling produces under such-and-such conditions.

When we think of proving in that way, what we see in it changes entirely. The intermediate steps become an uninteresting by-product. (Like a rattle in the insides of the automatic machine before it discharges its wares for us.)

9.   We say that a proof is a picture. But this picture stands in need of ratification, and that we give it when we work over it.—

True enough; but if it got ratification from one person, but not from another, and they could not *come to any understanding*—would what we had here be calculation?

So it is not the ratification by itself that makes it calculation but the agreement of ratifications.

For another game could quite well be imagined, in which people were prompted by expressions (similar perhaps to general rules) to let sequences of signs come to them for particular practical purposes, i.e. *ad hoc*; and that this even proved to pay. And here the 'calculations' if we choose to call them that, do not have to agree with one another. (Here we might speak of 'intuition'.)

The agreement of ratifications is the pre-condition of our language-game, it is not affirmed in it.

If a calculation is an experiment and the *conditions are fulfilled*, then we must accept whatever comes, as the result; and if a calculation is an experiment then the proposition that it yields such and such a result is after all the proposition that under such conditions this kind of sign makes its appearance. And if under these conditions one result appears at one time and another at another, we have no right to say "there's something wrong here" or "both calculations cannot be all right", but we should have to say: this calculation does not always yield the same result (*why* need not be known). But although the procedure is now just as interesting, perhaps even more interesting, what we have here *now* is no longer calculation. And this is of course a grammatical remark about the use of the word "calculation". And this grammar has of course a point.

What does it mean to reach an *understanding* about a difference in the result of a calculation? It surely means to arrive at a calculation that is free of discrepancy. And if we can't reach an understanding, then the one cannot say that the other is calculating too, only with different results.

10. Now how about this—ought I to say that the same sense can only have *one* proof? Or that when a proof is found the sense alters?

Of course some people would oppose this and say: "Then the proof of a proposition cannot ever be found, for, if it has been found, it is no longer the proof of *this* proposition". But to say this is so far to say nothing at all.—

It all depends *what* settles the sense of a proposition, what we choose to say settles its sense. The use of the signs must settle it; but what do we count as the use?—

That these proofs prove the same proposition means, e.g.: both demonstrate it as a suitable instrument for the same purpose.

And the purpose is an allusion to something outside mathematics.

I once said: 'If you want to know what a mathematical proposition says, look at what its proof proves'.[1] Now is there not both truth and falsehood in this? For is the sense, the point, of a mathematical proposition really clear as soon as we can follow the proof?

What Russell's '$\sim f(f)$' lacks above all is application, and hence meaning.

If we do apply this form, however, that is not to say that '$f(f)$' need be a proposition in any ordinary sense or '$f(\xi)$' a propositional function. For the concept of a proposition, apart from that of a proposition of logic, is only explained in Russell in its general conventional features.

Here one is looking at language without looking at the language-game.

When we say of different sequences of configuration that they shew e.g. that $25 \times 25 = 625$, it is easy enough to recognize what fixes the

---

[1] cf. *Philosophical Grammar*, p. 369 f; cf. also *Philosophical Remarks*, pp. 183, 184. (Eds.)

place of this proposition, which is reached by the two routes.

A new proof gives the proposition a place in a new system; here there is often a translation of one kind of operation into a quite different kind. As when we translate equations into curves. And then we realize something about curves and, by means of that, about equations. But what right have we to be convinced by lines of thought which are apparently quite remote from the object of our thought?

Well, our operations are not more remote from that object than is, say, dividing in the decimal system from sharing out nuts. Especially if one imagines (what is quite easy to imagine) that operation as originally invented for a different purpose from that of making divisions and the like.

If you ask: "What right have we?" the answer is: perhaps none.— What right have you to say that the development of this system will always run parallel with that one? (It is as if you were to fix *both* inch and foot as units, and assert that $12n$ inches will always be the same length as n feet.)

When two proofs prove the same proposition it is possible to imagine circumstances in which the whole surrounding connecting these proofs fell away, so that they stood naked and alone, and there were no cause to say that they had a common point, proved the same proposition.

One has only to imagine the proofs without the organism of applications which envelopes and connects the two of them: as it were stark naked. (Like two bones separated from the surrounding manifold context of the organism; in which alone we are accustomed to think of them.)

11. Suppose that people calculated with numbers, and sometimes did divisions by expressions of the form $(n - n)$, and in this way occasionally got results different from the normal results of multiplying etc. But that nobody minded this.—Compare with this: lists, rolls, of people are prepared, but not alphabetically as we do it; and in this way it happens that in some lists the same name appears more than once.—— But now it can be supposed that this does not strike anyone; or that people see it, but accept it without worrying. As we could imagine people of a tribe who, when they dropped coins on the ground, did not think it worth while to pick them up. (They have, say, an idiom for these occasions: "It belongs to the others" or the like.)

But now times have changed and people (at first only a few) begin to demand exactness. Rightly, wrongly?—Were the earlier lists *not* really lists?—

Say we quite often arrived at the results of our calculations through a hidden contradiction. Does that make them illegitimate?——But suppose that we now absolutely refuse to accept such results, but still are afraid that some might slip through.—Well then, in that case we have an idea which might serve as a model for a new calculus. As one can have the idea of a new game.

The Russellian contradiction is disquieting, not because it is a contradiction, but because the whole growth culminating in it is a cancerous growth, seeming to have grown out of the normal body aimlessly and senselessly.

Now can we say: "We want a calculus which more certainly tells us the truth"?

But you can't allow a contradiction to stand!—Why not? We do sometimes use this form in our talk, of course not often—but one could imagine a technique of language in which it was a regular instrument.

It might for example be said of an object in motion that it existed and did not exist in this place; change might be expressed by means of contradiction.

Take a theme like that of Haydn's (St. Antony Chorale), take the part of one of Brahms's variations corresponding to the first part of the theme, and set the task of constructing the second part of the variation in the style of its first part. That is a problem of the same kind as mathematical problems are. If the solution is found, say as Brahms gives it, then one has no doubt;—that is the solution.

We are agreed on this route. And yet, it is obvious here that there may easily be different routes, on each of which we can be in agreement, each of which we might call consistent.

'We take a number of steps, all legitimate—i.e. allowed by the rules—and suddenly a contradiction results. So the list of rules, as it is, is of no use, for the contradiction wrecks the whole game!' Why do you have it wreck the game?

But what I want is that one should be able to go on inferring *mechanically* according to the rule without reaching any contradictory results. Now, what kind of provision do you want? One that your present calculus does not allow? Well, that does not make that calculus a bad piece of mathematics,—or not mathematics in the fullest sense. The meaning of the word "mechanical" misleads you.

12. When, for some practical purpose, you want to avoid a contradiction mechanically, as your calculus so far cannot do, this is e.g. like looking for a construction of the . . .-gon, which you have up to now only been able to draw by trial and error; or for a solution of a third degree equation, to which you have so far only approximated.

What is done here is not to improve bad mathematics, but to create a new bit of mathematics.

Suppose I wanted to determine that the pattern '777' did not occur in the expansion of an irrational number. I might take π and settle that if that pattern occurs, we replace it by 'ooo'. Now I am told: that is not enough, for whoever is calculating the places is prevented from looking back to the earlier ones. Now I need another calculus; one in which I can be assured in advance that it cannot yield '777'. A mathematical problem.

'So long as freedom from contradiction has not been proved I can never be quite certain that someone who calculates without thinking, but according to the rules, won't work out something wrong.' Thus so long as this provision has not been obtained the calculus is untrustworthy.—But suppose that I were to ask: "*How* untrustworthy?" —If we spoke of degrees of untrustworthiness mightn't this help us to take the metaphysical sting out of it?

Were the first rules of the calculus not good? Well, we gave them only *because* they were good.—If a contradiction results later,—have they *failed* in their office? No, they were not given for this application.

I may want to supply my calculus with a particular kind of provision. This does not make it into a *proper* piece of mathematics, but e.g. into one that is more useful for a certain purpose.

The idea of the mechanization of mathematics. The fashion of the axiomatic system.

13.   But suppose the 'axioms' and 'methods of inference' are not just some kind of construction, but are absolutely convincing. Well, this means that there are cases in which a construction out of these elements is *not* convincing.

And the logical axioms are in fact not at all convincing if for the propositional variables we substitute structures which no one originally foresaw as possible values, when, that is, we began by acknowledging the truth of the axioms absolutely.

But what about saying: the axioms and methods of inference surely ought to be so chosen that they cannot prove any false proposition?

'We want, not just a fairly trustworthy, but an *absolutely* trustworthy calculus. Mathematics must be *absolute*.'

Suppose I had erected rules for a game of 'hare and hounds'—fancying it to be a nice amusing game.—Later, however, I find that the hounds can always win once one knows how.

Now, let's say, I am dissatisfied with my game. The rules which I gave brought forth a result which I did not foresee and which spoils the game for me.

14. "N. came upon the fact that in their calculations people had often reduced by expressions of the form '$(n - n)$'. He pointed out the consequent discrepancy of results and shewed how this way of calculating had led to the loss of human life."

But let us suppose that other people too had noticed these contradictions, only they had not been able to give any account of their source. They calculated as it were with a bad conscience. They had chosen *one* among contradictory results but with uncertainty, whereas N's discovery would have made them quite certain.—But did they tell themselves: "There's something wrong with our calculus"? Was their uncertainty of the same kind as ours when we do a physical calculation but are not certain whether these formulae really give the correct result here? Or was it a doubt whether their calculating was really calculating? In this case: what did they do to get over the difficulty?

So far these people have only rarely made use of reduction by expressions of values. But some time somebody discovers that they can actually arrive at any arbitrary result in this way.—What do they do now? Well, we could imagine very different things. They may now, e.g., state that this kind of calculation has lost its point, and that in future people are not to calculate in *this* way any more.

'He believes that he is calculating'—one would like to say—'but as a matter of fact he is not calculating.'

15.   If the calculation lost its point for me as soon as I knew I could work out any arbitrary result—did it have none so long as I did *not* know that?

I may of course now declare all these calculations to be null—for I have given up doing them now——but does that mean that they weren't calculations?

I at one time inferred *via* a contradiction without realizing it. Is my result then wrong, or at any rate wrongly got?

If the contradiction is so well hidden that no one notices it, why shouldn't we call what we do now proper calculation?

We say that the contradiction would *destroy* the calculus. But suppose it only occurred in tiny doses in lightning flashes as it were, not as a constant instrument of calculation, would it nullify the calculus?

Imagine people had fancied that $(a + b)^2$ must be equal to $a^2 + b^2$. (Is this a fancy of the same kind as that there must be a trisection of the angle by ruler and compass?) Is it possible, then, to fancy that two ways of calculating had to yield the same result, if it is not the same?

I add up a column, doing it in a variety of ways (e.g. I take the numbers in a different order), and I keep on getting random different results.—I shall perhaps say: "I am in a complete muddle, either I am making random mistakes in calculating, or I am making certain mistakes in particular connexions: e.g. always saying '$7 + 7 = 15$' after '$6 + 3 = 9$'."

Or I might imagine that suddenly, once in the sum, I subtract instead of adding, but don't think I am doing anything different.

Now it might be that I didn't find the mistake and thought I had lost my wits. But this would not have to be my reaction.

'Contradiction destroys the calculus'—what gives it this special position? With a little imagination, I believe, it can certainly be shaken.

To resolve these philosophical problems one has to compare things which it has never seriously occurred to anyone to compare.

In this field one can ask all sorts of things which, while they belong to the topic, still do not lead through its centre.
A particular series of questions leads through the centre and out into the open. The rest get answered incidentally.
It is enormously difficult to find the path through the centre.

It goes *via new* examples and comparisons. The hackneyed ones don't shew us it.

Let us suppose that the Russellian contradiction had never been found. Now—is it quite clear that in that case we should have possessed a false calculus? For aren't there various possibilities here?

And suppose the contradiction had been discovered but we were not excited about it, and had settled e.g. that no conclusions were to be drawn from it. (As no one does draw conclusions from the 'Liar'.) Would this have been an obvious mistake?

"But in that case it isn't a proper calculus! It loses all *strictness*!" Well, not *all*. And it is only lacking in full strictness, if one has a particular ideal of rigour, wants a particular style in mathematics.

'But a contradiction in mathematics is incompatible with its application.

'If it is consistently applied, i.e. applied to produce arbitrary results, it makes the application of mathematics into a farce, or some kind of superfluous ceremony. Its effect is e.g. that of non-rigid rulers which permit various results of measuring by being expanded and contracted.' But was measuring by pacing not measuring at all? And if people worked with rulers made of dough, would that of itself have to be called wrong?

Couldn't reasons be easily imagined, on account of which a certain elasticity in rulers might be desirable?

"But isn't it right to manufacture rulers out of ever harder, more unalterable material?" Certainly it is right; if that is what one wants!

'Then are you in favour of contradiction?' Not at all; any more than of soft rulers.

There is *one* mistake to avoid: one thinks that a contradiction *must* be senseless: that is to say, if e.g. we use the signs 'p', '$\sim$', '.' *consistently*, then '$p. \sim p$' cannot say anything.—But think: what does it mean to continue such and such a use 'consistently'? ('A consistent continuation of this bit of a curve.')

16.   What does mathematics need a foundation for? It no more needs one, I believe, than propositions about physical objects—or about sense impressions, need an *analysis*. What mathematical propositions do stand in need of is a clarification of their grammar, just as do those other propositions.

The *mathematical* problems of what is called foundations are no more the foundation of mathematics for us than the painted rock is the support of a painted tower.

'But didn't the contradiction make Frege's logic useless for giving a foundation to arithmetic?' Yes, it did. But then, who said that it had to be useful for this purpose?

One could even imagine a savage's having been given Frege's logic as an instrument with which to derive arithmetical propositions. He derived the contradiction unawares, and now he derives arbitrary true and false propositions from it.

'Up to now a good angel has preserved us from going *this* way.' Well, what more do you want? One might say, I believe: a good angel will always be necessary, whatever you do.

17. One says that calculation is an experiment, in order to shew how it is that it can be so practical. For we do know that an experiment really does have practical value. Only one forgets that it possesses this value in virtue of a technique which is a fact of natural history, but whose rules do not play the part of propositions of natural history.

"The limits of empiricism."[1]—(Do we live because it is practical to live? Do we think because thinking is practical?)

He knows that an experiment is practical; and so calculation is an experiment.

Our experimental activities have indeed a characteristic physiognomy. If I see somebody in a laboratory pouring a liquid into a test tube and heating it over a Bunsen burner, I am inclined to say he is making an experiment.

Let us suppose that people, who know how to count, want—just as we do—to know numbers for practical purposes of various kinds. And to this end they ask certain people who, having had the practical problem explained to them, shut their eyes, and let the appropriate number occur to them——here there wouldn't be any calculation, however trustworthy the numbers given might be. This way of determining numbers might be even more trustworthy in practice than any calculation.

[1] cf. p. 197 n.

A calculation—it might be said—is perhaps a part of the technique of an experiment, but is by itself not an experiment.

Do we forget that a particular *application* is part of a procedure's being an experiment? And the calculation is an instrument of the application.

For would anyone *think* of calling the translation of a cipher by means of a key an experiment?

When I doubt whether *n* and *m* multiplied yield *l*, my doubt isn't about whether our calculating is going to fall into confusion, and e.g. half of mankind say one thing is right and the other half another.

An action is an 'experiment' only as seen from a certain point of view. And it is *obvious* that the action of calculating can also be an experiment.

I may for example want to test what this man calculates, in such-and-such circumstances, when set this question.—But isn't that exactly what you are asking when you want to know what 52 × 63 is? I may very well ask that—my question may even be expressed in these words. (Compare: is the sentence "Listen, she's groaning!" a proposition about her behaviour or about her suffering?)

But suppose I *work over* his calculation?—'Well, then I am making a further experiment so as to find out with complete certainty that all normal human beings react like that.'—And if they do *not* react uniformly—which one is the mathematical result?

18.   "If calculation is to be practical, then it must uncover facts. And only experiment can do that."

But what things are 'facts'? Do you believe that you can shew what fact is meant by, e.g., pointing to it with your finger? Does that of itself clarify the part played by 'establishing' a fact?—Suppose it takes mathematics to define the *character* of what you are calling a 'fact'!

'It is interesting to know *how many* vibrations this note has! But it took arithmetic to teach you this question. It taught you to see this kind of fact.

Mathematics—I want to say—teaches you, not just the answer to a question, but a whole language-game with questions and answers.

Are we to say that *mathematics* teaches us to count?

Can mathematics be said to teach us experimental *methods of investigation*? Or to help us to discover such methods of investigation?

'To be practical, mathematics must tell us facts.'—But do these facts have to be the *mathematical* facts?—But why should not mathematics, instead of 'teaching us facts', create the forms of what we call facts?

"Yes but surely it remains an empirical fact that men calculate like this!"—Yes, but that does not make the propositions used in calculating into empirical propositions.

"Yes, but surely our calculating must be founded on empirical facts!" Certainly. But what empirical facts are you now thinking of? The psychological and physiological ones that make it possible, or those that make it a useful activity? The connexion with *the latter* consists in the fact that the calculation is the picture of an experiment as it practically always turns out. From the former it gets its point, its physiognomy; but that is certainly not to say that the propositions of mathematics have the functions of empirical propositions. (That would almost be as if someone were to believe that because only the actors appear in the play, no other people could usefully be employed upon the stage of the theatre.)

There are no causal connexions in a calculation, only the connexions of the pattern. And it makes no difference to this that we work over the proof in order to accept it. That we are therefore tempted to say that it arose as the result of a psychological experiment. For the psychical course of events is not psychologically investigated when we calculate.

'There are 60 seconds to a minute.' This proposition is very *like* a mathematical one. Does its truth depend on experience?—Well, could we talk about minutes and hours, if we had no sense of time; if there were no clocks, or could be none for physical reasons; if there did not exist all the connexions that give our measures of time meaning and importance? In that case—we should say—the measure of time would have lost its meaning (like the action of delivering check-mate if the game of chess were to disappear)—or it would have some quite different meaning. But suppose our experience were like that—then would experience make the proposition false; and the contrary experience make it true? No; *that* would not describe its function. It functions quite differently.

'Calculating, if it is to be practical, must be grounded in empirical facts.'——Why should it not rather determine what empirical facts *are*?

Consider: 'Our mathematics turns experiments into definitions'.

19.   But can't we imagine a human society in which calculating quite in our sense does not exist, any more than measuring quite in our sense?—Yes.—But then why do I want to take the trouble to work out what mathematics is?

Because we have a mathematics, and a special conception of it, as it were an ideal of its position and function,—and this needs to be clearly worked out.

Don't demand too much, and don't be afraid that your just demand will dwindle into nothing.

It is my task, not to attack Russell's logic from within, but from without.

That is to say: not to attack it mathematically—otherwise I should be doing mathematics—but its position, its office.

My task is, not to talk about (e.g.) Gödel's proof, but to by-pass it.

20. The problem: find the number of ways in which we can trace the joins in this wall:

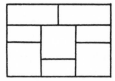

continuously and without repetition, will be recognized by everyone as a *mathematical* problem.—If the drawing were much bigger and more complicated, and could not be taken in at a glance, it could be supposed to change without our noticing; and then the problem of finding that number (which perhaps changes according to some law) would no longer be a mathematical one. But even if it does not change, the problem is, in this case, still not mathematical.——But even when the wall can be taken in at a glance, that cannot be said to make the question mathematical, as when we say: *this* question is now a question in embryology. Rather: *here* we need a mathematical solution. (Like: here what we need is a *model*.)

Did we 'recognize' the problem as a mathematical one because mathematics treats of making tracings from drawings?

Why, then, are we inclined to call this problem straight away a 'mathematical' one? Because we see at once that here the answer to a *mathematical* question is *practically* all we need. Although the problem could easily be seen as, for example, a psychological one.

Similarly with the task of folding a piece of paper in such-and-such a way.

It may look as if mathematics were here a science that makes experiments with *units*; experiments, that is, in which it does not matter what kind of units they are, whether for instance they are peas, glass marbles, strokes and so on.—Mathematics discovers only what holds for *all* these things. And so it does not discover anything about e.g. their melting point, but that 2 and 2 of them are 4. And the first problem of the wall is a mathematical one, i.e. can be solved by means of *this* kind of experiment.—And what does the mathematical experiment consist in? Well, in setting things out and moving them about, in drawing lines, writing down expressions, propositions, etc. And we must not be disturbed by the fact that the outward appearance of these experiments is not that of physical or chemical experiments, etc.; they just are of a different kind. Only there is a difficulty here: the procedure is easy enough to see, to describe,—but *how* is it to be looked at as an experiment? What is the head and what the tail of the experiment here? What are the conditions of the experiment, what its result? Is the result what is yielded by the calculation; or the pattern of calculation; or the assent (whatever that consists in) of the person doing the calculation?

But does it make the principles of dynamics, say, into propositions of pure mathematics if we leave their interpretation open, and then use them to produce a system of measurement?

'A mathematical proof must be perspicuous'—this is connected with the perspicuousness of that figure.

21. Do not forget that the proposition asserting of itself that it is unprovable is to be conceived as a *mathematical* assertion——for that is not *a matter of course*.

It is not a matter of course that the proposition that such-and-such a structure cannot be constructed is to be conceived as a mathematical proposition.

That is to say: when we said: "it asserts of itself"—this has to be understood in a special way. For here it is easy for confusion to occur through the variegated use of the expression "this proposition asserts something of . . .".

In this sense the proposition '625 = 25 × 25' also asserts something about itself: namely that the left-hand number is got by the multiplication of the numbers on the right.

Gödel's proposition, which asserts something about itself, does not *mention* itself.

'The proposition says that this number cannot be got from these numbers in this way.'—But are you also certain that you have translated it correctly into English? Certainly it looks as if you had.—But isn't it possible to go wrong here?

Could it be said: Gödel says that one must also be able to trust a mathematical proof when one wants to conceive it practically, as the proof that the propositional pattern can be constructed according to the rules of proof?

Or: a mathematical proposition must be capable of being conceived as a proposition of a geometry which is actually applicable to itself. And if one does this it comes out that in certain cases it is not possible to rely on a proof.

The limits of empiricism[1] are not assumptions unguaranteed, or intuitively known to be correct: they are ways in which we make comparisons and in which we act.

22.   'Let us assume that we have an arithmetical proposition saying that a particular number . . . cannot be obtained from the numbers . . ., . . ., . . ., by means of such and such operations. And let us assume that a rule of translation can be given according to which this arithmetical proposition is translatable into the figures of the first number—the axioms from which we are trying to prove it, into the figures of the other numbers—and our rules of inference into the operations mentioned in the proposition.—If we had then derived *the arithmetical proposition* from the axioms according to our rules of inference, then *by this means* we should have demonstrated its derivability, but we should also have proved a proposition which, by that translation rule, can be expressed: this arithmetical proposition (namely ours) is not derivable.'

What would have to be done here? I am supposing that we trust our *construction* of the *propositional sign*; i.e. we trust the *geometrical* proof. So we say that this 'propositional pattern' can be obtained from those in such and such ways. And, merely translated into another notation, this means: this number can be got from those by means of these operations. So far the proposition and its proof have nothing to do with any special *logic*. Here the constructed proposition was simply another way of writing the constructed number; it had the *form* of a proposition but we don't compare it with other propositions as a sign *saying* this or that, making *sense*.

But it must of course be said that that sign need not be regarded either as a propositional sign or as a number sign.—Ask yourself: what makes it into the one, and what into the other?

---

[1] cf. note p. 197. (Eds.)

If we now read the constructed proposition (or the figures) as a proposition of mathematical language (in English, say) then it says the opposite of what we regard as proved. Thus we have demonstrated the falsity of the real sense of the proposition and at the same time *proved* it—if, that is, we look on its construction from the admitted axioms by means of the admitted rules of inference as a proof.

If someone objects to us that we couldn't make such *assumptions*, for they would be *logical* or *mathematical* assumptions, then we reply that we need only assume that someone has made a mistake in calculating and so has reached the result we 'assume', and that for the time being he cannot find the mistake.

Here once more we come back to the expression "the proof convinces us". And what interests us about conviction here is neither its expression by voice or gesture, nor yet the feeling of satisfaction or anything of that kind; but its ratification in the use of what is proved.

It might justly be asked what importance Gödel's proof has for our work. For a piece of mathematics cannot solve problems of the sort that trouble *us*.—The answer is that the *situation*, into which such a proof brings us, is of interest to us. 'What are we to say now?'—That is our theme.

However queer it sounds, my task as far as concerns Gödel's proof seems merely to consist in making clear what such a proposition as:

"Suppose this could be proved" means in mathematics.

23. We take it much too much for granted that we ask "How many?" and thereupon count and calculate.

Do we count because it is practical to count? We count!—And in the same way we calculate.

An experiment—or whatever one likes to call it—can be what we go on, sometimes in determining the measurement of the thing measured, and sometimes even in determining the appropriate measure.

Then is the unit of measurement in this way the result of measurements? Yes and no. Not the result reached in measuring but perhaps the *consequence* of measurements.

"Has experience taught us to calculate in *this* way?" would be one question and: "Is calculation an experiment?" another.

24. But isn't it possible to derive anything from anything according to some rule or other—nay, according to *any* rule with a suitable interpretation? What does it mean for me to say, for example: this number can be got from that pair of numbers by multiplying? Ask yourself: When does one use this proposition? Well, it isn't, e.g., a psychological proposition saying what humans will do under certain conditions;

what will satisfy them; nor is it a physical proposition concerning the behaviour of marks on paper. That is, it will be applied in a surrounding other than a psychological or physical one.

Assume that human beings learn to calculate, roughly as they in fact do; but now imagine different 'surroundings' which turn the calculating, now into a psychological experiment, now into a physical experiment with the marks used in calculating, now into something else!

We assume that children learn counting and the simple kinds of sum by means of imitation, encouragement and correction. But now, from a certain point of view, the non-agreement of the one who is doing the sums (i.e., the mistakes) get treated, not as something bad, but as something psychologically interesting. "So you took that for correct then, did you? The rest of us did it like *this*."

I want to say that what we call mathematics, the *mathematical* conception of the proposition $13 \times 14 = 182$, hangs together with the special position that we assign to the activity of calculating. Or, the special position that the calculation . . . has in our life, in the rest of our activities. The language-game in which it is found.

One may learn a piece of music by heart in order to be able to play it correctly; but also as part of a psychological experiment, in order to investigate the working of musical memory. But one might also impress it on one's memory in order thereby to judge some alterations in the score.

25.   A language-game: I am doing multiplication and I say to the other: if you calculate right you will get such-and-such a result; whereupon he carries out the calculation and is pleased at the correctness, and sometimes the incorrectness, of my prediction. What does this language-game presuppose? That 'mistakes in calculating' are easy to discover, and that agreement about the rightness or wrongness of the calculation is always quickly achieved.

"If you agree with each step, you will arrive at this result."

What is the criterion for a step in the calculation's being right; isn't it that the step seems right to me, and other things of the same sort?

What is the criterion for my working out the same figure twice? Isn't it things like the figures' *appearing* to me to be the same?

What is the criterion for my having followed the paradigm here?

"If you say that each step is correct, this is what will come out."

The prediction really is: where you hold what you do to be right, *this* is what you will do.

Where you hold each step to be right, you will go this way.—And so you will reach this end.

A *logical* conclusion is being drawn, when no experience can contradict the conclusion without contradicting the premises. I.e., when the inference is only a movement within the means of representation.

26.   In some language-game sentences are used; reports, orders and so on. And now the people also employ calculating propositions. They say them to themselves perhaps, in between the orders and the reports.

A language-game, in which someone calculates according to a rule and places the blocks of a building according to the results of the calculation. He has learnt to operate with written signs according to rules.—Once you have described the procedure of this teaching and learning, you have said everything that can be said about acting correctly according to a rule. We can go no further. It is no use, for example, to go back to the concept of agreement, because it is no more certain that one proceeding is in agreement with another, than that it has happened in accordance with a rule. Admittedly going according to a rule is also founded on an agreement.

To repeat, what the correct following of a rule consists in cannot be described *more closely* than by describing the *learning* of 'proceeding according to the rule.' And this description is an everyday one, like that of cooking and sewing, for example. It presupposes as much as these. It distinguishes one thing from another, and so it informs a human being who is ignorant of something particular. (Cf. the remark: Philosophy doesn't use a preparatory language, etc.)

For if you give me a description of how people are trained in follow-ing a rule and how they react correctly to the training, you will yourself employ the expression of a rule in the description and will presuppose that I understand it.

We have, then, taught someone the technique of multiplying. So we employ expressions of acquiescence and rejection. We shall also sometimes write down the goal of the multiplication: "You must get this, if it is to be right," we may say to him.

But now, can the pupil contradict and say: "How do you know that? And what do you want?—Do you want me to follow the rule, or to get this result? For there's no need for the two to coincide." Well, we do not assume that the pupil can say that; we assume that he accepts the rule as valid when approached from either side. That he conceives both the individual step *and* the multiplication-pattern—and therefore the result of the multiplication—as criteria of correctness, and if these are not in accord with one another, he believes there is some confusion of his senses.

27.   Now is it imaginable for someone to follow the rule right and nevertheless to work out different results at different times in multi-plying 15 × 13? It all depends on what criteria one allows to count for correct following of the rule. In mathematics the result itself is also a criterion for correct calculation. Here then it is unthinkable that one should follow the rule right and should produce different patterns of multiplication.

Not letting a contradiction stand is something that characterises the technique of our employment of our truth-functions. If we do let the contradiction stand in our language-games, we alter that technique— as, if we departed from regarding a double negative as an affirmative. And this alteration would be significant, because the technique of our logic is connected in its character with the conception of the truth-functions.

"The rules compel me to . . ."—this can be said if only for the reason that it is not all a matter of my own will what seems to me to agree with the rule. And that is why it can even happen that I memorize the rules of a board-game and subsequently find out that in this game whoever starts *must* win. And it is something like this, when I discover that the rules lead to a contradiction.

I am now compelled to acknowledge that this is not a proper game.

'The rules of multiplication, once adopted, compel me to acknowledge that . . . × . . . = ...' Suppose it were disagreeable for me to acknowledge this proposition. Am I to say: "Well, this arises from that type of training. Human beings who are so trained, so conditioned, then get into this kind of difficulty"?

'How does one count in the decimal system?'—"We write 2 after 1, 3 after 2, . . . 14 after 13 . . . 124 after 123 *and so on*."—That is an explanation for someone who, while there is indeed something he doesn't know, does understand 'and so on'. And understanding it means not understanding it as an abbreviation: it does *not* mean that he now sees a much longer series in his mind than that of my examples. That he understands it comes out in his now making certain applications, in his saying *this* and acting *so* in particular cases.

"How do we count in the decimal system?"—. . . . . — Now is that not an answer?—But it isn't one for someone who did not understand the 'and so on'.—But may our explanation not have made it intelligible to him? May he not, through it, have got hold of the idea of the rule?—Ask yourself what are the criteria for his having got hold of the idea now.

What is it that compels me?—the expression of the rule?—Yes, once I have been educated in this way. But can I say it compels me to follow it? Yes: if here one thinks of the rule, not as a line that I trace, but rather as a spell that holds us in thrall.

((	"plain nonsense, and bumps . . ."))

28.   Why shouldn't it be said that such a contradiction as: 'heterological' ϵ heterological $\equiv \sim$ ('heterological' ϵ heterological), shews a logical property of the concept 'heterological'?

" 'Two-syllabled' is heterological", or " 'Four-syllabled' is not heterological" are empirical propositions. It might be important in some contexts to find out whether adjectives possess the properties they stand for or not. The word "heterological" would in that case be used in a language-game. But now, is the proposition "'b' ϵ b" supposed to be an empirical proposition? It obviously is not one, nor should we admit it as a proposition in our language-game even if we had not discovered the contradiction.

'b' ϵ b $\equiv$ $\sim$ ('b' ϵ b) might be called 'a true contradiction'.—But this contradiction is not a significant proposition! Agreed, but the tautologies of logic aren't either.

"The contradiction is true" means: it is proved; derived from the rules for the word "b". Its employment is, to shew that "'b'" is one of those words which do not yield a proposition when inserted into 'ξ ϵ b'.

"The contradiction is true" means: this really is a contradiction, and so you cannot use the word "'b'" as an argument in 'ξ ϵ b'.

29.   I am defining a game and I say: "If you move like this, then I move like *this*, and if you do that, then I do *this*.—Now play." And now he makes a move, or something that I have to accept as a move and when I want to reply according to my rules, whatever I do proves to conflict with the rules. How can this have come about? When I set the rules up, I *said* something: I was following a certain use. I did not foresee what we should go on to do, or I saw only a particular possibility. It was just as if I had said to somebody: "Give up the game; you can't mate with these pieces" and had overlooked an existing possibility of mating.

The various half joking guises of logical paradox are only of interest in so far as they remind anyone of the fact that a serious form of the paradox is indispensable if we are to understand its function properly. The question is: what part can such a logical mistake play in a language-game?

You may instruct someone what to do in such-and-such a case; and these instructions later prove *nonsensical*.

30.   Logical inference is part of a language-game. And someone who carries out logical inferences in the language-game follows certain instructions which were given him in the actual learning of the language-game. If, say, a builder's mate is building a house in accordance with certain orders, he has to interrupt his cartage of materials etc. from time to time and carry out certain operations with signs on paper; and then he takes up his work again in conformity with the result.

Imagine a procedure in which someone who is pushing a wheel-barrow comes to realize that he must clean the axle of the wheel when the wheelbarrow gets too difficult to push. I don't mean that he says to himself: "Whenever the wheelbarrow can't be pushed . . .", but he simply *acts* in this way. And he happens to shout to someone else: "The wheelbarrow won't push; clean the axle", or again: "The wheel-barrow won't push. So the axle needs cleaning." Now this is an inference. Not a logical one, of course.

Can I now say: "Non-logical inference can prove wrong; but logical inference not"?

Is logical inference correct when it has been made according to rules; or when it is made according to *correct* rules? Would it be wrong, for example, if it were said that p should always be inferred from $\sim p$? But why should one not rather say: such a rule would not give the signs '$\sim p$' and 'p' their usual meaning?

We can conceive the rules of inference—I want to say—as giving the signs their meaning, because they are rules for the use of these signs. So that the rules of inference are involved in the determination of the meaning of the signs. In this sense rules of inference cannot be right or wrong.

In the course of building A has measured the length and breadth of an area and gives B the order: "bring 15 × 18 slabs". B is trained to multiply and to count out a number of slabs in conformity with the result.[1]

The sentence '15 × 18 = 270' need of course never be uttered.

It might be said: experiment—calculation are poles between which human activities move.

31. We condition a man in such-and-such ways; then bring a question to bear on him; and get a number-sign. We go on to use

[1] cf. *Philosophical Investigations*, § 2, § 8. (Eds.)

this for our purposes and it proves practical. That is calculating.—No, it isn't enough! It might be an eminently *sensible* procedure—but need not be what we call 'calculating'. As one could imagine sounds being emitted for purposes now served by language, which sounds yet did not form a language.

It is essential to calculating that everyone who calculates right produces the same pattern of calculation. And 'calculating right' does not mean calculating with a clear understanding or smoothly; it means calculating *like this*.

Every mathematical proof gives the mathematical edifice a new leg to stand on. (I was thinking of the legs of a table.)

32. I have asked myself: if mathematics has a purely fanciful application, isn't it still mathematics?—But the question arises: don't we call it 'mathematics' only because e.g. there are transitions, bridges from the fanciful to non-fanciful applications? That is to say: should we say that people possessed a mathematics if they used calculating, operating with signs, *merely* for occult purposes?

33. But in that case isn't it incorrect to say: the *essential* thing about mathematics is that it forms concepts?—For mathematics is after all an anthropological phenomenon. Thus we can recognize it as the essential thing about a great part of mathematics (of what is called 'mathematics') and yet say that it plays no part in other regions. This insight by itself will of course have some influence on people once they learn to see mathematics in this way. Mathematics is, then, a family; but that is not to say that we shall not mind what is incorporated into it.

We might say: if you did not understand *any* mathematical proposition better than you understand the Multiplicative Axiom,[1] then you would *not* understand mathematics.

34. —There is a contradiction here. But we don't see it and we draw conclusions from it. E.g. we infer mathematical propositions; and wrong ones. But we accept these inferences.—And now if a bridge collapses, which we built on the basis of these calculations, we find some other cause for it, or we call it an Act of God. Now was our calculation wrong; or was it not a calculation?

Certainly, if we are explorers observing the people who do this we shall perhaps say: these people don't calculate at all. Or: there is an element of arbitrariness in their calculations, which distinguishes the nature of their mathematics from ours. And yet we should not be able to deny that these people have a mathematics.

What kind of rules must the king[2] give so as to escape henceforward from the awkward position, which his prisoner has put him in?—What sort of problem is this?—It is surely like the following one: how must I change the rules of this game, so that such-and-such a situation cannot occur? And that is a mathematical problem.

But can it be a mathematical problem to make mathematics into mathematics?

Can one say: "After this mathematical problem was solved, human beings began really to calculate"?

---

[1] I.e. the Axiom of Choice. (Eds.)

[2] Presumably the king who made the law that all who came to his city must state their business and be hanged if they lied. A sophist said he came to be hanged under that law.—(Eds.)

35.   What sort of certainty is it that is based on the fact that in general there *won't* actually be a run on the banks by all their customers; though they would break if it did happen?! Well, it is a *different* kind of certainty from the more primitive one, but it is a kind of certainty all the same.

I mean: if a contradiction were now actually found in arithmetic— that would only prove that an arithmetic with *such* a contradiction in it could render very good service; and it will be better for us to modify our concept of the certainty required, than to say that it would really not yet have been a proper arithmetic.

"But surely this isn't ideal certainty!"—Ideal for what purpose?

The rules of logical inference are rules of the *language-game*.

36.   What *sort* of proposition is: "The class of lions is not a lion, but the class of classes is a class"? How is it verified? How could it be *used*?—So far as I can see, only as a grammatical proposition. To draw someone's attention to the fact that the word "lion" is used in a fundamentally different way from the name of a lion; whereas the class word "class" is used like the designation of one of the classes, say the class *lion*.

One may say that the word "class" is used reflexively, even if for instance one accepts Russell's theory of types. For it is used reflexively there too.

Of course to say in this sense that the class of lions is not a lion etc. is like saying one has taken an "e" for an "a" when one has taken a ball for a bell.

The sudden change of aspect in the picture of a cube and the impossibility of seeing 'lion' and 'class' as comparable concepts.

The contradiction says: "Look out . . . .".

But suppose that one gives a particular lion (the king of lions) the name "Lion"? Now you will say: But it is clear that in the sentence "Lion is a lion" the word "lion" is being used in two different ways. (*Tractatus Logico-philosophicus*.[1]) But can't I count them as *one* kind of use?

But if the sentence "Lion is a lion" is used in this way: shouldn't I be drawing your attention to anything, if I drew your attention to the difference of employment of the two "lion"s?

One can examine an animal to see if it is a cat. But at any rate the concept cat cannot be examined in this way.

Even though "the class of lions is not a lion" seems like nonsense,

---

[1] Cf. *Tractatus* 3.323. (Eds.)

to which one can only ascribe a sense out of politeness; still I do not want to take it like that, but as a proper sentence, if only it is taken right. (And so not as in the *Tractatus*.) Thus my conception is a different one here. Now this means that I am saying: there is a language-game with this sentence too.

"The class of cats is not a cat."—How do you know?

The fable says: "The lion went for a walk with the fox", not a lion with a fox; nor yet the lion so-and-so with the fox so-and-so. And here it actually is as if the species lion came to be seen as a lion. (It isn't as Lessing[1] says, as if a particular lion were put in the place of some lion or other. "Reynard the Fox" does not mean: a fox of the name "Reynard".)

Imagine a language in which the class of lions is called "the lion of all lions", the class of trees "the tree of all trees", etc.—Because people imagine all lions as forming *one* big lion. (We say: "God created man".)

Then it would be possible to set up the paradox that there isn't a definite number of all lions. And so on.

---

[1] *Abhandlungen über die Fabeln*, in: G. E. Lessing, *Fabeln*, 1759. (Eds.)

But would it be impossible to count and calculate in such a language?

37.   We might ask: What role can a sentence like "I always lie" have in human life? And here we can imagine a variety of things.

38.   Is turning inches into centimetres logical inference? "The cylinder is 2 inches long.—So it is about 5 cm. long." Is that a *logical* inference?[1]

But isn't a rule something arbitrary? Something that I *lay down*? And could I lay it down that the multiplication 18 × 15 shall *not* yield 270?—Why not?—But then it just hasn't taken place according to the rule which I first laid down, and whose use I have practised.

Is something that follows from a rule itself in turn a rule? And if not,—what kind of proposition am I to call it?

"It is . . . impossible for human beings to recognize an object as different from itself." Well, if only I had an inkling how it is done,— I should try at once!—But, if it is impossible for us to recognize an object as different from itself, is it quite possible to recognize two objects as different from one another? I have e.g. two chairs before me and I recognize that they are *two*. But here I may sometimes believe that they are only *one*; and in *that* sense I can also take one for two.—

[1] Cf. Part I, § 9. (Eds.)

But that doesn't mean that I recognize the chair as different from itself! Very well; but then neither have I recognized the two as different from one another. If you think you can do this and you are playing a kind of psychological game, then translate it into a game with gestures. When you have two objects before you, point with each hand at one of them; as if, as it were, you wanted to indicate that they were independent. If you only have one object before you then you point to it with both hands in order to indicate that no difference between it and itself can be made.—But now, why should one not play the game the opposite way?

39. The words "right" and "wrong" are used when giving instruction in proceeding according to a rule. The word "right" makes the pupil go on, the word "wrong" holds him back. Now could one explain these words to a pupil by saying instead: "this agrees with the rule—that not"? Well yes, if he has a concept of agreement. But what if this has yet to be formed? (The point is how he reacts to the word "agree".)

One does not learn to obey a rule by first learning the use of the word "agreement".

Rather, one learns the meaning of "agreement" by learning to follow a rule.

If you want to understand what it means "to follow a rule", you have already to be able to follow a rule.

406   FOUNDATIONS OF MATHEMATICS   VII—40

"If you accept this rule you *must* do this."—This may mean: the rule doesn't leave two paths open to you here. (A mathematical proposition.) But I mean: the rule conducts you like a gangway with rigid walls. But against this one can surely object that the rule could be interpreted in all sorts of ways.—Here is the rule, like an order! And like an order too in its *effect*.

40.   A language-game: to bring something *else*; to bring the *same*. Now, we can imagine how it is played.—But how can I explain it to anyone? I can give him this training.—But then how does he know what he is to bring the next time as 'the same'—with what justice can I say that he has brought the right thing or the wrong?—Of course I know very well that in certain cases people would turn on me with signs of opposition.

And does this mean e.g. that the definition of "same" would be this: same is what all or most human beings with one voice take for the same?—Of course not.

For of course I don't make use of the agreement of human beings to affirm identity. What criterion do you use, then? None at all.

To use the word without a justification does not mean to use it wrongfully.

The problem of the preceding language-game exists also here: Bring me something red. For what shews me that something is red? The agreement of the colour with a sample?—What right have I to say: "Yes, that's red"? Well, I say it; and it cannot be justified. And it is characteristic of this language-game as of the other that all men consent in it without question.

An undecided proposition of mathematics is something that is accepted neither as a rule nor as the opposite of a rule, and which has the form of a *mathematical* statement.—But is this form a sharply circumscribed concept?

Imagine $\lim_{n \to \infty} \phi n = e$ as a property of a piece of music (say). But of course not as if the piece went on endlessly, but as a property that can be recognized by the ear (as it were an *algebraic* property) of the piece.

Imagine equations used as ornaments (wallpaper patterns), and now a test of these ornaments with a view to discovering what kind of curves they correspond to. The test would be analogous to that of the contrapuntal properties of a piece of music.

41. A proof that shews that the pattern '777' occurs in the expansion of π, but does not shew *where*.[1] Well, proved in this way this 'existential proposition' would, for certain purposes, not be *a rule*. But might it not serve e.g. as a means of classifying expansion rules? It would perhaps be proved in an analogous way that '777' does not occur in π^2 but it does occur in $\pi \times e$ etc. The question would simply be: is it reasonable to say of the proof concerned: it proves the existence

---

[1] Cf. Part V, § 27. (Eds.)

of '777' in this expansion? This can be simply misleading. It is in fact the curse of prose, and particularly of Russell's prose, in mathematics.

What harm is done e.g. by saying that God knows *all* irrational numbers? Or: that they are already all there, even though we only know certain of them? Why are these pictures not harmless?
For one thing, they hide certain problems.—

Suppose that people go on and on calculating the expansion of π. So God, who knows everything, knows whether they will have reached '777' by the end of the world. But can his *omniscience* decide whether they *would* have reached it after the end of the world? It cannot. I want to say: Even God can determine something mathematical only by mathematics. Even for him the mere rule of expansion cannot decide anything that it does not decide for us.

We might put it like this: if the rule for the expansion has been given us, a *calculation* can tell us that there is a '2' at the fifth place. Could God have known this, without the calculation, purely from the rule of expansion? I want to say: No.

42. When I said that the propositions of mathematics determine concepts, that is *vague*; for '2 + 2 = 4' forms a concept in a different sense from '$p \supset p$', '$(x) . fx \supset fa$', or Dedekind's Theorem. The point is, there is a family of cases.

The concept of the rule for the formation of an infinite decimal is—of course—not a specifically mathematical one. It is a concept connected with a rigidly determined *activity* in human life. The concept of this rule is not more mathematical than that of: following the rule. Or again: this latter is not less sharply defined than the concept of such a rule itself.—For the expression of the rule and its sense is only a part of the language-game: following the rule.

One has the *same* right to speak of such rules in general, as of the activities of following them.

Of course, we say: "all this is involved in the concept itself", of the rule for example—but what that means is that we incline to *these* determinations of the concept. For what have we in our heads, which of itself contains all these determinations?

A number is, as Frege says, a property of a concept——but in mathematics it is a mark of a mathematical concept. $\aleph_0$ is a *mark* of the concept of a cardinal number; and the *property* of a technique. $2^{\aleph_0}$ is a mark of the concept of an infinite decimal, but what is this number a property of? That is to say: of what kind of concept can one assert it empirically?

43. The proof of a proposition shews me what I am prepared to stake on its truth. And different proofs can perfectly well cause me to stake the same thing.

Something surprising, a paradox, is a paradox only in a particular, as it were defective, surrounding. One needs to complete this surrounding in such a way that what looked like a paradox no longer seems one.

If I have proved that $18 \times 15 = 270$, I have thereby also proved the geometrical proposition that we get the sign '270' by applying certain transformation rules to the sign '18×15'.—Now suppose that people, having their vision or memory impaired (as we now put it) by some harmful drug, did not get '270' when they did this calculation.—If we cannot use it to make a correct prediction of the result anyone is going to get under normal circumstances, isn't the calculation useless? Well, even if it is, that does not shew that the proposition '$18 \times 15 = 270$' is the empirical proposition: people in general calculate like *this*.

On the other hand it is not clear that the general agreement of people doing calculations is a characteristic mark of all that is called "calculating". I could imagine that people who had learned to calculate might in particular circumstances, say under the influence of opium, begin to calculate differently from one another, and might make use of these calculations; and that they were not said not to be calculating at all and to be deranged—but that their calculations were accepted as a reasonable procedure.

But must they not at least be trained to do the same calculations? Doesn't *this* belong essentially to the concept of calculating? I believe that we could imagine deviations here too.

44. Can we say that mathematics teaches an experimental method of investigation, teaches us to formulate empirical questions (cf. p. 381).

Can't it be said to teach me e.g. to ask whether a particular body moves according to the equation of a parabola?—What does mathematics do in this case? Without it, or without the mathematicians, we should of course not have arrived at the definition of this curve. But was defining this curve itself a piece of mathematics? Would it for instance imply mathematics for people to investigate the movement of a body so as to see whether its path can be represented by the construction of an ellipse with two pegs and a string? Was whoever invented this inquiry doing mathematics?

He did create a new *concept*. But was it in the same way as mathematics does? Was it like the way the multiplication $18 \times 15 = 270$ gives us a new concept?

45. Then *can't* one say that mathematics teaches us to count? But if it teaches us to count, then why doesn't it also teach us to compare colours?

It is clear that if someone teaches us the equation of an ellipse he is teaching us a new concept. But if someone proves to us that *this* ellipse and *this* straight line intersect at these points—he too is giving us a new concept.

Teaching us the equation of an ellipse is like teaching us to count. But it is also like teaching us to ask the question: "Are there a hundred times as many marbles here as there?".

Now if I had taught someone this question in a language-game, and a method of answering it, should I have taught him mathematics? Or would it have been that only if he operated with signs?

(Would that be like asking: "Would it be geometry, even if it *only* consisted of the Euclidian axioms?")

If arithmetic teaches us the question "how many?", then why doesn't it also teach the question "how dark?"?

Is a new conceptual connexion a new concept? And does mathematics create conceptual connexions?

But the question "are there a hundred times as many marbles here as there?" is surely not a mathematical question. And the answer to it is not a mathematical proposition. A mathematical question would be: "are 170 marbles a hundred times as many as 3 marbles?" (And this is a question of pure, not of applied mathematics.)

Now ought I to say that whoever teaches us to count etc. gives us new concepts; and *also* whoever uses such concepts to teach us pure mathematics?

The word "concept" is too vague by far.

Mathematics teaches us to operate with concepts in a new way. And hence it can be said to change the way we work with concepts.

But only a mathematical proposition that has been proved or that is assumed as a postulate does this, not a problematic proposition.

46.   But can we not experiment mathematically? for instance, try whether a square bit of paper can be folded into a cat's head, where the *physical* properties of the paper, such as stiffness or elasticity, don't come into the question? Now certainly we speak of trying here. And why not of experimenting too? This case is like one in which we substitute pairs of numbers in the equation $x^2 + y^2 = 25$ in order to find by trial and error one that satisfies the equation. And if one finally arrives at $3^2 + 4^2 = 25$, is this proposition now the result of an experiment? For why did we call our procedure "trying"? Should we also have called it that if someone always solved such problems first time off with complete certainty (giving the signs of certainty) but without calculating? What did the experiment consist in here? Suppose that before he gives the solution, he has a vision of it.—

47.   If a rule does not compel you, then you aren't *following* a rule.

But how am I supposed to be following it; if I can after all follow it as I like?

How am I supposed to follow a sign-post, if whatever I do is a way of following it?

But, that everything can (also) be *interpreted* as following, doesn't mean that everything is following.

But how then does the teacher interpret the rule for the pupil? (For he is certainly supposed to give it a particular interpretation.)—Well, how but by means of words and training?

And if the pupil reacts to it thus and thus; he possesses the rule inwardly.

But *this* is important, namely that this reaction, which is our guarantee of understanding, presupposes as a surrounding particular circumstances, particular forms of life and speech. (As there is no such thing as a facial expression without a face.)

(This is an important movement of thought.)

48.   Does a line compel me to trace it?—No; but if I have decided to use it as a model in *this* way, then it compels me.—No; then *I* compel myself to use it in this way. I as it were cleave to it.—But here it is surely important that I can form the decision with the (general) interpretation so to speak once for all, and can hold by it, and do not *interpret* afresh at every step.

The line, it might be said, intimates to me how I am to go. But that is of course only a picture. And if I judge that it intimates this or that to me as it were irresponsibly, then I would not say that I was following it *as a rule*.

"The line intimates to me how I am to go": that is merely a paraphrase for:—it is my *last* court of appeal for how I am to go.

49.   Imagine someone was following a line as a rule in this way: he holds a pair of compasses, one point of which he carries along the rule, while the other point draws the line that follows the rule. And as he goes along the rule-line in this fashion, he opens and closes the compasses, to all appearances with great exactness; as he does this, he keeps on looking at the rule, as if *it* determined what he was doing. Now we, who are watching him, can see no regularity of any kind in this opening and shutting. Hence we cannot learn his way of following the rule from him either. But we believe him when he tells us that the line intimated to him to do what he did.

Here we should perhaps really say: "The model seems to *intimate* to him how he has to go. But it isn't a rule."

50.   Suppose someone follows the series "1, 3, 5, 7, . . . in writing the series 2x + 1; and he asked himself "But am I always doing the same thing, or something different every time?"
If from one day to the next someone promises: "Tomorrow I will give up smoking," does he say the same thing every day, or every day something different?

How is it to be decided whether he always does the same, when the line intimates to him how he is to go?

51.   Didn't I want to say: Only the total picture of the use of the word "same" as it is interwoven with the uses of the other words, can determine whether he does use the word as we do?

Doesn't he always do the same, namely, let the line intimate to him how he is to go? But suppose he says that the line intimates now this to him and now that? Couldn't he now say: in *one* sense he is always doing the same thing, but still he isn't following a rule? And cannot the one who is following a rule nevertheless also say that in a certain sense he does something different every time? Thus whether he does the same thing or keeps on doing something different does not determine whether he is following a rule.

The procedure of following a rule can be described only like this: by describing in a different way what we do in the course of it.

Would it make sense to say: "If he did something *different* every time, we should not say he was following a rule"? That does *not* make sense.

52.   Following a rule is a particular language-game. How can it be described? When do we say he has understood the description?— We do this and that; if he now reacts in such-and-such a way, he understood the game. And this "this and that," "in such-and-such a way" doesn't contain an "and so on."—Or: if I used an "and so on" in the description, and were to be asked what that meant, I should have to explain that in turn by the narration of examples; or perhaps by means of a gesture. And I should then regard it as a sign of understanding, if

he, say, repeated the gesture with an intelligent expression; and in special cases acted in such-and-such a way.

"But then doesn't the understanding reach beyond all the examples?" A very remarkable expression, and one that is entirely natural.

When one recounts examples and then says "and so on", this latter expression does not get explained in the same way as the examples.

For the "and so on" might on the one hand be replaced by an arrow, which indicates that the end of the series of examples is not supposed to signify an end of their application. On the other hand "and so on" also means: that's enough, you've understood; we don't need any more examples.

If we replace the expression by a gesture, it might easily be that people only took our series of examples as they were supposed to (only followed it correctly) when we made this gesture at the end. Thus it would be quite analogous to pointing to an object or a place.

53.   Let us imagine a line intimating to me how I am to follow it; that is, as my eye travels along the line a voice within me says: "*This* way!"—What is the difference between this process of obeying a kind of inspiration and that of obeying a rule? For they are surely not

the same. In the case of inspiration I *await* direction. I shall not be able to teach anyone else my 'technique' of following the line. Unless, indeed, I teach him some way of hearkening, some kind of receptivity. But then, of course, I cannot require him to follow the line in the same way as I do.

It would also be possible to imagine such instruction in a sort of calculating. The children can calculate, each in his own way—as long as they listen to their inner voice and obey it. Calculating in this way would be something like composing.

For doesn't the technique (the *possibility*) of training someone else in following it belong to the following of a rule? To be sure, by means of examples. And the criterion of his understanding must be the agreement of their individual actions. Hence it is not as it is with instruction in receptivity.

54.   How do you follow the rule?—"I do it like *this*; . . ." and now there follow general explanations and examples.—How do you follow the voice of the line?—"I look at it, exclude all thoughts, etc., etc."

"I wouldn't say that it kept on intimating something else to me—if I were following it as a rule". Can one say that? "Doing the same" is tied up with "following the rule."

55.   Can you imagine having absolute pitch, if you don't have it? Can you imagine it, *if* you do?—Can a blind man imagine the seeing of red? Can *I* imagine it? Can I imagine spontaneously reacting in such-and-such a way if I don't do so? Can I imagine it better, if I do do so?

But can I play the language-game, if **I** don't react in this way?

56.   One does not feel that one must always be awaiting the tip-off of the rule. On the contrary. We are not excited about what it will tell us to do next, rather it always tells us the same thing, and we do what it says.

It might be said: we look at what we do in following according to the rule from the point of view: *always the same.*

You might say to someone you were beginning to train: "See, I always do the same: . . ."

57.   When do we say: "the line intimates this to me *as a rule*—always the same." And on the other hand: "It keeps on intimating to me what I have to do—it is not a rule."
   In the first case the story is: I have no further court of appeal for what I have to do. The rule does it all by itself; I need only follow it (and following just is *one thing*). I don't feel for example that it's queer that the line always tells me something.—

The other proposition says: I don't know what I shall do; the line will tell me.

Calculating prodigies, who reach the right result, but cannot tell how. Are we to say: they don't calculate? (A family of cases.)

These things are finer spun than crude hands have any inkling of.

58.   May I not *believe* I am following a rule? Doesn't this case exist? And if so, then may I not also believe I am *not* following a rule and yet be following a rule? Isn't there something that we should call *that*, too?

59.   How can I explain the word "same"?—Well, by means of examples.—But is that *all*? Isn't there a still deeper explanation; or must not the *understanding* of the explanation be deeper?—Well, have I myself a deeper understanding? *Have* I more than I give in the explanation?

But whence arises the feeling, as if I had more than I can say?

Is it that I interpret the not-limited as length which reaches further than any given length? (The permission that is not limited, as a permission for something limitless.)

The image that goes with the limitless, is of something so big that we can't see its end.

The employment of the word "rule" is interwoven with the employment of the word "same".

Consider: Under what circumstances will the explorer say: The word "..." of this tribe means the same as our "and so on"? Imagine the details of their life and their language, which would justify him in this.

"But I know what 'same' means!"—I have no doubt of that; I know it too.

60.   "The line intimates to me ..." Here the emphasis is on the *impalpability* of the intimating. On this: that *nothing* stands between the rule and my action.

One could however imagine that someone multiplied, multiplied correctly, with such feelings; kept on saying: "I don't know—now suddenly the rules intimates *this* to me!" and that we reply: "Of course; for you are going ahead perfectly in accordance with the rule."

Following a rule: this can be contrasted with various things. Among other things the explorer will also describe the circumstances under which someone of these people doesn't want to say he is following a rule. Even when in this or that respect it looks as if he were.

But might we not also calculate as we do calculate (all agreeing), etc., and yet at every step have the feeling of being guided by the rule as if by a spell; astonished maybe at agreeing with one another? (Thanking the deity perhaps for this agreement.)

From this you can just see how much there is to the physiognomy of what we call "following a rule" in everyday life!

One follows the rule *mechanically*. Hence one compares it with a mechanism.

"Mechanical"—that means: without thinking. But *entirely* without thinking? Without *reflecting*.

The explorer might say: "they follow rules, but it looks different from the way it looks among us."

"It—for no reason—intimates this or that to me" means: I can't teach you *how* I follow the line. I make no presumption that you will follow it as I do, even if you do follow it.

61.   An addition of shapes together, so that some of the edges fuse, plays a very small part in our life.—As when

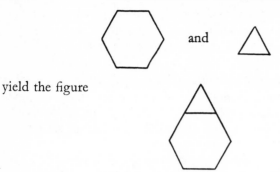

yield the figure

But if this were an *important* operation, our ordinary concept of arithmetical addition would perhaps be different.

It is natural for us to regard it as a geometrical fact, not as a fact of physics, that a square piece of paper can be folded into a boat or hat. But is not geometry, so understood, part of physics? No; we split geometry off from physics. The geometrical possibility from the physical one. But what if we left them together? If we simply said: "If you do this and this and this with the piece of paper then *this* will be the result"? What has to be done might be told in a rhyme. For might it not be that someone did not distinguish at all between the two possibilities? As e.g. a child who learns this technique does not. It does not know and does not consider whether these results of folding are possible only because the paper stretches, is pulled out of shape, when it is folded in such-and-such a way, or because it is *not* pulled out of shape.

And now isn't it like this in arithmetic too? Why shouldn't it be possible for people to learn to calculate without having the concepts of a mathematical and a physical fact? They merely know that this is always the result when they take care and do what they have learnt.

Let us imagine that while we were calculating the figures on paper altered erratically. A 1 would suddenly become a 6 and then a 5 and then again a 1 and so on. And I want to assume that this does not make any difference to the calculation because, as soon as I read a figure in order to calculate with it or to apply it, it once more becomes the one that we have in *our* calculating. At the same time, one would see how the figures change during the calculation; but we are trained not to worry about this.

Of course, even if we do not make the above assumption, this calculation could lead to useful results.

Here we calculate strictly according to rules, yet this result does not *have* to come out.—I am assuming that we see no sort of regularity in the alteration of the figures.

I want to say: this calculating could really be conceived as an experiment, and we might for example say: "Let's try what will come out now if I apply this rule".

Or again: "Let us make the following experiment: we'll write the figures with ink of such-and-such a composition ... and calculate according to the rule. . . ."

Now you might of course say: "In this case the manipulation of figures according to rules is not calculation."

"We are calculating only when there is a *must* behind the result."— But suppose we don't know this *must*,—is it contained in the calculation all the same? Or are we not calculating, if we do it quite naïvely?

How about the following: You aren't calculating if, when you get now this, now that result, and cannot find a mistake, you accept this and say: this simply shews that certain circumstances which are still unknown have an influence on the result.

This might be expressed: if calculation reveals a causal connexion to you, then you are not calculating.

Our children are not only given practice in calculation but are also trained to adopt a particular attitude towards a mistake in calculating.[1]

What I am saying comes to this, that mathematics is *normative*. But "norm" does not mean the same thing as "ideal".

62.   The introduction of a new rule of inference can be conceived as a transition to a new language-game. I can imagine one in which for example one person pronounces: '$p \supset q$', another 'p' and a third draws the conclusion.

63.   Is it possible to observe that a surface is coloured red and blue;

---

[1] [Variant]: . . . towards a departure from the norm. (Ed.)

and not to observe that it is red? Imagine that a kind of colour adjective were used for things that are half red and half blue: they are said to be 'bu'. Now might not someone be trained to observe whether something is bu; and not to observe whether it is also red? Such a man would then only know how to report: "bu", or "not bu". And from the first report we could draw the conclusion that the thing was partly red.

I am imagining that the observation happens by means of a psychological sieve, which for example only lets through the fact that the surface is blue-white-red (the French tricolour) or that it is not.

Now if it is a special observation that the surface is partly red, how can this follow logically from the preceding? Surely logic cannot tell us what to observe.

Someone is counting apples in a box; he counts up to 100. Someone else says: "so there are at any rate 50 apples in the box" (that is all that interests him). This is surely a logical conclusion; but isn't it also a special piece of experience?

64. A surface which is divided into a number of strips is observed by several people. The colours of the strips change every minute, all at the same time.

| red | green | blue | white | black | blue |

Now the colours are: red, green, blue, white, black, blue.

It is observed:

$$\text{red . blue} \supset \text{black .} \supset \text{. white.}$$

It is also observed:

$$\sim\text{green} \supset \sim\text{white}$$

and someone draws the conclusion:

$$\sim\text{green} \supset : \text{red . blue . } \sim\text{black.}$$

And these implications are 'material implications' in Russell's sense.

But then is it possible to *observe* that

$$\text{red . blue} \supset \text{black . } \supset \text{. white?}$$

Isn't one observing *arrangements* of colours, and so for example that red.blue.black.white; and then deducing that proposition?

But may not someone who is observing a surface be quite preoccupied with the question whether it is going to turn green or not green; and if he now sees: $\sim$green, need he be attentive to the particular colour that the surface is?

And might not someone be preoccupied with the aspect red.blue $\supset$ black . $\supset$. white? If, for example, he has been taught to forget everything else, and only to look at the surface from this point of view. (In particular circumstances it might be all one to people whether objects were red or green but important whether they had one of these colours or some third one. And in this case there might be a colour word for "red or green".)

But if one can observe that

$$\text{red . blue} \supset \text{black . } \supset \text{. white}$$

and

$$\sim\text{green} \supset \sim\text{white}$$

then one can also observe, and not merely infer, that

$$\sim\text{green} \supset : \text{red} . \text{blue} . \sim\text{black}.$$

If these are three observations then it must also be possible for the third observation not to agree with the logical conclusion from the first two.

Then is it imaginable that someone observing a surface should see the combination red-black (say as a flag), but if he now sets himself to see *one* of the two halves, he sees blue instead of red? Well, you have just described it.—It would perhaps be as if someone were to look at a group of apples and always see it as two groups of two apples each, but as soon as he tried to take the whole lot in at a glance, they seemed to him to be five. This would be a very remarkable phenomenon. And it is not one of whose possibility we take any notice.

Remember that a rhombus, seen as a diamond, does not look like a parallelogram. Not that the opposite sides seem *not* to be parallel, only the parallelism does not strike us.

65.   I could imagine someone saying that he saw a red and yellow star but did not see anything yellow—because he sees the star as, so to speak, a *conjunction* of coloured parts, which he cannot separate.

For example he had figures like these before him:

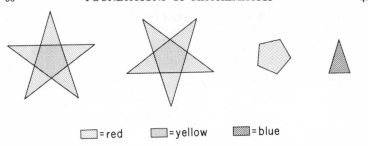

☐ = red   ☐ = yellow   ▨ = blue

Asked whether he sees a red pentagon he would say "yes"; asked whether he sees a yellow one, "no". In the same way he says that he sees a blue triangle but not a red one.—When his attention was drawn to it perhaps he said: "Yes, now I see it; I had not taken the star like that."

And it might seem to him that you can't separate the colours in the star, because you can't separate the shapes.

You cannot learn to view the geography of a landscape as a whole, if you move on in it so slowly that you have already forgotten one bit when you come to another.

66.   Why do I always speak of being compelled by a rule; why not of the fact that I can *choose* to follow it? For that is equally important.

But I don't want to say, either, that the rule compels me to act like this; but that it makes it possible for me to hold by it and let it compel me.

And if e.g. you play a game, you keep to its rules. And it is an interesting fact that people set up rules for the fun of it, and then keep to them.

My question really was: "How can one keep to a rule[1]?" And the picture that might occur to someone here is that of a short bit of hand-rail, by means of which I am to let myself be guided further than the rail reaches. [But there *is* nothing there; but there isn't *nothing* there!] For when I ask "How *can* one . . .", that means that something here looks *paradoxical* to me; and so a picture is confusing me.

"I never thought of its being red too; I only saw it as part of a multi-coloured ornament."

Logical inference is a transition that is justified if it follows a particular paradigm and its rightness is not dependent on anything else.

67.   We say: "If you really follow the rule in multiplying, you *must* all get the same result." Now if this is only the somewhat hysterical way of putting things that you get in university talk, it need not interest us overmuch.

It is however the expression of an attitude towards the technique of calculation, which comes out everywhere in our life. The emphasis of the *must* corresponds only to the inexorableness of this attitude both to the technique of calculating and to a host of related techniques.

The mathematical Must is only another expression of the fact that mathematics forms concepts.

---

[1] Cf. Part VI, § 47. (Eds.)

And concepts help us to comprehend things. They correspond to a particular way of dealing with situations.

Mathematics forms a network of norms.

68.   It is possible to see the complex formed of A and B, without seeing A or B. It is even possible to call the complex a "complex of A and B" and to think that this name points to some kind of kinship of this whole with A and with B. Thus it is possible to say that one is seeing a complex formed from A and B but neither A nor B. As for example one might say that there is a reddish yellow here but neither red nor yellow.

Now can I have A and B before me and also see them both, but only observe A v B? Well, in a certain sense this is surely possible. I was thinking of it like this: the observer is preoccupied with a particular aspect; for example, he has a special kind of paradigm before him; he is engaged in a particular routine of application.—And just as he can be adjusted to A v B, so he can also be adjusted to A.B. Thus only A.B strikes him, and not, for example, A. To be adjusted to A v B might be said to mean: to react to such-and-such a situation with the concept 'A v B'. And one can of course do exactly the same thing with A.B too.

Say someone is interested only in A.B, and so whatever happens he judges merely either "A.B", or "∼(A.B)"; then I can imagine his judging "A.B" and saying "No, I see A.B" when he is asked "Do you see B?" As for example some people who see A.B will not concede that they see A v B.

69.   But 'seeing' the surface 'blue all over' and 'seeing' it 'red all over' are surely 'genuine' experiences, and yet we say that a man could not have them at the same time.

Now suppose he assured us that he saw this surface really red all over and blue all over at the same time? We should have to say: "You aren't making yourself intelligible to us."

With us the proposition "1 foot = ... cm." is timeless. But we could imagine the case in which the foot and the metre gradually altered somewhat, and kept on having to be compared anew in order for us to calculate their translations into one another.

But have we not determined the relative length of foot and metre experimentally? Yes; but the result was given the character of a rule.

70.   In what sense can a proposition of arithmetic be said to give us a concept? Well let us interpret it, not as a proposition, as something that decides a question, but as a—somehow accepted—connexion of concepts.

The equating of 25^2 and 625 could be said to give me a new concept. And the proof shews what the position is regarding this equality.— "To give a new concept" can only mean to introduce a new employment of a concept, a new practice.

"How can the proposition be separated from its proof?" This question betrays a false conception.

The proof is part of the *surroundings* of the proposition.

'Concept' is a vague concept.

71. It is not in every language-game that there occurs something that one would call a concept.

Concept is something like a picture with which one compares objects.

Are there concepts in language-game (2)[1]? Still, it would be easy to add to it in such a way that "slab", "block" etc. became concepts. For example, by means of a technique of describing or portraying those objects. There is of course no sharp dividing line between language-games which work with concepts and others. What is important is that the word "concept" refers to one kind of expedient in the mechanism of language-games.

---

[1] *Philosophical Investigations*, § 2; here, above, p. 343n. (Eds.)

72.   Consider a mechanism. For example this one:

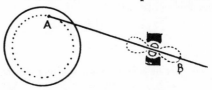

While the point *A* describes a circle, *B* describes a figure eight. Now we write this down as a proposition of kinematics.

When I work the mechanism its movement proves the proposition to me; as would a construction on paper. The proposition corresponds e.g. to a picture of the mechanism with the paths of the points *A* and *B* drawn in. Thus it is in a certain respect a picture of that movement. It holds fast what the *proof* shews me. Or—what it persuades me of.

If the proof registers the procedure according to the rule, then by doing this it produces a new concept.

In producing a new concept it convinces me of something. For it is essential to this conviction that the procedure according to these rules must always produce the same configuration. ('Same', that is, by our ordinary rules of comparison and copying.)

With this is connected the fact that we can say that proof must shew the existence of an internal relation. For the internal relation is the operation producing one structure from another, seen as equivalent to the picture of the transition itself—so that now the transition according to this series of configurations is *eo ipso* a transition according to those rules for operating.

In producing a concept, the proof convinces me of something: what it convinces me of is expressed in the proposition that it has proved.

Problem: Does the adjective "mathematical" always mean the same: when we speak of "mathematical" concepts, of "mathematical" propositions and of mathematical proofs?

Now what has the proved proposition got to do with the concept created by the proof? Again: what has the proved proposition got to do with the internal relations demonstrated by the proof?

The picture (proof-picture) is an instrument producing conviction.

It is clear that one can also apply an unproved mathematical proposition; even a false one.

The mathematical proposition says to me: Proceed like this!

73. "If the proof convinces us, then we must also be convinced of the axioms." Not as by empirical propositions, that is not their role. In the language-game of verification by experience they are excluded. Are, not empirical propositions, but principles of judgement.

A language-game: How have I to imagine one in which axioms, proofs and proved propositions occur?

Someone who hears a bit of logic for the first time at school is straightway convinced when he is told that a proposition implies itself, or when he hears the law of contradiction, or of excluded middle.— Why is he immediately convinced? Well, these laws fit entirely into the use of language that he is so familiar with. Then he learns perhaps to prove more complicated propositions of logic. The proofs are exhibited to him, and he is again convinced; or he invents proofs himself.

In this way he learns new techniques of inference. And also, what account to lay it to, if now errors appear.

The proof convinces him that he must hold fast to the proposition, to the technique that it prescribed; but it also shews him how he can hold fast to the proposition without running any risk of getting into conflict with experience.

74. Any proof in applied mathematics may be conceived as a proof in pure mathematics which proves that *this* proposition follows from *these* propositions, or can be got from them by means of such and such operations; etc.

The proof is a particular *path*. When we describe it, we do not mention causes.

I act on the proof.—But how?—I act according to the proposition that got proved.

The proof taught me e.g., a technique of approximation. But still it proved *something*, convinced me of something. *That* is expressed by the proposition: It says what I shall now do on the strength of the proof.

The proof belongs to the background of the proposition. To the system in which the proposition has an effect.

See, *this* is how 3 and 2 yield 5. Note this proceeding.

Every empirical proposition may serve as a rule if it is fixed, like a machine part, made immovable, so that now the whole representation turns around it and it becomes part of the coordinate system, independent of facts.

"This is how it is, if this proposition is derived from these ones. That you have to admit."—What I admit is, *this* is what I call such a procedure.

INDEX

ground
- recognize the ground that is before us as the ground, 333
grounds, 135

Heine–Borel theorem, 293
heterological, 206–7, 395–6

identity, law of, 89, 150, 244, 404
identity (equality), *cf.* same, agreement, 108, 109, 110, 187, 237, 247, 359
- of a word, 340
imagining (image), 68, 73, 88, 223, 224, 226, 264, 288
impossibility, *v.* possibility
impress, see memorable
inductive proof, *v.* recursive
inexorability, *cf.* compulsion, must, necessity, 37–8, 60–1, 82
inference, logical, 38–40, 41–2, 44–5, 48, 50, 75, 79, 80, 83, 93, 96, 164, 168, 172, 257, 261, 306, 308–10, 320, 364, 387, 392, 397, 400, 404, 425–30, 436
- difference between inferring wrong and not inferring, 352
- rule (law) of, 80, 96, 168, 172, 174, 364, 372–3, 387, 398, 401, 425
infinite, infinity, 141, 142, 260, 263–4, 266–270, 272–3, 278–9, 280
insight, *cf.* self-evidence, intuition, 241, 244
institution, 167–8, 334
instruction, 348–9
intensional, *v.* extensional
intention, 89
interpretation, 80, 267, 300, 332, 341–2, 352, 389, 414
intuition, 36, 152, 235, 237, 246, 247, 347, 365
invention (inventor), 99, 111, 136, 270
irrational number, *cf.* Dedekind cut, 129, 133–4, 267, 286–91, 371, 408

judgment, 298, 327, 329, 330, 337, 435
justification, 142, 171–2, 199, 305, 312, 325, 342, 406, 430

knowing, 356, 363

language, 38, 43, 60, 62, 90, 95, 96, 99, 116, 165–6, 168, 196, 209, 236
- function of, 333, 334
- phenomenon of, 209, 335, 342, 351
language-game, 43, 89, 117, 133, 196, 201, 207, 208, 220, 231, 236, 255, 278, 281, 284, 296, 299–300, 316, 318, 322, 327, 338, 343, 360–1, 363, 365, 367, 381, 390, 391, 392, 394, 395, 397, 401, 403, 406, 409, 411, 416, 425, 433, 435, 436
- at the bottom of our, 330
- description of a, 208, 320
law, *cf.* command, inference, rule,
- of excluded middle, 266–81, 287
- of thought, 90
Lessing, G. E., 403
letter
- number of letters of a word, 245, 338–340
Liar, The, 120, 255–6, 376, 404
licence, *cf.* command, 133, 420
life (form of, manner of), 335, 390, 409, 414, 421
limit, 288, 290, 294, 407
limits of empiricism, 197, 237, 379, 387
logic, *cf.* constants, inference, machine, must, Russell, 90, 115
- and arithmetic, 146, 170, 217
- curse of, 162, 281, 282, 284, 299, 300, 408
- and mathematics, 99, 174, 175, 185, 281–4
- the phenomenon of, 353
- more primitive, 105
- as ultra-physics, 40

machine, *cf.* calculating machine,
- logical, *cf.* mechanical, 83, 213, 249
- mathematical, *v.* logical machine
- as symbol, 84–7, 242, 249, 434
mathematics, 99, 176, 182, 201, 381, 383, 425
- and family of activities, 273
- and grammar, 234
- and measure, 201
- pure and applied, 219, 232, 265, 363, 412, 436
- without propositions, 93, 117, 233–4, 265, 398
meaning, *cf.* application, use, sense, 41, 42, 102, 104, 105, 106, 107, 108, 110, 141, 142, 257, 274, 367, 398
mean, to, 36, 41, 42, 53, 78, 103, 104, 105–6, 107–8
measure (measuring, measurement), 38–9, 40–1, 53, 71, 84, 91, 146–7, 167–8, 179, 182, 199–200, 236, 355–6, 377, 382, 389, 432